Learning to Teach Music in the Secondary School

Learning to Teach Music in the Secondary School is intended to support student teachers, newly qualified teachers and more experienced music teachers in their professional development.

Topics covered include:

- the place of music in the curriculum
- the nature of musical learning
- planning, managing and assessing musical learning
- music and individual needs
- school examinations and music
- music outside the curriculum.

One of the main premises of the book is that music needs to be taught musically. It is important that the nature of music itself guides what goes on in the music classroom if we are to motivate our pupils and help them to fulfil their potential as musicians.

This book will help student teachers to develop their subject knowledge, teaching skills, understanding of the wider issues and their ability to reflect on classroom practice.

Chris Philpott taught music and performing arts in secondary schools for sixteen years before moving into teacher education. He is currently responsible for the Secondary PGCE Music course at Canterbury Christ Church University College, and Programme Director for the Key Stage 2/3 PGCE.

Related titles

Learning to Teach Subjects in the Secondary School Series

Series Editors
Susan Capel, Canterbury Christ Church University College; Marilyn Leask, De Montfort University, Bedford; and Tony Turner, Institute of Education, University of London.

Designed for all students learning to teach in secondary schools, and particularly those on school-based initial teacher training courses, the books in this series complement *Learning to Teach in the Secondary School* and its companion, *Starting to Teach in the Secondary School*. Each book in the series applies underpinning theory and addresses practical issues to support students in school and in the training institution in learning how to teach a particular subject.

Learning to Teach English in the Secondary School
Jon Davison and Jane Dowson

Learning to Teach Modern Foreign Languages in the Secondary School
Norbert Pachler and Kit Field

Learning to Teach History in the Secondary School
Terry Haydn, James Arthur and Martin Hunt

Learning to Teach Physical Education in the Secondary School
Edited by Susan Capel

Learning to Teach Science in the Secondary School
Tony Turner and Wendy DiMarco

Learning to Teach Mathematics in the Secondary School
Edited by Sue Johnston-Wilder, Peter Johnston-Wilder, David Pimm and John Westwell

Learning to Teach Religious Education in the Secondary School
Edited by Andrew Wright and Ann-Marie Brandom

Learning to Teach Art and Design in the Secondary School
Edited by Nicholas Addison and Lesley Burgess

Learning to Teach Geography in the Secondary School
David Lambert and David Balderstone

Learning to Teach Design and Technology in the Secondary School
Edited by Gwyneth Owen-Jackson

Learning to Teach Music in the Secondary School
Edited by Chris Philpott

Learning to Teach Music in the Secondary School

A companion to school experience

Edited by
Chris Philpott

RoutledgeFalmer
Taylor & Francis Group

LONDON AND NEW YORK

First published 2001 by RoutledgeFalmer
2 Park Square, Milton Park, Abingdon, Oxon OX14 4RN

Simultaneously published in the USA and Canada
by RoutledgeFalmer
270 Madison Ave, New York, NY 10016

Reprinted 2003 , 2006

RoutledgeFalmer is an imprint of the Taylor & Francis Group

Typeset in Bembo and Myriad by
Curran Publishing Services Ltd, Norwich
Printed and bound in Great Britain by
TJ International Ltd, Padstow, Cornwall

British Library Cataloguing in Publication Data
A catalogue record for this book is available from the British Library

Library of Congress Cataloging in Publication Data
Learning to teach music in the secondary school: a companion to school
experience/edited by Chris Philpott.
    p. cm.
Includes bibliographical references and index.
1. School music – Instruction and study – United States. I. Philpott, Chris, 1956–
MT1.l52 2001
780`71   2--dc21   00-062724

ISBN 0–415–15833–8

Contents

Illustrations

Figures

Tables

Boxes

Tasks

Contributors

Chris Philpott is Principal Lecturer in music education at Canterbury Christ Church University College, and taught for sixteen years in secondary schools before moving into higher education.

Pauline Adams is Senior Lecturer in music education at The Institute of Education, University of London.

Charles Plummeridge is Senior Lecturer in music education at The Institute of Education, University of London. He has written and edited much significant work in the field of music education.

Bill Crow is Senior Lecturer in music education at Middlesex University

Chris Carden-Price is head of music at Highworth Grammar School for Girls in Ashford, Kent. He has composed many works for performance by his pupils.

Mike Lewis was formerly head of music at Simon Langton Boys Grammar School in Canterbury, Kent. He has now retired to the delights of organ building.

Acknowledgements

I should like to thank Tony Turner for his support and comments during the editing process, the other authors for their ideas and prompt writing, my wife for her patience, Routledge for much of the same and Canterbury Christ Church University College for allowing me time to complete the volume when in its final stages.

The Roland Fiddy cartoon reproduced as Figure 9.1 is taken from from *The Fanatic's Guide to Computers,* © Roland Fiddy 1991, and is reprinted by kind permission of Exley Publications Ltd.

The Agbadza is © R. M. Kwami 2000, and is reprinted by kind permission.

Chris Philpott

Series Editors' Preface

This book *Learning to Teach Music in the Secondary School* is the twelfth in a series of books entitled *Learning to Teach (subject name) in the Secondary School: A Companion to School Experience*, covering most subjects in the secondary school curriculum. The books in this series support and complement *Learning to Teach in the Secondary School: A Companion to School Experience*, (Capel, Leask and Turner, 2nd edn 1999). These books are designed for student teachers learning to teach on different types of initial teacher education courses and in different contexts. However, it is hoped that they will be equally useful to tutors and mentors in their work with student teachers. A complementary book was published in 1997 entitled *Starting to Teach in the Secondary School: A Companion for the Newly Qualified Teacher* (Capel, Leask and Turner 1997). This second book was designed to support newly qualified teachers in their first post, and addressed aspects of teaching which are likely to be of concern in the first year of teaching.

The information in the subject books does not repeat that in *Learning to Teach*; rather, the content of that book is adapted and extended to address the needs of student teachers learning to teach a specific subject. In each of the subject books, therefore, reference is made to the generic book *Learning to Teach in Secondary School*, where appropriate. It is recommended that you have both books so that you can cross-reference when needed.

The positive feedback on *Learning to Teach*, particularly the way it has supported the learning of student teachers in their development into effective, reflective teachers, has encouraged us to retain the main features of that book in the subject series. Thus, the subject books are designed so that elements of appropriate theory introduce each topic or issue. Recent research into teaching and learning is also incorporated into these texts. This material is interwoven with tasks designed to help you identify key features of topics and issues and apply these features to your own practice.

Although the basic content of each subject book is similar, each book is designed to address the unique nature of each subject. This book begins by exploring the place of music in the curriculum as an important mode of human knowledge and understanding. Indeed, while music is one of the foundation subjects in the national curriculum, music educators have always needed to vigorously argue a case for inclusion in the school timetable. Part of making this case needs to be based on a firm understanding of what counts as musical knowledge, how we acquire it and how it develops. Defenders of music need to understand how it is possible to bring about musical achievement and to recognise when it happens. Finally, music is important to the extra curricular dimension of schools, all of which places many challenges on the music teacher to plan and manage a coherent and integrated set of experiences for pupils. This book is designed to accompany your learning in each of these areas, within a framework which is committed to teaching music musically.

We as editors have found this project to be exciting. We hope that, whatever the type of initial teacher education course you are following and wherever you may be following that course, you find that this book is useful and supports your development into an effective, reflective music teacher. Above all, we hope you enjoy teaching music.

Susan Capel, Marilyn Leask and Tony Turner

Introduction

Learning to teach music

Chris Philpott

LEARNING HOW TO TEACH MUSIC

This book is a companion to learning how to teach music. It is intended to provide support, guidance, ideas and challenges for student teachers, mentors, trainers and teacher educators of all types. By the time the book is published there will be a variety of routes into music teaching including full time study, part-time study, graduate teacher, registered teacher and modular PGCEs. Student teachers and teacher educators in these wide variety of circumstances do not require a manual, for their needs are all very different. This book therefore does *not* take you stage by stage through the process of learning how to teach music (even if this were possible); instead, it is intended to be used after you have 'audited' your own particular needs in your own specific circumstances.

You are unlikely to want to read this book from cover to cover, and are more likely to dip into it and use it selectively. The tasks, for example, can be used as part of a 'training plan' in school or college by tutor, mentor or student. They do not, however, represent a systematic action plan for becoming a music teacher. The chapters can be read in preparation for, or as a response to learning sessions inside or outside the classroom.

The book is not explicitly linked to the 'standards', nor is it an apologist for the national curriculum or examination board syllabi. However, the text does cover the skills, knowledge and understandings which allows you to embrace the national curriculum and to address targets in your progress towards the standards for QTS. Ultimately, the quest for a 'musical' education transcends standards and published curricular, although teacher educators cannot abdicate their statutory responsibilities. In any case the two demands are not mutually exclusive, and we suggest that this book has a role to play in helping you and your tutors to achieve both goals. Readers will find important areas such as planning, assessment, individual needs, ICT and examinations are covered in some depth, but always from a perspective of 'behaving' musically.

There are many aspects of learning how to teach which are covered in the generic book (*Learning to Teach in the Secondary School: A Companion to School Experience* – Capel, Leask and Turner 1999) and do not necessarily need a musical spin here. We concentrate on those aspects of learning how to teach which have significant implications for the music teacher. For example, some aspects of behaviour management have cross subject implications and are covered more than adequately in the generic book.

Some of the chapters are unashamedly theoretical in outlook. We believe that theory and practice are inextricably linked for theory always underpins practice. We do not use the concept of theory here to mean anything distinct from practice, but as the *rational* basis for practice. *All* teachers have theories about the nature of children, the importance of the subject, and the nature of learning in their subject upon which they base their everyday work. These theories often remain intuitive and Swanwick makes the same point when he suggests that:

> no human mind is free from the impulse towards theorising, any more than human physiology can get by for long without breathing – (teachers) are implicitly working to theories about music and educational processes, whether or not they declare them publicly.
>
> (Swanwick 1988: 6–7)

Much of the theory which underpins this book has been derived from many years of teaching in both the secondary music classroom and as teacher educators. In addition some of the chapters have been influenced by *many* eminent writers in the field of music education, *and* in particular the work of Keith Swanwick.

Learning how to teach any subject involves a willingness to become open and to reflect on and evaluate practice. Indeed, the cycle of *plan – act – reflect* has been important in the development of many teachers. Quite apart from needing to improve in order to gain QTS, all teachers have a professional obligation to both their pupils and themselves to become better practitioners. It is the aim of this book to be part of that cycle for student teachers, mentors, NQTs and experienced teachers. In this sense learning to teach music is a 'lifelong' process.

In offering to be a 'companion for learning how to teach music' this book adopts certain positions about the nature of music, the nature of musical knowledge, the nature of musical learning and the nature of musical development; that is, it expounds particular theories of music education. This is inevitable given the impossibility of being neutral over how to teach a subject as complex and ephemeral as music. Hopefully, these 'positions' will constantly confront you with the problems, difficulties and issues which surround the messy job that is music teaching, and require that you reflect on teaching and learning. This process of reflection is important for there are many areas of music and arts education which remain problematic for example, the assessment of composition. Thus, in learning how to teach music you also learn how to engage with these issues on a regular basis, as part of your planning and practice. You may not agree with each and every position adopted in this book but it is important that you reflect on and review what you *do* believe in. This process may help you underpin your beliefs with a sound philosophy of music education.

In this book the positions adopted often revolve around the principles which suggest that

- music is an important symbolic mode for expression, knowledge and understanding
- pupils should be given opportunities to learn how to use and understand musical expression
- knowing and understanding is about building *meaningful relationships* with music both in and out of school
- musical knowledge embraces many different traditions,
- music needs to be taught musically.

These principles are 'fleshed out' as the book progresses. You may embrace some or all of the implications of these as part your cycle of reflection, or develop well reasoned principles (theories) of your own. This is important for experience suggests that strong music teachers (from many different ideologies) are those who have developed for themselves sound and well reasoned positions. The strength of such teachers is enhanced if, at the same time, they are receptive to the theories which underpin the good practice of other music teachers.

Task 0.1 An initial statement

Remember a music teacher from any part of your music education: for example, their personal characteristics, gossip, nickname, physical features.

Now ask yourself the following questions:

- Was s/he a good or bad music teacher in your opinion?
- Try to identify why they were good or bad and make a list of features.
- Try to recall one good lesson from your music education and one bad lesson/experience. Now try to evaluate what makes a good lesson in music and what makes a poor one.
- What do you feel are the priorities for music education? Are these the same or different from the priorities you experienced as a pupil?
- If you have already taught music in some way try to recall one good lesson and one bad lesson/experience, then try to evaluate, as earlier, what makes a good lesson and a poor one.

Compare your experiences with other student teachers.

Write an initial statement which identifies the sort of music teacher you would like to become, drawing on evidence from the tasks.

An important starting point for learning how to teach music is your own experience as a pupil, student or teacher. It is likely that your biography will be an important influence on the way you think about the music and the teaching of music. If you are to reflect on these influences, then you will need to recall events from past experience. Task 0.1 prepares you for this reflective process through a consciousness-raising exercise.

From the background of your experience, intuitive beliefs and ideas there are at least two very good reasons for developing a personal philosophy of music education. First, your theories will underpin the successful planning and execution of your lessons. Second, it seems that music will always be under pressure in the curriculum and if you are armed with a well reasoned rationale for what you do, then you can argue the case for music education with headteachers, governors, advisors and government! To have no reasoned philosophy diminishes your power to convince others of the value of music at school and of its importance in the wider society.

FURTHER READING

Elliot, D. J. (1995) *Music Matters: A New Philosophy of Music Education*, Oxford: Oxford University Press

Swanwick, K. (1988) *Music, Mind, and Education*, London: Routledge. In the early chapters of both of these books the authors make a strong claim for the importance of theory in music education and also the need for a coherent philosophy to underpin and inform our practice.

1 The place of music in the school curriculum

Charles Plummeridge

INTRODUCTION

School programmes have evolved over a long period of time, and current curriculum issues and debates can often be more clearly illuminated and better understood when viewed initially from an historical perspective. It is perhaps not always appreciated that music is, in fact, one of the oldest of curriculum subjects and was probably included in the first formal systems of education designed for the ruling elite in ancient Egypt. The Greeks valued musical studies for intellectual, cultural and moral reasons, and the strong connections between singing and Christian worship have ensured a place for music in educational institutions over the past two thousand years.

Class music teaching, as we know it today, has its origins in the nineteenth century. With the establishment of a national educational system, choral activity and music reading were encouraged in schools, partly in the hope that such action would eventually lead to an improved standard of musical performance in church services. It was with this aim in mind that legendary teachers like Sarah Glover and John Curwen devised systematic and successful schemes of class teaching based on singing and the acquisition of aural and literacy skills. How far they realised their main aim is unclear, but as Simpson (1975) has pointed out, these early music educators were highly imaginative and influential teachers, and many of their ideas and methods are firmly embedded in contemporary practices. The Victorian educational reformers were also committed to Classical ideals. They had a belief in the power of music as a civilising force, and maintained that it should therefore be taught as part of an education which would instil a sense of decorum and in due course foster a more stable and harmonious social order.

In the English independent (or 'public') schools of the nineteenth century, music was largely 'extra-curricular', the focus being mainly on individual instrumental tuition and the formation of choirs, orchestras, bands and various ensembles.

Concerts and other artistic events came to be valued as public celebrations of a school's corporate achievements and a visible sign of its social cohesion. Nowadays, music in most maintained (state) and independent schools is both a curriculum subject and an extra-curricular pursuit, and represents a fusion of the two sectors' traditions, values and practices.

Music education has become a broad enterprise, and as a music teacher you will find that you are responsible for a range of both formal and informal activities. The purpose of this chapter is to identify and examine some of the theoretical and practical issues associated with the present position of music as a subject within the curriculum. Extra-curricular or extended musical activities and the relationship between the two 'dimensions' of school music are considered further in Chapter 13.

OBJECTIVES

After studying the content of the chapter you should be able to:

- describe the evolution of music in schools
- discuss different conceptions of music in the curriculum
- provide an account of musical knowledge and understanding
- define the main features of the national curriculum for music and school leaving examinations
- discuss the similarities and differences between the various arts disciplines
- describe different ways of organising music within the curriculum.

THE POSITION OF MUSIC

In a comprehensive and fascinating survey outlining the growth of music in schools, Bernarr Rainbow (1989) shows that in spite of the importance frequently attached to the subject, its position within the curriculum has never been altogether secure. Enthusiastic proponents have often had to contend with sceptics who express serious doubts about music's educational value. From numerous reports on the state of music teaching (see for example Rogers 1998) it would appear that to some extent these conflicting views continue to permeate curriculum thinking and practices. And one only has to talk to a group of serving teachers to appreciate that attitudes towards music and the arts, and provision for these subjects in schools, are extremely variable.

It is sometimes suggested that because of music's seemingly weak and threatened curriculum status, teachers have spent an inordinate amount of time attempting to justify their subject. If that has been the case in the past, one might reasonably assume that with the advent of the national curriculum there is no longer any need to worry so much about justification. Surely, it would be more sensible to concentrate on *how* to teach music rather than dwell too much on the *why* questions. Indeed, some teachers may well argue that in those schools where music is being taught effectively there is seldom any mention of its justification. There is actually much to be said in support of this latter view but it would, of course, be quite wrong to think that the introduction of the national curriculum has led to a curtailment of discussions about the content of the curriculum. There have been major changes since the passing of the Education Reform Act (1988), differences of opinion remain, and some teachers still feel that they have to confront their 'opponents' and 'defend' their subject areas. But these points aside, there are three closely related reasons why it is necessary for the practitioner to provide a sound rationale for music in the curriculum. First, it is a statutory requirement that schools produce, and keep under review, written statements about their curricula; teachers of all subjects will need to be involved in such exercises. Second,, it is part of an educator's role to be able to give a public account of his or her actions. Teachers are not compliant 'operatives' who simply 'deliver' curricula according to some set of externally imposed rules and instructions. They are autonomous professionals, engaged in a complex value-laden process concerned with the intellectual and moral well being of young people. In this process they have to make independent practical judgements and explain their intentions and decisions, in different ways, to a variety of audiences: students, colleagues, governors, parents, inspectors and members of the general public. Third, how teachers conceive music within the curriculum will have a bearing on their choice of content and mode of implementation. For example, if one is of the opinion that the main purpose of teaching music is to introduce students to their 'cultural heritage' then this implies a particular kind of curriculum content and activities and almost certainly a concern for the past. Alternatively, if emphasis is placed on the relationship between music and self-realisation or the development of students' creativity, then practical activities are more likely to be those that encourage forms of musical experience in which creative expression, investigation and exploration become centrally important. It might be possible to combine these two approaches which would, in turn, lead to yet another type of curriculum content and design. Prior to the national curriculum, individual teachers devised their own schemes of work and class music teaching in English schools was characterised by its diversity. Teachers now have a professional responsibility to take notice of the prescribed framework. However, this does not mean that there is an absolute conformity since any curriculum specification is inevitably open to alternative interpretations. These are determined, to some degree, by teachers' conceptions of music as a component of a general education.

JUSTIFICATIONS, AIMS AND PRACTICES

Some contemporary observers seek to justify music in terms of its extrinsic values. There are those who uphold the view that musical studies are educationally beneficial since they foster worthy dispositions and qualities of mind, and equip students with a range of transferable skills. As indicated earlier, this sort of assertion is by no means new, but it has been highlighted in recent years by the publication of various research reports purporting to show a positive correlation between musical studies and general academic performance. The idea that music makes students more generally proficient is obviously attractive and is given much prominence in a popular pamphlet issued by the Campaign for Music in the Curriculum (1998). It may be the case that any number of desirable personal and academic outcomes arise from participating in musical activities, but it could be unwise to put too much faith in such claims. Furthermore, we need to make sure that possible non-musical benefits are not seen as one of the main reasons for including music in the curriculum. There are two points to bear in mind. First, the logical outcome of adopting this position would be to evaluate music programmes in terms of students' achievements in activities other than music. It is not hard to see that apart from being a rather odd procedure it would also be one that could lead to very awkward problems. Second, in all areas of the curriculum there will be outcomes which are not subject specific. It might be that musical activities help develop, say, imaginative thinking and a sense of co-operation, but these would be general educational aims and applicable to all curriculum subjects.

In considering the place of music in the curriculum it is necessary to recognise that the selection of curriculum content is inevitably related to a particular conception of education. And it is readily apparent that there are alternative views of education, or educational ideologies, which will have implications for what and how students are expected to study. Martin Skilbeck (1976) describes three ideologies: classical humanism, progressivism and reconstructionism. These are 'ideal' types and, in reality, almost certainly never found in a 'pure' form. However, they do provide a useful starting point when thinking about the complicated issues of how music is to be justified, what the aims of music programmes might be, and how the subject is to be taught in the classroom.

Classical humanism can be traced back to the Platonic view that education should be partly concerned with preserving the 'best' elements of the culture. This is an ideology that has subsequently appeared in different forms. Typical modern interpretations are reflected in the writings of Rhodes Boyson (1974) and Nicholas Tate (1996) both of whom favour introducing children to the 'great masters' whose works represent the highest accomplishments in the 'world' of (Western) music. Very few educationists would want to justify music solely in these terms, but it is a position associated with what has come to be regarded as a 'traditional' conception of music education in which children develop a working knowledge and appreciation of the post-Renaissance classical tradition. It was the standard approach to music education in the early post-war years and one that underpinned a number of class music teaching schemes. A good example would be the Oxford School Music Books (Fiske and Dobbs 1956). These were carefully chosen and beautifully designed materials for class singing, musical appreciation, skill development and recorder playing. The books were widely used for over twenty years.

The classical humanist or traditional conception of education is often contrasted with the *progressive* ideal. Instead of concentrating on the past, the progressive educator, inspired by the theories of Rousseau and Froebel (and Dewey to some extent) is more concerned with fostering, in students, certain types of qualities: creativeness, imagination, sensitivity and the ability to express thoughts and ideas in personal ways. On this view of education, experiences in music and the arts are ways of promoting these general educational aims and also cultivating an 'aesthetic awareness'. These ideas were particularly influential during the 1960s and 1970s and were disseminated through the writings of Robert Witkin (1974), Malcolm Ross (1975) and John Paynter (1982). One of the central pedagogical principles arising from progressivism has been the importance attached to children creating or composing their own music. Although more traditional educators also advocated composing, many progressive innovators encouraged a style of classwork based on experience of contemporary music and a freer exploration of sound itself. In some ways, they were influenced by the theories and practices of earlier visual arts educators such as Herbert Read and Marion Richardson. Progressive music educators would be inclined to see themselves as facilitators who provide an environment for students' creative exploration of expressive media. There can be little doubt that these innovations have had a marked effect on the ways in which music is presented and taught in schools, and greatly extended ideas as to what 'counts' as music in an educational context. One of the finest publications of this period was Paynter and Aston's (1970) *Sound and Silence* which although now thirty years old contains a wealth of ideas about musical materials and teaching strategies that are still relevant for classroom teachers.

At this point it should again be noted that traditional and progressive conceptions of music education, like the general educational ideologies outlined by Skilbeck, are not realities. They are theoretical constructs used for the purpose of analysing different approaches to music in education. In actuality, teachers are likely to adopt strategies that are both traditional and progressive. In a rather crude sense this is the essence of *reconstructionism* which has its roots in the educational philosophy of John Dewey. Those who subscribe to the reconstructionist ideal, see education as a process, which focuses on the betterment of both the individual and society. For Denis Lawton this is to be achieved through a common curriculum. He bases his position on two main precepts. First, the curriculum is to be a range of worthwhile pursuits that represent a 'selection from the culture'. Second, in a democratic society it is morally just that all children of compulsory school age should have access to the whole curriculum. According to Lawton, selection from the culture is determined by the existence of 'cultural invariants' or sub-systems: socio-political, economic, communication, rationality, technology, morality, belief, aesthetic, maturation. Music and the arts have a place in a common curriculum, derived from the sub systems, the aim of which is to develop students' understanding of the various 'meanings' that constitute the living culture (Lawton 1988).

This type of thinking about education, areas of experience and the curriculum, provides a framework for a view of music and the arts as a 'way of knowing' that has been advanced by certain aestheticians over a period of some fifty years and more recently by music educationists. The theory of music as a unique form of knowledge, or realm of meaning, into which students will be 'initiated' through the inter-related activities of performing, listening and composing, is at the heart of numerous curriculum models and schemes. This theory, which has had a significant influence on the design of the national curriculum, the GCSE and the A level examination, is further considered in the following section

Task 1.1 Alternative approaches to class music teaching

Discuss with colleagues the class teaching practices you have observed in schools. Do music programmes differ very much from school to school? Consider similarities and differences in practices with particular reference to:

- aims and objectives
- curriculum content
- teaching strategies
- pupil assessment.

Make a table in which you list features of classical humanism, progressivism and reconstructionism based on your observations of school practices.

MUSICAL MEANING AND KNOWING

One of the reasons why music and the arts disciplines have often occupied only a peripheral place in education is that they are regarded as lacking in cognitive content, being to do with 'feeling' rather than 'thinking'. To a practising musician this sort of attitude seems extremely uninformed, yet it is surprising how many people are still content to accept Cardinal Newman's famous statement that playing a musical instrument is an 'elegant pastime' but not educational since it does not 'cultivate the intellect'. However, these ideas are really very dated. Developments in the theory of knowledge and the emergence of new theories regarding the nature of intelligence, have led to a very different view of the arts and their place in the curriculum.

One theorist who has contributed to the newer thinking is the American philosopher Suzanne Langer. In a celebrated book, *Philosophy in a New Key* (Langer 1957) she rejects the long held assumption that experiences of an artistic kind are nothing more than pleasurable sensations. Langer outlines convincing (although difficult) philosophical arguments to support the theory of an arts semantic. The arts are symbolic forms of human feeling; they are just as meaningful, in their own ways, as those types of knowledge, such as science and mathematics, that are stated in propositions and rely on empirical proof or logical verification. The British philosopher and educationist, Louis Arnaud Reid (1986) has developed a similar theoretical position, and maintains that the arts are powerful forms of experience and meaning that embody human values in a unique way. For Reid, artistic knowledge is closer to the knowledge we have of people through personal relationships; artistic knowledge is 'by acquaintance'. Of course, the strength and import of these philosophers' writings cannot be adequately conveyed in a brief summary and their works need to be carefully studied over a period of time. Building on these philosophical foundations, Peter Abbs (1987, 1994) refers to the 'six great arts' of music, literature, drama, visual art, dance and film. He sees the disciplines as comprising a 'generic community' united by the processes of making, performing, presenting and evaluating. Through taking part in these artistic processes people develop a special type of perceptual understanding that is the basis of artistic knowledge.

In the field of music education itself, the notion of music as a realm of meaning and a way of knowing has been explored by a number of writers (e.g. Plummeridge 1991, Swanwick 1994, Aspin 1990, Paynter 1992). These educators certainly do not speak with one voice, but there is a fairly common agreement that musical knowledge and understanding are developed not as a result of learning 'about' music but through direct contact with music in three experiential modes: performing, composing and listening. It is recognised that meaningful engagement in music is dependent on the acquisition of skills and related information, that but these are a means to a growing practical competence that enhances musical experience and understanding. The activities of performing, composing and listening can take many forms and may be based on a variety of musical styles and genres. But it is through participation in these activities that people come to understand the structures and workings of the discipline. Like any other discipline, music has its own procedures, 'rules' and 'grammars', which are internalised by engaging in genuine musical encounters.

Theories of knowledge are closely related to theories of intelligence. Traditionally, a display of musical competence has often been thought of as a sign of a talent or special ability, and something separate from intelligence. For many people, it would not seem incongruous to refer to an individual as intelligent but unmusical or to another as musically able but not particularly intelligent. There was a time when certain psychologists, musicians and educationists were greatly interested in measuring students' musical ability or aptitude. In many studies it was concluded that there was little correlation between scores on musical ability tests and those designed to measure general intelligence. However, the notion of general intelligence is now regarded as being an unsatisfactory descriptor of human behaviour. The American psychologist, Howard Gardner (1993) has revived and extended the notion of multiple intelligences; he proposes at least six distinct types of cognitive operations: logical–mathematical, linguistic, bodily-kinaesthetic, spatial, personal, musical. The theory receives widespread support and is founded on the premise that human beings have developed different cognitive processes in the course of evolution. People in all cultures are 'programmed' to think and behave musically just as they have an inbuilt capacity for language and other operations. Gardner's *Frames of Mind* (1993) is an optimistic account of human abilities and one that will be of the greatest interest to all teachers.

Current views of music as a way of knowing and a form of intelligence provide a rationale for music in a curriculum that is line with a reconstructionist ideal. It would be unwise to assume that these theoretical principles have always been directly applied to curriculum planning and practice. Nevertheless, they have clearly been influential as can be seen through a review of the development and present structure of the national curriculum.

THE NATIONAL CURRICULUM

The introduction of a statutory national curriculum for England and Wales is one of the most significant pieces of educational legislation in modern times. When the Secretary of State for Education announced that music was to be one of the

Task 1.2 Your musical development

Think about your own education in music in relation to what you have just read and consider how it fits into some of the 'positions' identified thus far. Consider how your teachers developed your skills in:

- performing
- composing
- listening.

It might be worthwhile revisiting Task 1.1 as part of this exercise.

foundation subjects, many teachers concluded that this was (at long last) an 'official' confirmation of its importance within the curriculum. Working Groups for each subject were appointed by the government to provide provisional specifications which would constitute the basis of the curriculum Statutory Orders. The Subject Working Group for Music submitted an *Interim Report* in January 1991 (DES 1991a) and a *Final Report* (DES 1991b) in August of the same year. On the whole, teachers welcomed the Working Group's proposals which emphasised practical activity and wide-ranging musical experiences. The subsequent decision by the Secretary of State to make music compulsory only until the end of Year 9 caused many teachers to feel that once again the subject was being marginalised. However, other foundation subjects have also been made optional after key stage 3; it would seem that government policy over the past fifteen years has been to prioritise the raising of standards in the core subjects.

The Music Order was first published in 1992(DES 1992); it was revised three years later (DFE 1995) and the most recent version (DfEE 1999b) will be implemented in September 2000. The earlier reports of the Subject Working Group, referred to earlier, have been largely forgotten. This is a pity because both contain many good ideas about practice and can be very useful resources; they are certainly worth consulting. Three main principles (which have actually evolved from within the music education community) inform the national curriculum for music. The first is the notion of a generalist rather than specialist form of musical education that is available to all and not merely those who display a particular aptitude or talent. Second, musical understanding is to be developed through performing, composing and listening. The third principle is that music is a broad discipline which encompasses many styles and genres; it is far more than the 'Great' tradition. An education in and for a pluralist society is to be one in which students come to an awareness of the diverse nature of music as an art form. As indicated earlier, most teachers will be in sympathy with these principles and their subsequent pedagogical challenges. The Order sets out a programme of study based on composing, performing and appraising, and is designed to ensure that students follow a curriculum that has continuity and progression, allows for differentiation in teaching and provides a framework for regular assessment. The implementation of the national curriculum is discussed in Chapter 4.

It is well known that the national curriculum has been the subject of much professional controversy and debate. When the *Interim Report* first became available there was a strong reaction from certain groups of philosophers and musicians against what they saw as a move away from 'classical' values in favour of popular culture. Numerous articles appeared in national newspapers and there were heated exchanges about the content of the music programme. Although these public debates have been largely abandoned the issues remain disputatious. This is not altogether surprising when one considers the previously diverse practice of music teaching in this country. Some people have objected to the national curriculum on the grounds that the government has assumed too much control of education. Others argue that it provides a framework which allows for all children between the ages of five and fourteen to have access to an ordered and consistent musical education. To what extent one 'model' of music teaching and learning can be applied to all schools is, of course, open to question. However, it has to be remembered that the Order is no more than a basic outline which sets out certain principles and parameters. Teachers themselves are required to design their own detailed schemes of work which then have to be translated into meaningful educational encounters. And it is the act of translation that presents the real challenge. No matter how elegant and convincing a scheme or specification looks on paper it is only through the actions and interactions of teacher and students that the curriculum comes 'alive'. It is then that the curriculum becomes a dynamic process and not merely an 'inert' document.

MUSIC AND COMBINED ARTS

Although music is a discrete component of the national curriculum, in some schools it is taught within the context of an arts grouping. Such groupings normally comprise visual arts, drama, music and dance, but may also include film and media studies and literature. Several different terms are used to describe arts departments or faculties: creative arts, performing arts, or expressive arts, each indicating a particular type of curriculum organisation. The theoretical basis for bringing subjects together is that the arts form a unity in virtue of their common elements, procedures and techniques. Reference has already been made to Peter Abbs' (1994) conception of the 'generic community', which is but one version of the thesis that the arts constitute a distinct area of experience or realm of meaning. How far curriculum organisation is underpinned by these sorts of theoretical principles is far from certain since curriculum decisions are determined by many factors. On some occasions arts teachers themselves may choose to work closely together; in other circumstances senior managers will see the grouping of the subjects as a convenient and economical way of utilising staffing resources.

Nevertheless, there is a growing interest in and movement towards 'arts education'. Following a report on the provision for the arts in educational institutions from the Calouste Gulbenkian Foundation (1982), the Schools Curriculum and Development

Committee (SCDC) set up a national project, The Arts in Schools, under the direction of Professor Ken Robinson. (As a result of governmental changes in educational advisory bodies the project was taken over by the National Curriculum Council (NCC)). The project team produced three excellent reports (NCC 1990a, 1990b, 1990c) which contain a large number of ideas and suggestions for curriculum planning, practice and development. The project is based on the principle that the arts have common characteristics and should be considered together as a major curriculum component. There is no suggestion that the separate disciplines should always be taught as a unity, but one of the tasks of the team was to investigate various approaches to collaborative arts teaching. This type of work has been going on for many years often under the heading of 'integrated arts'. However, the term is used to describe many different sorts of practice and the team suggest that it would be more helpful to talk about 'combined arts'. In the report *The Arts 5–16: A Curriculum Framework* (NCC 1990a), four types of combined arts programmes are outlined:

- Mixed media: the use of more than one medium such as the combination of musical performance, dance and lighting.
- Multi-disciplinary: teachers of the separate disciplines pursue a common theme.
- Interdisciplinary: work involving close interaction between disciplines and possible overlapping of subject activities.
- Integration: working in a way that leads to the fusion of the disciplines into a new form as may be found in some non-European arts practices.

Actual examples of these practices are given in the document.

Although there is much effective collaborative arts practice it should be noted that the notion of arts education is not always greeted with approval. The philosopher and educator David Best (1992) is one of several outspoken critics of the idea of the generic community. Best is not opposed to combined arts initiatives, where these seem appropriate, but he strongly argues that the disciplines do *not* have some common characteristics that bind them together. Furthermore, he argues that to base curriculum structures and practices on what he regards as no more than a 'myth' is an unaccept-able and unsafe educational policy. To what extent the arts do have a unifying 'essence' is a philosophical issue over which aestheticians disagree and no doubt will continue to do so.

A more practical objection to the idea of arts education is that it leads to a type of curriculum organisation that may well further marginalise the individual disciplines. There are two points here. First, if the arts are seen as a unity then it might be argued that arts education can be achieved through any of the several disciplines; there will be no need for students to study the range of subjects. Second, an amount of allotted time for the arts as a whole is likely to result in less time for the individual subjects thereby again undermining their position in the curriculum. Teachers express different views on these matters. While some would share the concerns referred to earlier, others argue that the existence of an arts team actually strengthens the status of the arts and provides the basis for more effective teaching. Ultimately, these sorts of general arguments have to be related to particular schools, their organisational styles and modes of operation. An objection to combined arts may come from teachers who are concerned about their personal standing within the school community. It is always necessary to be aware of the fact that school subjects are social as well as academic systems. The teacher who has a sole responsibility for a subject area is in a different professional position from the one who works as a member of a team. Arts education and combined arts teaching have a bearing not only on the status of subjects but also on the status of teachers themselves. It is interesting to note that these organisational and professional concerns have been similarly expressed by science teachers, especially in the 1970s and 1980s when integrated science often replaced the separate science disciplines.

No matter how music is organised in the school, one of the big advantages of arts teachers working co-operatively is that it can provide for more imaginative curriculum planning. There are clearly links between arts activities and if these can be acknowledged then this will hopefully lead to a richer form of music education. It also has to be recognised that music relates in some way to every other subject on the curriculum. A common educational aim would be to assist students in the making of meaningful connections between all the disciplines; this has further implications for curriculum design and development strategies.

Task 1.3 Combined arts

Discuss the issue of arts education with colleagues in school with particular reference to:

- some of the similarities between the arts subjects
- differences between the arts
- the advantages and disadvantages of combined arts teaching.

You will find it helpful to read Chapter 5 of *The Educational Imperative* by Peter Abbs (1994) in which the author deals with some of the philosophical issues.

MUSIC BEYOND 14

Although music is not a compulsory curriculum subject for students after the end of key stage 3, many continue to receive instrumental tuition and participate in extra-curricular activities. Some follow examination courses, and a brief overview of these courses serves to further reveal something of the place of music in the curriculum and changing views regarding the nature of music and musical studies.

In most schools, music is offered as an option in the General Certificate of Secondary Education (GCSE). Overall, the numbers taking GCSE courses in music are small which in itself may be an indicator of how the subject is perceived by students, teachers and parents. Traditionally, music as an examination subject was often thought of as being only for those with a particular musical interest; this attitude was reflected in school leaving examinations and especially the old GCE 'O' level. But the GCSE is in no way a specialist examination; it is suitable for all students who have followed a five-year course in curriculum music

Syllabuses are issued under the authority of three unitary bodies (see Chapter 11) and have to be designed in accordance with regulations and criteria as set out by the Qualifications and Curriculum Authority (QCA). It is a requirement that syllabuses build on the knowledge, understanding and skills contained in the national curriculum, and provide for courses in performing, composing and listening that will foster musical sensitivity, promote cultural development and support personal and social development.

In recognition of the diverse nature of musical interests and experiences, students are offered a wide range of choices. For example, in the area of composing, students may work in any style, use the full range of existing technology, or they can, if they so wish, develop the techniques of 'old fashioned' melody writing and Lovelockian harmony. The task for the teacher is to direct students to the type of work which best suits their abilities and aspirations and allows them to demonstrate positive achievements; a task which naturally requires careful planning and preparation. As with the national curriculum, teachers need to have a broader acquaintance with music than some might have had during their formal studies in higher education. Obviously, nobody can be an 'expert' in every musical tradition, but part of developing as a school music teacher is widening one's musical experience and knowledge of different styles and genres. This is an ongoing and never-ending process.

While A level courses are still within the context of a general certificate of education, and normally taken with one or more subjects, they represent a high standard of musical achievement. Again, they are taken by relatively small numbers. The A level syllabuses retain the principle that courses should provide for wide academic and practical experience and make provision for different musical interests. This reflects the contemporary view that music is a multi-dimensional discipline and that to be musically educated can be interpreted in a number of different ways.

An alternative programme of study for post-16 students is that offered as a General National Vocational Qualification (GNVQ). These courses are intended to provide a broad education and training as a preparation for employment or higher education. The inclusion of music as part of a GNVQ Performing Arts course is another indicator of changing attitudes towards musical studies and a recognition that music can have both academic and vocational relevance for a growing number of students.

SUMMARY AND CONCLUSIONS

It is important for you as a teacher to have a properly formulated rationale for music in the curriculum since this is the foundation for your practice. Additionally, you will

Task 1.4 Developing musical expertise

Music teachers are required to be extremely versatile musicians although obviously nobody can be an authority on every aspect of music. There are numerous ways in which teachers can further their musical experiences and you will be able to find information on this in schools and your training institution.

As a first step, study the content of the national curriculum and the requirements of the GCSE and A level examinations. Make a list of the areas in which you feel you need to develop your own musical expertise. See also the ideas for auditing subject knowledge in Appendix C.

be frequently required to give public accounts of aims, policies and practices, and the ability to do so has become a necessary part of your professional knowledge and expertise.

It is possible to find several different types of justification for music as a curriculum subject. At the present time, there appears to be a measure of agreement that it is as a way of knowing or realm of meaning that music has a place in a broad and balanced curriculum. This view leads to a form of music education in which students come to understand the 'workings' of the discipline through direct participation in musical activities. These principles are embedded in the national curriculum and courses leading to school-leaving examinations.

While there are those who favour the inclusion of music within combined arts programmes there are differences of opinion regarding the theoretical and organisational reasons for this type of curriculum structure. Even so, for the purposes of

Task 1.5 A public presentation

You are asked to speak to a group of parents about music as a subject in the curriculum. Consider how you would approach this presentation with reference to:

- an account of aims and objectives
- practical demonstrations
- audience participation.

Some points to bear in mind:

Most parents are not educational theorists and will not want to sit through an 'academic' lecture. However, they are likely to have views about music education and will probably ask questions or make statements. Be prepared! What sort of topics do you think will be of particular interest?

curriculum planning and development there is much to be said in support of arts teachers working together. You will also want to consider links between music and all other areas of the curriculum since helping children to make connections between the disciplines is a general aim of education.

Teaching music in schools is a demanding occupation and one which requires much imagination and determination. The constant challenge for you is how to transform ideas, principles and materials into live and enjoyable musical encounters, so that students come to an understanding of the meanings and procedures that constitute the discipline. A strong rationale for music in the curriculum can never be a sufficient condition for effective music education. But it is a necessary condition, since the rationale embodies the ideals, values and aims which, in turn, underpins all practical action and gives point and direction to your work as a professional educationalist.

FURTHER READING

Campaign for Music in the Curriculum (1998) *The Fourth 'R'*, London: Campaign for Music in the Curriculum. This pamphlet reviews research into 'instrumental' justifications for music in the curriculum.

Abbs, P. (1989b) *A is for Aesthetic: Essays on Creative and Aesthetic Education*, London: Falmer. This book offers a wider justification for the arts in the curriculum. The arts are seen as vital symbolic modes of our aesthetic consciousness.

Metcalfe, M. (1987) 'Towards the Condition of Music' in Abbs, P. (ed.), *Living Powers*, London: Falmer. This chapter offers an excellent overview of the place of music in the curriculum from a historical perspective.

2   Musical learning

Chris Philpott

INTRODUCTION

Musical learning is a difficult and complex process. However, it is of fundamental importance for the music teacher to formulate an understanding of the nature of learning in music if they are to plan lessons and schemes of work which enable pupils to become progressively better performers, listeners and composers.

In this chapter we address three broad issues in order to help you build an understanding of how pupils can become better musicians:

- What is there to learn? What is the nature of musical knowledge?
- How do pupils learn? How do they learn what there is to know?
- What is the sequence of this learning? How do pupils develop musically?

OBJECTIVES

By the end of this chapter you should understand:

- how music can be differentiated into different types of knowledge
- how these knowledge types can inform your objectives for the music lesson
- that musical knowledge can develop in both formal and informal settings
- the potential sequences of this development both in the short term and over time
- that the successful musician is able to integrate different types of musical knowledge
- how to maximise continuity and progression over different phases of education
- how learning in music is potentially transferable to other areas of the school curriculum.

Task 2.1 Musical knowledge 1

What different types of musical knowledge have you needed to learn in order to become a successful musician? Think back to your own musical development and try to place these into categories? Discuss this with a colleague and compare ideas.

Music teachers are always engaging with these questions (consciously or not) when deciding what to teach, how to frame learning objectives, how to bring about learning and how to measure learning. To a large extent the learning objectives you choose for your lessons will be dictated by the assumptions behind your answers to the questions above. Much of the work in this chapter has important links with other chapters on language, learning, planning and assessment where we also consider:

- the essential nature of music
- readiness for learning
- the sequence of learning
- the relationship between formal and informal learning
- continuity and progression between phases of music education.

WHAT IS LEARNING?

For the purposes of this chapter learning is defined as having taken place when a change has occurred in pupil behaviour, attitudes or values through the development of knowledge. Learning is not a one dimensional concept; it can be differentiated into types of knowledge. Teaching constitutes the strategies which are used to motivate and sustain an environment to bring about learning, in other words, creating the optimum conditions for learning. Given the complexity of musical learning, there is no more important professional duty for the teacher than that of making meaningful connections between their teaching and pupil learning.

THE NATURE OF MUSICAL KNOWLEDGE

What is there for the musician to learn? What is the nature of musical knowledge? Answers to these questions are particularly important when you are setting objectives for learning in your classroom. Three different types of musical knowledge can be identified, which have been adapted from Reid (1986).

Knowledge 'about' music

This might be referred to as factual knowledge, that is, factual knowledge about composers, about style, about theory, about musical concepts. In the context of the national curriculum for music it is difficult to see how this knowledge type could furnish *all* of the programmes of study. Indeed, the national curriculum with its emphasis on practical engagement, is part of a movement away from an emphasis on factual musical knowledge. However, it is clear that 'facts' have an important role to play in informing our practical engagement with music. Knowing *that* a movement is in sonata form or *that* Mozart was a prodigy or *that* a diminished seventh is a pile of minor thirds can enhance our understanding and enjoyment of music. However, facts about music are only *musical* in as much as they are derived from and related to the sound of music itself. Facts about music are given meaning by real music, without which they are not distinguishable from historical or theoretical (albeit interesting) trivia.

Knowledge 'how'

This could be termed 'know how' and is clearly an important dimension of musical knowledge. Musicians might have 'know how' in the following areas:

- technical know how (knowing how to do this or that on an instrument)
- technical skill (the physical ability to carry this out)
- aural discrimination (knowing how to distinguish between sounds)
- perceptual know how (knowing how to recognise a 'drone')
- presentational know how (how to present a piece to an audience)
- notational know how (reading and writing music)
- craft skills (knowing how to make music sound in a particular way).

Clearly some of these skills are closely linked, for example, an aural dictation exercise can test discrimination, perception and notational know how. It is also clear that learning facts 'about' music without the 'know how' to recognise their embodiment in music can be a sterile process. Some writers such as Fletcher (1987) suggest that the only way to genuine musical understanding is via the development of performing/instrumental skills, that is, learning the craft. This position echoes the views of many writers music educators who feel that 'know how' should form the meat of music education.

Knowledge 'of' music

This form of musical knowledge is a knowledge 'of' music by direct acquaintance (Reid 1986). It implies the building of an understanding relationship with the music (in the same way that we get to know a person or a face). We might not be able to say what we know or even demonstrate it yet the relationship with 'this' piece of music cannot be denied. Indeed, this is the only way that we can account for pupils developing musically *without* any formal music education. Some pupils arrive in Year 7 with a great deal of intuitive understanding; in particular they understand 'their' music and use it to make sense of the world. Clearly our knowledge 'of' music (our understanding relationship with it) is differentiated by 'how' and 'about'. Knowing *that* we are listening to an Irish rebel folk song and knowing *how* to identify the structural elements of course enhances our understanding of the work. However, formal know how and factual knowledge are not *essential* to this understanding. Pupils (indeed all humans) build significant relationships with pieces of music without any formal understanding about the music or how it is put together. This is not to say that their relationship, their knowledge 'of' the music is not underpinned by much *intuitive* 'know how' (see also the chapter on music, language and learning).

Task 2.2 Musical knowledge 2

Complete the following with examples from your own musical knowledge:

1 I know that (Stravinsky was a Russian composer) ....

2 I know that..

3 I know that..

4 I know how to (recognise a tri-tone)...

5 I know how to ....

6 I know how to..

7 I know (Wagner's 'Ring' cycle in the same way I know a person)

    ....

8 I know..

9 I know..

Is it possible to rank these types of musical knowledge in any order of importance? How are they related? Do we need to learn 'know how' before we can really build meaningful relationships with music?

Musical knowledge and objectives for the music lesson

When designing lesson objectives in relation to the knowledge types discussed above Swanwick (1979) argues for the following priorities to be observed:

- Category 1 objectives: for pupils to recognise, identify, understand and use expressive gestures and structures in a range of styles (primarily knowledge 'of' music).
- Category 2 objectives: for pupils to engage in skill acquisition and literature

studies; to assemble and categorise information (mainly concerned with knowing 'how' and knowing 'about').

- Category 3 objectives: for pupils to develop skills in human interaction (co-operation and sharing).

Swanwick is quite clearly saying that developing knowledge 'of' music is the ultimate aim of music education. While he recognises the interrelationships between the knowledge types, he believes that categories 2 and 3 service category 1 objectives, that is, those objectives which aim to develop pupils' meaningful relationships with music. It has been notoriously difficult to plan for category 1 objectives in the classroom. While many music educators have placed knowledge 'of' as an ultimate aim of music education, there has been less agreement on how to achieve it. Metcalfe (1987) has shown that the history of music education is littered with good intentions, yet many music curricula have become reductionist about musical knowledge, that is, assuming that the only way we can teach music is by breaking down the holistic experience into chunks of knowledge 'about' and knowledge 'how'. Writers such as Reimer (1989) have suggested that in order to plan for knowledge 'of' music we must return to the nature of music itself. He asks us to consider how we understand music; what do we mean when we say we know a piece of music? Clearly, such knowledge does not merely amount to knowledge 'about' or 'how' for this would exclude the intuitive musical understandings which pupils bring with them to the classroom.

Task 2.3 Swanwick's hierarchy

How do you feel about Swanwick's hierarchy? To what extent can category 1 develop without 2 or 3? Do we need to learn 2 and 3 before we can achieve in 1? Is it possible to have 1 your overriding priority? What are the priorities of the department in which you are working? Discuss this with your group and/or mentors.

It is difficult to imagine a 'musical' curriculum which only deals with knowledge 'about' music. While some traditional theory classes come pretty close to this the national curriculum, GCSE and A level music courses assume that knowledge 'about' music will be fully integrated with 'know how' at the very least. For example, while it is possible to know about the compositional techniques used by Stravinsky the modern music examination will expect the pupil to recognise these aurally.

The knowledge types in action

Our observations on the different types of musical knowledge and their relationship are clearly important when planning objectives and understanding the potential of

Table 2.1 The knowledge types in action

Knowledge 'about'	Know 'how'	Knowledge 'of'
Rounds, minor, 4 time, counterpoint etc.	Signing in parts, breathing technique, how to recognise minor and counterpoint, beat in 4 time, ensemble skills, performing on an instrument.	The expressive character of the music e.g. the shaping of phrase, rising and falling; potential of different expressive characters, e.g. major and minor, sung as a strident march, sung as a lament.

different activities for delivering these. For example, the simple traditional song (Figure 2.1) can be used with pupils to develop knowledge 'about' music, knowledge 'of' music and the 'know how' of music.

As can be seen from Table 2.1 you can develop your pupils' technical musical knowledge (factual and know how) as well as their knowledge 'of' the music, that is, when building an understanding relationship with the expressive nature of the music.

Task 2.4 The knowledge types in action

Using the example in Figure 2.1 and Table 2.1 as a model, take a simple musical activity such as a song and try to analyse which aspects of the knowledge types can be learned when pupils engage with this work. Try to turn this analysis into a lesson plan with specific objectives in relation to all of the knowledge types.

HOW DO PUPILS GAIN THEIR MUSICAL KNOWLEDGE?

There is little agreement and much controversy on how pupils learn their musical knowledge. However, what is certain is that such learning is complex. Important

Figure 2.1 Traditional song

themes in the debate centre around the role of the 'culture' in musical learning, in other words, what pupils learn in spite of any formal 'instruction'. The following questions have exercised music educators for many years:

- is there any significant relationship between informal, intuitive learning and formal training and instruction?
- is a pupil's informal learning derived from experience of the culture important to music teachers when planning for future learning?
- is it possible to have instruction or training in anything but knowledge 'about' and 'know how'?
- can knowledge 'of' music form meaningful and measurable objectives in a teaching programme?

Some strands in the psychology of musical learning

In order to address some of these questions we can turn to mainstream psychology for guidance.

For example, behavioural psychology can offer us some insight as to how pupils learn knowledge 'about' and 'how'. According to this school of thought behaviour can ultimately be reduced to sets of learnt associations between stimuli and responses. A learning task can be broken down into a series of hierarchically organised stages, and progress through the stages acts as motivation to further success. Feedback, via assessment, is vital to the system as learning is rewarded and reinforced. The main criticism of this work is that while the approach seems to apply to skills ('know how') it fails to account for creativity, composition and improvisation. Behavioural psychology would lead us to value a skills-based ('know how' and 'about') music course, building up an increasingly complex competence reinforced by success.

Task 2.5 Behavioural psychology and technical skills

Devise a lesson on these principles, for example when playing five consecutive notes with the right hand on a keyboard. What activities, tasks and strategies would you use to encourage learning. Share the lesson plan with colleagues.

Writers in the field of cognitive psychology have attempted to deal with all aspects of musical knowledge though a more integrated notion of musical learning. One of the concerns for a cognitive psychology of musical development is the relationship between 'intuitive/cultural' learning and 'formal/instructional' learning (see Table 2.2).

Table 2.2 Some dichotomies of musical learning

'Intuitive/cultural' learning	*'Formal/instructional' learning*
Enculturation	Training
Encounter	Instruction
Informal	Formal
Knowledge of	Know how, knowledge about
Intuition	Analysis
Osmosis, culture is 'caught'	Induction into the culture

Several writers have tried to explain and solve the problematic relationship between the formal and the informal dimensions to musical learning. Sloboda (1985) refers to intuitive musical learning as 'enculturation' which he maintains happens in 'waves' without conscious effort or instruction in the early years of life. The 'formal' aspects of music education are, he maintains, concerned with training and skill acquisition. Skills are formed out of habits which become automatic after repetition. Goals are set which rely on motivation derived from positive feedback. The development of skills is based upon the *if and then* conditions; what he calls a production system. For example, *if* the goal is to play a G on the recorder *and* the fingers of the left hand are on the top three holes, *then* blow and the goal is achieved.

Sloboda deals with the two aspects of musical learning quite separately. He tries to embrace our knowledge 'of' music through our intuitive 'enculturation' and skills ('know how') through training. Sloboda suggests that we cannot progress significantly from the encultured state unless we engage with high level skill development and the role of formal education is to provide this training at various levels. While he does not suggest that we leave knowledge 'of' music behind (indeed he might argue that skills enhance it) it is clear that, for him, a new type of learning takes precedence after initial immersion in the culture.

Swanwick (1988) has also developed a cognitive theory of musical learning which tries to heal the formal/intuitive split in which the knowledge types are integrated into a spiral of musical development. Knowledge 'of', 'about' and 'how' are learned along side each other, hand in hand. However, as we have seen, for him, the first of these is the ultimate goal of all music education at *all* levels. Thus, for Swanwick formal instruction is not merely about the teaching and learning of skills (or know how). Music lessons should contain a productive tension between musical encounters and instruction and between intuitive response and analysis. Unlike Sloboda he believes that enculturation and intuition can be planned for in the classroom and can develop alongside training for skills (see Figure 2.1). For Swanwick knowledge 'of' music is always an essential and fundamental element of all musical learning, that is, we can only make sense of 'know how' and knowledge 'about' music by building meaningful relationships with it.

Implicit in the work of both Sloboda and Swanwick is the important dimension of *social learning*. The role of social learning has crucial implications for music teachers. Clearly all learning, both formal and intuitive, takes place within specific cultural contexts. We are subjected to *models* of musical practice as part of both enculturation and formal instruction. Elliot calls this learning 'procedural knowledge', in other words how to behave musically within a particular culture, and for him, this learning can only develop in conditions where 'real' music is being made in 'real' circumstances. That is, where 'the heart of the music curriculum (is) a musical teacher inducting students in to musical practices through active music making' (Elliot 1995: 285). Plummeridge also takes up this point when he maintains that:

> the central aim of music education is to engage pupils in practical activities through which they will come to learn and internalise the procedures of the discipline. In this way they develop musical thinking. . . . Procedures have to be taught . . . but there is a sense in which they are 'caught' . . . people come to understand the methods, or procedures, of music by working with others who are on the inside of that discipline.
>
> (Plummeridge 1991: 29)

Indeed, in much 'community' based music education, such as brass bands and church choirs learning is based upon a healthy mixture of formal induction into musical practices and the 'catching' of musical learning by 'osmosis', by just being there! The tension between formal and intuitive learning in community music-making is also reflected in the work of Vygotsky who emphasises the importance of social interaction and instruction in learning. Crucial to this theory of learning is what Vygotsky calls the *zone of proximal development*. This term refers to the gap between what a learner can do on her own and what she is able to do with the help of a *significant other* (Vygotsky 1986). In this way, learners move from co-operation to independence. It is the role of the teacher to plan strategies to help move pupils on from an existing knowledge base, towards autonomy in learning.

The implications of social learning for music teachers are as follows:

- the music teacher is a model for his/her pupils which informs their learning
- the models we provide need to be musical and as authentic possible
- pupils bring much social (formal and intuitive) learning with them
- pupils also can be musical models for the learning of others (pupils and teacher)
- the school/classroom can been seen as a community of musical learning.

Many of the musical traditions adopted by recent developments in music education, for example music such as the Gamelan, African music and so on, assume a community, socially based learning model.

The implications of work in cognitive psychology and social learning is for a *constructivist* approach to pupil learning. This approach assumes that learning takes place when existing knowledge interacts with new learning experiences. Learning

Task 2.6 Social learning

What are the implications of social learning for music education and how might the theory influence the way you teach? What are the implications of placing pupils of similar abilities in the same groups for class and extra curricular work? Prepare some notes as the basis for a seminar/discussion.

is not seen as a passive process but an active one in which the learner has a stake in the construction of personal meanings. Pupils need to feel responsible for their learning, and their teachers need to plan learning experiences which support both meaningful development and positive relationships with curriculum content. Constructivism is an integrated approach to the intuitive – formal dichotomy exposed in this chapter.

THE SEQUENCE OF MUSICAL LEARNING

Why do we need a theory of musical development?

We have explored the types of musical knowledge and how these might be learned. We now turn to how pupils develop musically. Why is a theory of musical development important to music teachers? It is your job to develop pupils musically and every time you plan a curriculum your notions of musical development are made explicit, for example in your objectives for a scheme or lesson, when moving from one topic to another (within a particular year) and when planning over a longer period of time (from one year to the next). You can use your theory of musical development (intuitive or otherwise) to

- recognise what it means to be musical
- recognise that some pupils are more or less musically mature than others
- evaluate your teaching: have the pupils made progress? Have they developed?
- help you assess pupils both formatively and summatively, at what levels are your pupils functioning musically?
- understand the relationship between the various knowledge types.

We have identified that musical learning can be both intuitive and formal. Theories of musical development provide you with a framework for understanding the role of both the intuitive and the formal in the musically educated pupil. There is much evidence that intuitive learning seems to precede more formal learning especially in younger pupils and thus a theory of development helps you to decide if you are 'putting the cart before the horse'. It is important to understand when it is most appropriate to teach certain skills or use particular content, for if you get the sequence wrong pupils can become de-motivated and alienated.

The tasks in Task 2.7 asks you to engage with some influential models of development, apply them to practice in your schools and to reflect upon their usefulness.

Task 2.7 Musical development

In Table 2.3 there is a summary of some models of musical and artistic development (these have been simplified for the purposes of the task). After carrying out the following tasks, prepare answers to share with other student teachers in a seminar.

- Identify any broad similarities between the theories.
- Identify any contradictions.
- Does any of the theory confirm or contradict your own experience thus far?
- List some of the musical differences you have noticed among your pupils thus far.

Compare pupils of the same age and also pupils of 11, 14, 16 and 18 years old. Can you characterise their efforts at composition, performance and appraisal? Discuss your observations with the group and draw up a table summarising your findings.

Despite the differences in emphasis between the theories, it does seem that there is sequence to musical development; it is not random. It is, however, important to emphasise that the ages attached to musical development need to be read with considerable caution. You are likely to find pupils of vastly different developmental stages in the same class.

Musical development and the national curriculum for music

There is, of course, an important model of musical development contained within the national curriculum for music, that is, the attainment target for Music. While this is a statutory document it is interesting to see how it has been influenced by other models of musical development from the wider field of music and arts education. For example, there is a sequence of development which moves from the sheer sensory feel for sound (Swanwick's 'materials' phase), to the use of sound for expressive purposes ('expression'), to the conscious patterning of expressive ideas into structure ('form'), through to music having a personal philosophical significance ('value'). We have analysed the statements which make up the national curriculum levels into four themes which can be seen in Table 2.4. Hopefully this will allow you to see the different types of progress pupils can make in the national curriculum.

Each new level shows how pupils have developed a greater range and complexity

Table 2.3 Some models of musical and artistic development

Ages	0–4	5–9	10–15	15 +
Swanwick (1988)	Materials: impressed by the use of extremes of sound, for example dynamics, timbre. Rambling exploration of instruments.	Expression: gross musical gestures for example of loudness to express the words of songs. Later on musical conventions appear, for example metrical 4-bar units.	Form: experiment with structure for example surprise and contrast. Later a desire and empathy with authentic structures from immediate culture, e.g. the pop song.	Value: music becomes special with personal significance. May even become discursive on own and others' work.
Parsons et al. (1978)		Children see artistic objects in terms of their own experience.	Understanding the 'rules' of public use of artistic symbols.	Understanding that a wide variety of traditions and styles exist.
Shuter–Dyson and Gabriel (1981)	Very young children (0–1) react to sounds. Older children (2–3) reproduce bits of songs.	Beginning to understand basic sound elements; discriminating pitch and rhythmic perception.	Perception and skill improvement i.e. tonal and rhythmic. Harmonic sense is established.	Increase in the cognitive and emotional response to music.
Sloboda (1985)	Enculturation: spontaneous acquisition of musical skill. Lack of self-conscious effort and explicit instruction.	Enculturation: children do not aspire to improve their ability to pick up songs yet they do improve.	Training is self-consciously engaged with. Experiences are specific to a subculture but based on the foundation of enculturation.	Training: contributing to a depth of knowledge and accomplish-ment in a narrow skill area. Developed through instruction.
Ross (1982)	Sensory engagement; early relationships to the mood of the music.	Doodling and mastery of sound patterns.	Emergence of musical procedures, conventional competence and association with idiom.	Personal expression, embodying meaning, a vision and significance.

of knowledge. Indeed, the model has been criticised for assuming that musical development can be judged by the acquisition of a greater range and complexity of musical knowledge. It is debatable whether musicianship can be measured in this way. Does this mean, for example, that minimalist 'dance' composers are poor musicians? However, like other models the national curriculum model does provide an important reference point for planning learning objectives and, most crucially, criteria for assessing pupils' work in the difficult areas of listening, performing and composing.

Collecting evidence for the levels

In the chapter on assessment we examine formative and summative assessment in more detail. At this stage it is important to realise that evidence for musical achievement and development can come from a wide variety of sources. You will need to account for the levels of each of your pupils (especially at the end of key stage 3) and write a report summarising their achievement and development. When collecting evidence for the level of your pupils' development you can draw on:

- recordings of pupils' work
- work in books
- pupils' self-assessments
- marks or grades
- comments on notable features of pupils' work when appraising, composing and performing
- worksheets completed
- graphic scores and other 'notations'
- video evidence
- ICT evidence
- other evidence.

Given the ephemeral nature of musical development it is important that you draw on a wide variety of evidence in coming to 'know' your pupils such that you can 'capture' their level of musical achievement. You are now ready to attempt Task 2.8 (overleaf).

Continuity from key stage 2 to key stage 3

The musical development of pupils is important when considering the transition of pupils from one phase of education to another. Progression is dependent upon past learning and at the time of transfer, pupils with diverse experiences of informal and formal education will be in the same class. As secondary teachers you need to manage this transition in learning carefully and sensitively. Mills (1996) has suggested that many secondary music teachers have not facilitated a smooth transition due to their assumptions about the state of primary school music and

Task 2.8 Using the national curriculum levels

Examine the national curriculum attainment targets (Table 2.4). What similarities and differences can you notice in relation to other models of development you have examined.

Use the table to assess the levels of learning in three of your pupils in Years 7, 8 and 9. Draw on all of the evidence you have collected when coming to 'know' these pupils, and remember that pupils might be at different levels in each of the themes. Try to use the language of the levels when writing a sentence or two about their levels of listening, composing and performing. Share your 'reports' with other students or your mentor. (An example might be: 'Alice is able to identify how musical ideas are used for different purposes (level 4), and is developing a useful musical vocabulary when talking and writing about both her own music and the music of others (level 4). Alice is also able to sing in tune and play in time (level 3) from simple notations (level 4).')

What levels do you think are realistic for pupils in each of these years? Does having instrumental lessons make a difference to their achievement?

the musical learning of primary school pupils. She has identified that many secondary music teachers respond to new pupils in one or more of the following ways:

- 'Sheep and goats': music teachers try to identify the musical pupils from the 'non musicians', often in order to furnish extra curricular work.
- 'They do nothing at primary school': music teachers assume that little has happened before secondary school and thus expectations are low.
- 'Back to basics': this is often linked to response no. 2, and some music teachers feel that pupils need a grounding in basic musicianship, usually in notation.
- 'Praise them regardless': again expectations are low and poor levels of work are accepted.
- 'No keyboards before Christmas': the new intake require 'training up' and do not have the necessary skills (social or musical) to cope with practical sessions.

Mills accepts that many secondary music teachers realise that starting at secondary school can be a time of great musical opportunity for pupils and yet according to inspection evidence pupils are often taught by a teacher who expects little of them and who does not provide adequate challenges. There is, she maintains a drop in the quality of teaching which is greater than in any other subject (Mills 1996). This assertion, it must be said, is a reverse of current wisdom found in many secondary school music departments.

There are ways in which the learning opportunities can be maximised in the secondary school following the primary–secondary transfer. The following questions are important to your understanding of this process:

- What can you assume of Year 7 pupils (skills, knowledge)?
- What work might they have they done?
- What activities are they likely to have experienced?
- With which resources are they liable to be familiar?
- What documentation is available in relation to musical learning?
- How do non-specialists feel about teaching music in the primary schools?
- What can I do to help our feeder schools?
- What sorts of things are possible at secondary school but not primary (perhaps for developmental reasons)?
- To what extent does 'enculturation' develop pupils before and after they get to secondary school?

As secondary teachers you need to be proactive in addressing these issues of transfer. You can visit primary feeder schools to observe primary pupils making music. You can develop relationships with primary music co-ordinators. Indeed, some schools take part in joint INSET programmes to set up shared common understandings about teaching and learning in music. It is also possible to encourage joint appointments at both secondary and primary schools, for example through peripatetic staff. Even if records of musical achievement are few, there are other records which can be searched for and welcomed by the secondary school music department, for example schemes of work, lesson plans, materials and so on. Most of all it is important for the secondary music teacher to plan lessons which are suitably demanding and *musical* from day one.

Task 2.9 Primary–secondary transfer

What links are there between the music department in your school and local feeder schools? List the activities and staff concerned. Is there a departmental policy?

What are the first lessons in music like at your school (for example in Year 7)?

What are your views on Mills' evidence?

Discuss these issues and share views and data with your colleagues.

We turn finally to an aspect of musical learning which seems to take on an increasing importance, that is the transfer of learning in music to other areas of human knowledge, skill and understanding.

Table 2.4 Music in the national curriculum – the attainment target

	General statement	Performing skills	Composing skills	Appraisal skills
level 1	Pupils recognise and explore how sounds can be made and changed.	They use their voices in different ways such as speaking, singing and chanting, and perform with awareness of others.	They repeat short rhythmic and melodic patterns and create and choose sounds in response to given starting points.	They respond to different moods in music and recognise well-defined changes in sounds, identify simple repeated patterns and take account of musical instructions.
level 2	Pupils recognise and explore how sounds can be organised.	They sing with a sense of the shape of the melody, and perform simple patterns andaccompaniments to a steady pulse.	They choose carefully and order sounds within simple structures such as beginning, middle, end, and in response to given starting points.	They represent sounds with symbols and recognise how the musical elements can be used to create different moods and effects. They improve on their own work.
level 3	Pupils recognise and explore the ways sounds can be combined and used expressively.	They sing in tune with expression and perform rhythmically simple parts that use a limited range of notes.	They improvise repeated patterns and combine several layers of sound with awareness of the combined effect.	They recognise how the different musical elements are combined and used expressively and make improvements to their own work, commenting on the intended effect.
level 4	Pupils identify and explore the relationship between sounds and how music reflects different intentions.	While performing by ear and from simple notations they maintain their own part with awareness of how the different parts fit together and the need to achieve an overall effect.	They improvise melodic phrases as part of a group performance and compose music by developing ideas within musical structures.	They describe, compare and evaluate different kinds of music using an appropriate musical vocabulary. They suggest improvements to their own and others' work, commenting on how intentions have been achieved.
level 5	Pupils identify and explore musical devices and how music reflects time and place.	They perform significant parts from memory and from notations with awareness of their own contribution such as leading others, taking a solo part and/or providing rhythmic support.	They improvise melodic and rhythmic material within given structures, use a variety of notations and compose music for different occasions using appropriate musical devices such as melody, rhythms, chords and structures.	They analyse and compare musical features. They evaluate how venue, occasion and purpose affects the way music is created, performed and heard. They refine and improve their work.

level 6	Pupils identify and explore the different processes and contexts of selected musical genres and styles.	They select and make expressive use of tempo, dynamics, phrasing and timbre. They make subtle adjustments to fit their own part within a group performance.	They improvise and compose in different genres and styles, using harmonic and non-harmonic devices where relevant, sustaining and developing musical ideas and achieving different intended effects.	They use relevant notations to plan, revise and refine material. They analyse, compare and evaluate how music reflects the contexts in which it is created, performed and heard. They make improvements to their own and others' work in the light of the chosen style.
level 7	Pupils discriminate and explore musical conventions in, and influences on, selected genres, styles and traditions.	They perform in different styles, making significant contributions to the ensemble and using relevant notations.	They create coherent compositions drawing on internalised sounds and adapt, improvise, develop, extend and discard musical ideas within given and chosen musical structures, genres, styles and traditions.	They evaluate, and make critical judgements about, the use of musical conventions and other characteristics and how different contexts are reflected in their own and others' work.
level 8	Pupils discriminate and exploit the characteristics and expressive potential of selected musical resources, genres, styles and traditions.	They perform, improvise and compose extended compositions with a sense of direction and shape, both within melodic and rhythmic phrases and overall form.	They explore different styles, genres and traditions, working by ear and by making accurate use of appropriate notations and both following and challenging conventions.	They discriminate between musical styles, genres and traditions, commenting on the relationship between the music and its cultural context making and justifying their own judgements.
level 9	Pupils discriminate and develop different interpretations.	They give convincing performances and demonstrate empathy with other performers.	They produce compositions that demonstrate a coherent development of musical ideas, consistency of style and a degree of individuality	They express their own ideas and feelings in a developing personal style exploiting instrumental and/or vocal possibilities. They discriminate and comment on how and why changes occur within selected traditions including the particular contribution of significant performers and composers.

THE TRANSFER OF MUSICAL LEARNING

One of the justifications for music in the curriculum is that learning *in* the discipline leads to a good deal of learning *through* it, in other words much can be transferred to other areas of the curriculum and to general development. While you should exercise caution in being over reliant on justifying music in terms of its influence on learning in other subjects, there is some evidence for such effects. It has been claimed that music education might have positive transferable effects in the following areas of the curriculum (Campaign for Music in the Curriculum 1998):

- spoken and written English
- performance in mathematics
- spatial reasoning
- problem-solving and creativity
- performance under pressure
- memory
- team work
- social skills
- morality and attitude
- physical and psychomotor skills
- psychological health
- self-esteem
- perceptual skills
- behaviour.

Task 2.10 The transfer of learning

Can you to add to the list of transferable learning?

Have you experienced/observed any of these transferable effects of learning through your experience of music? How and why do you think this effect has occurred? Try to give specific examples from your own learning or that of pupils at your school. Record what you have noticed and discuss this with another student teacher or with your mentor.

Research into the transfer of learning is in its early stages and thus evidence needs to be read critically, especially in relation to methodology and conclusions.

SUMMARY

- We have suggested in this chapter that musical knowledge is complex.
- Knowledge 'of' music is particularly important in a constructivist approach

to musical learning, when pupils build meaningful relationships with their own music and the music of others.

- It is possible to plan for knowledge 'of' music within an integrated approach to musical development.
- The musical learning of pupils can be both formally and informally developed in all situations and while the relationship between these two is complex it cannot be ignored.
- Studies in the psychology of musical development show us that the teacher is an important model in a constructivist approach to pupil learning.
- An understanding of musical development is vital if you are to plan and assess the development of musical understanding in your pupils.
- Understanding musical development is important when moving pupils from one educational phase to another.
- Finally, learning in music can have important transferable effects to learning in other areas of pupil development, that is, learning through music.

FURTHER READING

Elliot, D. J. (1995) *Music Matters: A New Philosophy of Music Education*, Oxford: Oxford University Press. An important book which explores the role of the classroom as a community in the development of musical knowledge.

Hallam, S. (1998) *Instrumental Teaching*, London: Heinemann. Although aimed at instrumental teaching and learning this book has some vital insights into the complexity of musical learning.

Hargreaves, D. J. (1986) *The Developmental Psychology of Music*, Cambridge: Cambridge University Press. Hargreaves offers a comprehensive overview of psychological issues which impinge on musical learning.

Swanwick, K. (1979) *A Basis for Music Education*, Windsor: NFER-Nelson.

—— (1988) *Music, Mind, and Education*, London: Routledge. These seminal publications develop an influential theory of musical knowledge, learning and development.

3 The national curriculum for music and planning

Chris Philpott

INTRODUCTION

At the beginner teacher stage it is crucial for you to plan thoroughly; researching, selecting and adapting material. To do this you will need to be familiar with the national curriculum for music and there will be times, for example during inspections, when you are held to account for your work in the classroom in relation to this statutory document. Having said this there is much scope for interpretation and you can find many 'flavours' in different schools. There is a sense in which the whole of this book is about planning and the next two chapters deal with this in some detail both from the perspective of the national curriculum (NC) and the needs of particular pupils in a particular context. Themes which arise here are also dealt with elsewhere, such as the use of ICT and differentiation.

THE NATIONAL CURRICULUM FOR MUSIC IN CONTEXT

The national curriculum for music caused a stir during its gestation and subsequent revisions, which we referred to briefly in Chapter 1. There was something of a paradox in that a discipline which had only just 'squeezed in' to the foundation subjects, caused much press coverage with eminent philosophers (O'Hear and Scruton) and musicians (Boulez, Solti and Rattle), joining a high profile debate. The debate was caused by:

- questions about the importance of music in the curriculum
- questions about the nature of music and how we experience it
- wider educational questions about what to learn and the ways in which we learn.

OBJECTIVES

By the end of this chapter you should:

- understand the context of the national curriculum for music
- understand the structure and nature of the current national curriculum for music
- understand a planning framework work in relation to the national curriculum for music
- be clear about the terminology related to planning.

An amusing account of the development of the NC for music has been written by Vincent (1992). However, the main protagonists took up serious stances broadly along the following lines:

> *Music is a highly skilled and noble discipline that not all can fully engage with; however, the best way to develop musically is through studying the Western canon of 'classical' music, learning skills for performance and reading notation, leaving composition to the 'experts'.*

versus

> *Music is an expressive medium for all; the best way to learn is through actively engaging in listening, composing and performing in a wide range of styles and genre and developing technical and notational skills on a need to know basis in the process.*

These two positions mirror debates which have raged through the history of music education (see Metcalfe 1987), and are also linked to wider educational debates which surround progressivism and traditionalism (see Chapter 1), which have a similar long history. The positions are also linked to similar debates in other subjects during the formation of the national curriculum. In English education the debate centred around the literary canon/grammar versus wide-ranging texts/appropriate expression. In History the debate centred on empathy/interpretation versus facts/dates/British history.

As the national curriculum developed, these two positions in music education managed to swing the pendulum of policy back and forth in terms of emphasis, although in fairness the national curriculum for music has always been fundamentally eclectic. These developments in the music national curriculum can be seen in Box 3.1.

It is interesting to note the ways in which the debate influenced the music NC and in particular the changing status of factual/theoretical knowledge. Other notable changes include an apparent simplification (and slimming down) of the document, and the introduction for the first time of prescriptive 'levels', to be used for reporting pupil progress. What is also apparent is the move towards viewing composing, performing and appraising as *skills* rather than activities, and that 'knowledge' needs

Box 3.1 The development of the national curriculum in music

1991 (draft)

Profile component 1: making music
Attainment target (AT) 1 – Performing
AT 2 – Composing

Profile component 2: Understanding music
AT 3 – Listening
AT 4 – Knowing
(At this stage there were levels in each AT)

1991 (later)

AT1 – Performing
AT2 – Composing
AT3 – Appraising

(This represents a position that many found acceptable and which the Welsh Office finally adopted. However, the government were concerned to reduce and simplify, and had taken seriously the call for more 'knowledge' and Western cultural heritage. The levels in each AT had been dropped)

1992

AT1 – Performing and composing: the development of the ability to perform and compose music.
AT2 – Knowledge and understanding: the development of knowledge and understanding of musical history and theory, including the ability to listen to and appraise music.

(A new emphasis on factual knowledge. However, the debate convinced the secretary of state to change his mind and, following professional advice from quarters, we arrive at another version.)

1992 (a little later)

AT1 – Performing and composing: the development of the ability to perform and compose music with understanding.
AT2 – Listening and understanding: the development of the ability to listen to and appraise music, including knowledge of musical history.

(Knowledge and understanding is subsumed into rather more 'practical' version of AT2)

1995

In the 1992 version AT1 was given a weighting of 2:1 in its favour although explicit

Box 3.1 (continued)

reference to this was lost in the slimming down commissioned by Dearing for 1995. End of key stage descriptions are used as levels (3) with non-statutory exemplifications published.

1999

The 'new' national curriculum for music has one attainment target (music) and the 'levels' return for the first time since 1991. These levels are statutory for the first time in music.

Some definitions

Attainment target (AT): defining the knowledge, skills and understandings which might be expected of pupils
Programmes of study (POS): what pupils should be taught to achieve the ATs and the level statements.

Task 3.1 The development of the national curriculum for music

From your knowledge of how the national curriculum came about and by reading Chapter 1, examine the current national curriculum document to identify the influences that shaped it. While it is clearly an eclectic model of music education, trace the elements of other ideologies and positions on (music) education. Use your findings as the basis of a discussion or reflection activity.

---

to be applied across the attainment target in a curriculum which takes an integrated approach to the development of these skills.

THE 'NEW' NATIONAL CURRICULUM FOR MUSIC

The national curriculum (NC) for music has had an important influence on planning for teaching and learning in the music classroom. While open to many interpretations the requirements for music are subject to external accountability, that is when OFSTED inspect school music, and the preparation of teachers in training. Music teachers need to be able to audit their lesson plans and schemes in terms of the NC requirements and teachers in training need to show that they have the knowledge, skills and understanding to deal with them. However, while the NC for music sets *an* agenda for planning, it is by no means the whole picture, for there is still such scope for flexibility. We now turn to an analysis of the nature and structure of the 'new' national curriculum for music.

Common elements in all subject documents

The 'new' national curriculum for music (1999a) contains elements which are common to all subject specific documents, and has statements on:

1   The importance of music.
2   The contribution of music to spiritual, moral, social and cultural education (SMSC).
3   The contribution of music to key skills that is, communication, application of number, ICT, working with others, improving ones own performance and problem solving.
4   The contribution of music when promoting other aspects of the curriculum such as thinking skills, enterprise and entrepreneurial skills and work-related learning.
5   The use of language across the curriculum, that is, writing, speaking, listening, reading in both subject-specific and generic use of language.
6   The application of ICT to support learning when finding out, developing ideas, exchanging and sharing information, reviewing and modifying work.

Task 3.2 The 'common' elements of the national curriculum

Read the sections of the music national curriculum which deal with the common elements of the national curriculum and then complete the following tasks.

- Try to categorise phrases in the statement on 'importance' under the headings of 'learning in music' and 'learning through music'
- What other contributions can music make to SMSC education?
- Create a table in which you audit the contribution of music to the key skills.
- In what circumstances might music contribute to the development of writing, speaking, listening and reading?
- Make a table of how the use of ICT in music might contribute to finding out, developing ideas, sharing information and reviewing work.

Use your findings as the basis for a discussion with other student teachers, mentors and/or tutors.

Another common aspect of all documents is the emphasis on inclusion and the access of *all* pupils to musical achievement (this is dealt with in more detail in Chapter 8). This statement requires that you are proactive in three ways. These are:

Setting suitable learning challenges

'Teachers should aim to give every pupil the opportunity to experience success in learning and to achieve as high a standard as possible' (DFEE 1999b: 24)

- through differentiation
- through suitable challenge
- through flexibility of the POS.

Responding to pupils' diverse learning needs

'Teachers should plan their approaches to teaching and learning so that all pupils can take part in lessons fully and effectively' (ibid.: 25):

- through equality of opportunity
- through a variety of teaching and learning styles
- through sensitivity.

Overcoming potential barriers to learning and assessment for individuals and groups of pupils

'A number of pupils may need access to specialist equipment and approaches or to alternative or adapted activities' (ibid.: 27):

- through accessibility
- through the use of all available senses and experiences
- through adaptation of the learning environment.

These 'principles for inclusion' are a strong statement about the entitlement of *all* pupils to musical experience, achievement and development.

Finally, while there is no explicit reference to citizenship in the music document, music does feature briefly in the national curriculum for citizenship at key stage 3. The latter document requires that 'pupils study, reflect upon and discuss topical political, spiritual, moral, social and cultural issues, problems and events' (DFEE 1999a: 14). Furthermore, pupils should be taught about 'the diversity of national, regional, religious and ethnic identities in the UK and the need for mutual respect and understanding' (ibid.: 14). The cross-reference to music is to the requirement that pupils should study 'a range of live and recorded music from different times and cultures' (ibid.: 21).

While the statutory requirements for citizenship do not commence until September 2000, it is clear that music teaching can have a significant role to play here.

Task 3.3 Citizenship and music

Read the citizenship document and make a list of other possible contributions that music can make to development in this area.

The music-specific content of the national curriculum

The programmes of study (POS) in the music national curriculum, set out what should be taught in music. The NC requires that pupils should be taught the skills, knowledge and understandings such that they learn how to:

- control sounds through singing and playing (performing skills)
- create and develop musical ideas (composing skills)
- respond to and review music (appraising skills).

Pupils should be taught how to listen and apply their knowledge and understanding across these skill areas and 'teachers should ensure that listening, and applying knowledge and understanding, are developed through the interrelated skills of performing, composing and appraising' (DFEE 1999b: 20).

Pupils also need to be taught through a broad range of learning opportunities which include:

- activities in the three skill areas
- activities which integrate the three skill areas
- responding to musical and non-musical stimuli
- working in different sizes of group
- using ICT
- engaging with a wide range of music.

In the margins of the NC document there is 'further information' as a summary of the key stage expectations. There are also comments on links with other subjects, technical definitions and opportunities for ICT, and statutory and non-statutory requirements.

There is one attainment target for music, which sets out the 'knowledge, skills and understandings that pupils of different abilities and maturities are expected to have by the end of each key stage' (DFEE 1999b: 36). As in all subject areas these are described through eight levels with one for exceptional performance. The levels are an assessment tool and a reporting device, which enables you to describe, monitor and report the progress of your pupils. We return to these at other points in this book.

The type of content for the POS for music at all key stages can be seen in Table 3.1. Pupils are expected to develop knowledge and understanding through the three skill areas and to apply this knowledge while engaging with them.

The level of content in each of these areas is, of course, dependent upon the key stage. Indeed, it is important that you become familiar with the other key stages in the music document in order to understand where your pupils have come from. It is also the case that some pupils who are chronologically at Key Stage 3 might need to engage with earlier POS. Task 3.4 will help you to read and understand the change, continuity and progression of content across the key stages.

Task 3.4 Understanding the programmes of study

Use Table 3.2 to plot the change in content across the key stages. Do changes in the level of the content in the POS follow on smoothly from each other?

The QCA are currently publishing exemplar units of work for the NC at all key stages, which they hope will be practical, manageable teaching plans. These documents are non–statutory and if used in school they will need to be adapted for the particular needs of your pupils, as is the case with any published materials or resources. However, it is expected that the practice exemplified will include the following principles:

Table 3.1 The detail of the programmes of study

Performing skills in:
a	singing
b	playing on instruments
c	practising, rehearsing and presenting

Composing skills in:
a	improvisation
b	composition

Appraising skills in:
a	analysis, evaluation and comparison
b	communicating ideas and feelings (musical vocabulary)
c	adapting and refining own and others' work

Listening and applying knowledge and understanding when:
a	discriminating and internalising
b	identifying the 'elements'
c	identifying the musical resources of style, tradition and genre
d	identifying the context of music.

- that lessons and units of work should integrate the skill areas of performing, composing and appraising
- that knowledge and understanding is the basis of the skill areas
- that the skill areas are the means by which knowledge and understanding can develop.

We shall spend some time exploring musical knowledge throughout this book and the ways in which you can develop listening, composing and performing skills. We now turn to some of the 'nuts and bolts' of planning of which the NC for music is an important component.

A PLANNING FRAMEWORK FOR THE NATIONAL CURRICULUM

The detail of the planning framework in Figure 3.1 is given more flesh in subsequent chapters. Advice can also be sought from both the generic book on *Learning to Teach in the Secondary School* (1999), and from the planning documents in your placement school(s).

Short, medium and long-term planning

Long-term planning involves designing the overall content which covers a music programme across an age group *(scheme of work)*. It also involves planning between Years 7–9 such that there is coherent continuity and progression and suitable

Figure 3.1 A framework for planning lessons/units

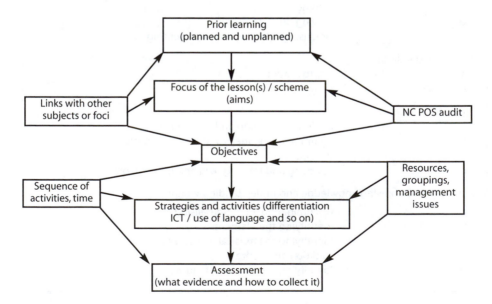

Table 3.2 Auditing the programmes of study

The national curriculum for music			
Knowledge, skills and understanding	*Key Stage 1*	*Key Stage 2*	*Key Stage 3*
Controlling sounds through singing and playing 1 (a) 1 (b) 1 (c)			
Creating and developing musical ideas 2 (a) 2 (b)			
Responding and reviewing others' and own work 3 (a) 3 (b)			
Listening and applying knowledge and understanding 4 (a) 4 (b) 4 (c) 4 (d)			
Breadth of study 5 (a) 5 (b) 5 (c) 5 (d) 5 (e)	*Key Stage 1*	*Key Stage 2*	*Key Stage 3*

coverage of the national curriculum for music. While you will see evidence of this in your placement schools, it is unlikely that you will actually be involved in year planning during the course of your training. Medium-term planning involves designing the individual *units* of work which go into making up the whole year plan (*scheme*). These may last anything from two to eight weeks (maybe longer), and you need to design these in the context of the programme for a particular year group. At first you will need to adapt a school's schemes of work. Both long and medium term planning is relatively inflexible, but the short term plan of the individual lesson is the way in which you can be responsive to the unique developments within each class or group. It is important that the *lesson plan* takes into account the ever changing (and unpredictable) musical development of pupils, and thus is a vehicle for flexibility, individuality and teacher creativity.

Box 3.2 introduces some basic terminology for planning which is taken up in more detail elsewhere.

SUMMARY

> Good planning means that the teaching in a lesson or a sequence of lessons has clear objectives for what pupils are to learn and how these objectives will be achieved. It will take account of the differing needs of the pupils.
>
> (OFSTED 1995: 72)

Plans only become a reality in the classroom and the good lesson, in action, will have many of the following characteristics:

- it is purposeful and has pace
- it has high expectations for pupils
- it allows the pupils to organise some of their own learning, including problem solving and creativity

---

Box 3.2 Planning terminology

Prior interests and learning: an often much neglected area of planning (see Chapter 4).

Lesson/unit focus: this should be short and precise, for example exploring musical change and variation through cover versions, developing compositions based around features of the Javanese gamelan, exploring the influence of social context on the expression and form of the blues.

Objectives: what you expect the pupils to have learned by the end of the lesson/unit (see Chapter 2), for example, to be able to recognise the use of ostinato in a piece of music.

Strategies: the ways in which you bring about learning; the tactics employed (see Chapters 6, 7, 8 and 9).

Sequence: the most appropriate order for activities and strategies (see Chapter 2) and how long these should take.

Management: planning for the organisation of the music lesson for example group size and transition between activities (see chapter 5)

Resources and materials: used to stimulate and support learning.

Assessment: how to recognise the evidence for learning and how to collect and record it (see Chapters 2 and 10).

- it elicits and sustains interest
- it is relevant and challenging
- it develops and extends the pupils
- it is matched to the ability and needs of the pupils
- it includes a variety of strategies and activities
- it is well organised
- it allows pupils to understand the nature of their involvement and the nature of the assessment procedures
  (adapted from Kyriacou 1991, 1998).

Such qualities can only occur on the back of thorough planning, and intelligent adaptation during the process of the lesson itself and the next chapter explores these issues in more depth.

In this chapter we have seen that:

- the national curriculum for music has been influenced by many different sources in its development
- the national curriculum for music is an important framework planning
- the national curriculum for music is open to interpretation.

FURTHER READING

Swanwick, K. (1992) 'Music Education and the National Curriculum', from *London File*, Papers from the Institute of Education, London: Tufnell. This paper offers a critical analysis of the development of the national curriculum for music.

4   Planning to teach music musically

Pauline Adams

Researcher: 'So what's it like to be a pupil?'
Pupil: 'I don't know. I ain't never been a teacher.'
(Kushner 1991: 12)

INTRODUCTION

In order for teachers to plan and implement relevant and effective schemes of work within the classroom, consideration needs to be given to the different ways in which pupils learn, how they relate to teacher-provided materials and respond to varying curriculum approaches.

Since 1992, teachers in maintained schools have provided a music curriculum which has met the statutory requirements of the national curriculum for Music. The revised orders of 1995, and those of 2000, have continued to engage teachers in an ongoing curriculum debate. The design of the national curriculum for Music, with its programmes of study and end of key stage descriptions, has also influenced the way in which teachers plan their schemes of work, although there has been room for flexibility of interpretation regarding teaching content and methodology.

During your teaching experience you are expected to familiarise yourself with the requirements of both the national curriculum and of the schemes of work in your placement school. It is also important that you create opportunities to plan your own units and individual lessons in consultation with your subject tutor and mentor.

TAKING ACCOUNT OF PUPILS' PRIOR EXPERIENCE AND INTERESTS

OFSTED (1993) reported the following findings from observing a number of music lessons in feeder primary schools and their local secondary schools:

OBJECTIVES

By the end of this unit you should:

- be aware of the need to take into account pupils' previous experiences when planning your schemes of work and lesson content
- understand how teaching methodology runs parallel to thorough planning
- be clear about terminology related to planning, such as 'aims', 'objectives', 'progression' and 'differentiation'
- be able to plan a unit of work reflecting a balance of musical activities
- know how to devise effective lesson plans with clearly stated methodology
- be able to evaluate pupil learning and the effectiveness of your teaching.

Some schools involved Year 7 pupils in challenging and exciting opportunities to perform, compose, listen and appraise. Lessons were organised so that pupils could achieve at a high standard, and so that everyone could take part, whatever their previous experience. In these schools the pupils worked with confidence, enthusiasm, and soon started to move beyond the achievement that HMI had observed in the primary schools from which they were drawn. Elsewhere, lessons were often marred by the teachers' underestimation of the pupils' abilities and skills. The teachers had very little knowledge of the pupils' previous experiences, and sometimes set tasks lacking in challenge so that the pupils could not show the same standard of achievement as observed by HMI in the primary schools from which they were drawn.

(OFSTED 1993:10)

The issue of continuity and progression is raised again by Mills in *The Arts Inspected*:

Starting at secondary school often brings pupils new experiences, including the opportunity to work with new resources, in special accommodation, and with some new musicians, both pupils and teachers. However, where the transition between the primary and secondary music curriculum is not managed well, a move to a new school carries a risk that pupils will cease to achieve as highly as they did at primary school, and not make adequate progress during Key Stage 3.

(OFSTED 1998: 68)

Mills also makes some recommendations for schools to consider in relation to the transfer of pupils from primary to secondary school, suggesting 'spreading the good practice found in some primary and secondary schools so that more teachers can benefit from it' and 'promoting a dialogue between primary and secondary schools which takes account of the achievements and difficulties of teachers in both phases, and increases continuity in children's experience of music when they change schools' (Mills 1994: 196).

Although it can be unrealistic for secondary music teachers to gain an awareness of curriculum approaches and content within every one of their feeder primaries, opportunities can be created which allow the exchange of relevant information through meetings, musical encounters, hosted visits and cross-phase projects.

Pressure on primary teachers to give adequate time to the core subject areas of mathematics and English, plus the recently introduced curriculum area of Information and Communications Technology (ICT), may well lead to a reduction in time spent on other subject areas of the curriculum, in particular the arts. Indeed it is the view of some music educators and inspectors that music is 'at risk' within the primary curriculum. Primary schools vary in their commitment to the arts and music, and your Year 7 pupils arrive at secondary school with differing degrees of musical skills and expertise.

When you embark on planning and teaching units of work, it is important for you to set up opportunities for pupils to demonstrate what they already know, and can do, particularly in Year 7, thus giving full value to prior learning. Issues of prior learning are illustrated in the following scenario:

A teacher decides that in the first term Year 7 pupils will focus on the use of ostinato, and so plans a unit of work incorporating some singing and composing activities which use rhythmic and melodic repetition. The first lesson begins with the teacher explaining what an ostinato is, writing the word on the board, demonstrating this device with a musical example, and then teaching a song with an ostinato line. The teacher decides, as this is only Year 7, that the composing task will not include melodic work ('Forget the keyboards, they are not used until Year 8!' or 'We don't start melody percussion work until term 3!') and gives out only untuned percussion. There is no questioning of whether or not the pupils have experienced singing or playing rhythmic and melodic ostinatos before, and no attempt to find out if they have already acquired a way of verbally expressing how this musical device works, or if some possibly know the correct musical terminology for it.

There is no value in the secondary teacher taking the view that children come from primary school with nothing: the 'empty vessels' model. As Mills says in her paper, secondary music teachers should 'focus on what primary pupils can do, and not on what primary teachers can or cannot do when they are teaching music' (Mills 1996: 12).

TAKING ACCOUNT OF PUPILS' MUSICAL EXPERIENCES WITHIN THE WIDER COMMUNITY

Musical concepts, skills and knowledge can be acquired in a variety of settings outside the classroom. Pupils, in their everyday life experiences, tap into the culture of the wider community in a number of ways: instrumental lessons (as individuals or learning within a group), Saturday music centres (run by LEAs and independent bodies), community and cultural centres, clubs, places of religious worship, and so on. Local communities may provide some common and relevant musical experi-

Task 4.1 Finding out what pupils know and can do

Think about an inclusive way of involving pupils when planning for a lesson which introduces, for example, ostinato, graphic notation, contrasts and gradations within dynamics. Consider:

- devising a practical activity which allows pupils to demonstrate musically what they already know,
- setting up appraisal tasks and using open ended questioning to encourage pupils to share knowledge.

Write your notes up as a lesson plan and discuss your thinking and planning with your mentor.

ences on which the teacher can draw. For example, a locally run tap and ballet or Asian dance class allows for musical engagement in precise rhythm work and fosters the keenly focused listening required of dancers to synchronise movement with music.

Ethnic diversity within some communities also plays a part in pupils' arts experiences, often providing them with opportunities to learn something from unfamiliar cultural traditions. Further, pupils may have acquired instrumental and other musical skills which reflect regional or ethnically influenced music enculturalisation, for example: Northumbrian bagpipe playing, or tabla playing. Nor must we forget the influences of newly emerging contemporary styles of music, such as Bhangra music created by British Asians, and crossover styles, as is found in the music of Steve Reich.

TAKING ACCOUNT OF THE WORLD OF MEDIA AND INFORMATION

We can choose the road to discovery in many new and interesting ways, including stepping on to the 'super highway'. Such adventures are available for any of us to explore or ignore. The fact that many teenagers are great consumers of both 'technological' inventions and 'popular' culture can open up musical avenues and possibilities for engaging them in classroom music. The use of music software programmes means that near authentic sound can now be realised when creating music within some styles and genres.

Information and ideas gathered from books, CD ROMs, the Internet, television and radio, friends, visits to various places both local and in a wider geographical sense, all contribute to an individual's body of knowledge and experience. What pupils have sifted from such encounters may be muddled, forgotten, partially accurate or totally inaccurate (Bennett and Dunne 1994: 51), but such media exposure enables them to express their current ideas about a number of topics, including music.

On the other hand pupils may have formed an accurate body of knowledge, and be able to express ideas about their experiences when offered the opportunity. For example, a primary teacher played an extract from Vivaldi's *Four Seasons* to a class of five and six year olds without introducing it by name. She then asked the children what they thought about it, at which point a child volunteered the information that the music was called *Spring*, that it was written by Vivaldi and that his mum played 'that music in the car'. The Nigel Kennedy recording of Vivaldi's *Four Seasons* had brought popularity to this music of another time and place. Such music can now even enter the charts! It can register in the mind of a five year old who has as yet no historical or stylistic concept of Vivaldi's music but who knows that music can have a title, that people can create music, and that the same music can be heard in different places: in this case in the car and at school. The teacher was surprised by the response, but commented on how much this exchange had taught her in terms of allowing children to tell us what they already know.

School is only one setting in which young people gain their knowledge, experience and view of the world. Pupils' voices need to be heard and teachers need to listen.

It might be argued that it is hard enough to design a meaningful and relevant curriculum within the constraints of changing political dogma. The challenge too for the secondary teacher is to reconcile their own teaching agenda with the different life perspectives of the teenager and emerging adult. Perhaps such reconciliation is not totally possible, but an awareness of the wider issues surrounding the school curriculum should influence the way in which teachers approach curriculum design. While a teacher's job is to educate in the true sense of the word, leading pupils to new areas of learning and discovery, space needs be created for their own process of continuing education to run alongside that of their pupils. Teachers too can be led to new and exciting places.

TAKING ACCOUNT OF PUPIL DIFFERENCES

Planning for learning requires a recognition of differences in pupils' abilities, experiences, cultural backgrounds, interests and motivation across different classes and year groups.

You also need to consider gender and equal opportunity issues in order to ensure equal access to learning and resources.

Each pupil is a unique individual and the challenge for the teacher is to try to ensure that each can develop their full potential. The development of sensitivity and awareness, when working with groups of pupils, is crucial to gaining a sense of the needs of individuals.

Schools group pupils in a variety of ways, working to different educational agendas. Those which emphasise the minimising of differences may opt for mixed-ability grouping, with a range of ability, experience and interest spread across each group. Some schools use setting by ability for subjects such as English and mathe-

Task 4.2 The formative musical experiences of adults

Discuss the former musical experiences of colleagues, both those who have undergone music degree training and others who have not. Make a note of musical interests and skills gained from school-based activities and those acquired in some other way. Tease out the key influences which have been formative in creating a desire to pursue music further in some way. These could include:

- being influenced by a particular teacher
- being offered instrumental tuition at school
- participating in a school ensemble/ band
- participating in and/or enjoying live music at concerts and gigs
- attending a borough-led music centre for extra instrumental lessons
- being a member of a county youth ensemble/ steel band/ choir
- learning an instrument through private tuition/ from a teach-yourself tutor/ from listening to radio, cassettes and CDs
- interactive music software programmes.

You can make further additions to this list.

Relate your findings to your own experiences.

In order to gain a broader picture it may be useful to share your findings with other beginning music teachers or with other student teachers in your school.

matics, but retain mixed ability grouping for some other subjects, often including the arts. Banding is another way of grouping pupils, placing them in broad ability groupings. Streaming places pupils in particular ability bands for all subjects, the high achieving pupils in the top band graduating to the lowest achievers in the bottom band. There are arguments for and against streaming, the strongest argument against being the 'vicious circle of lowered teacher and pupil expectations concerning what they (the pupils) are capable of' (Kyriacou 1998: 42). One obvious example of pupils of (so-called) low ability achieving in music is when other subject teachers express surprise at a 'labelled' low achiever performing well in the school concert, with comments such as, 'I didn't know he could concentrate for that long' or 'I didn't know she could play the guitar, and quite well too'.

The inclusive music room can provide a haven for some of those pupils who feel disqualified from achieving in other areas of the curriculum. It can be a place where both self respect and self confidence through musical activity are positively encouraged. Promoting inclusivity across a whole range of ability and experience within any group requires careful planning, with differentiated teaching approaches and support materials prepared in advance of the lesson.

Table 4.1 may be helpful to you when planning for differentiated learning. The

Table 4.1 Differentiation in planning

Kyriacou (1998: 43) draws on the work Stradling and Saunders (1993) to define five different types of differentiation	Comparative musical examples phrased in the context of learning about the blues
Differentiation by task, where pupils cover the same content but at different levels.	Differentiation by task, where in a whole class arrangement, some pupils play a simple bass line, some play chords and others play the melody.
Differentiation by outcome, where the same general task is set, but is flexible enough for pupils to work at their own level.	Differentiation by outcome, where all pupils improvise over the blues chord sequence but at their individual levels; or as a group, creating their own arrangement of the blues.
Differentiation by learning activity, where pupils are required to address the same task at the same level but in a different way.	Differentiation by learning activity, where pupils are encouraged to move from playing block chords to using arpeggio techniques; or developing rhythmic interest in the bass line.
Differentiation by pace, where pupils can cover the same content at the same level but at a different rate.	Differentiation by pace where pupils, once they are secure playing the simple bass line, are then introduced to the technique of playing two or three note chords.
Differentiation by dialogue, where the teacher discusses the work with individual pupils in order to tailor the work to their needs.	Differentiation by dialogue, where the teacher discusses pupils' ideas and musically demonstrates models for further development, for example, learning a better technique in order to play chords more fluently.

generic statements in the left hand column have been used as the basis for a range of activities within a 'blues' unit.

In music lessons pupils' learning experiences can be approached and structured in a number of ways, taking into account different ways in which pupils learn. Interest and engagement can be fostered by talking, questioning and explaining, demonstrating and presenting musical models on which pupils can base their own work, and by creating opportunities for pupil-based practical music-making, where different kinds of tasks and challenges are designed to help them to consolidate and build on what they already know and make sense of what is new to them. There has to be room too for innovation and discovery, and for what is novel to the pupil. Your planning should consist of all of these approaches, applying the maxim 'Music education should be mainly concerned with bringing children into contact with the musician's fundamental skills of performing, composing and listening' (DES 1985:2).

PLANNING FOR WHOLE CLASS, GROUP OR INDIVIDUAL ACTIVITIES

Whole class

Whole group activity is often a good way to start a lesson. Songs, circle activities, fixed arrangements with improvisation opportunities, ensure that you can observe all the pupils. Circle activities in particular give opportunity for eye contact with every pupil, a recognition and acknowledgement of each individual's presence in the room. Such activities can also revise, recap and extend material already being undertaken as work in progress, or introduce new material and ideas. Whole class involvement with an arranged piece, or an interpretation of a graphic score, can allow for different skills and levels of learning and promote discussion about interpretation, as well as critical analysis of performance. Such activities may be set up so that all can succeed.

A useful model of whole class teaching is the brass band tradition found within former mining communities, where beginners were involved from the outset by being given simple and manageable parts, learning at weekly rehearsals from more experienced players. Indonesian gamelan players learn in much the same way. As Swanwick remarks, 'music education is only one strand of experience in a web of social activities and community values' (Swanwick 1988: 90). The value we place on such communal pursuits allows us to celebrate engagement in pleasurable human activity.

The construction of meaning is related closely to shared learning experience as viewed by Bruner (1986): 'I have come increasingly to recognise that most learning in most settings is a communal activity, a sharing of the culture'. Vygotsky's (1986) concept of the 'zone of proximal development' refers to the gap between what an individual can do unaided and alone and what is possible if help is given by those more knowledgable. Such theories clearly favour the shared music curriculum, where pupils can engage in group composing, arranging and conducting, whole class singing and performing, and where the teacher participates fully as musician and musical model.

Small group

Small group work is one way of allowing pupils to experiment with and develop their own ideas, share their knowledge and skills, and discuss the effectiveness of their music. Pupils in such group settings are permitted to take ownership of their creations. It is, however, the responsibility of the teacher to monitor such activities carefully, taking on an advisory role. Encouraging experimentation, developing and refining ideas, and guiding practice and rehearsal techniques are all important features to be considered when planning for teaching, particularly when the teacher is circulating around the different groups, and pupils are left to work on their own.

When planning for group work you need to think carefully about how you are going to build progression into a group task which may span two or three weeks. In her paper 'Reframing curriculum design', Major warns against pupils viewing group work as 'just another task' and thinking that 'any solution will do'(Major 1996:185). Progression may be interpreted in a number of ways, for example: learning specific musical skills; refining a performance by listening to the overall balance of the different parts; developing compositional ideas in terms of structure and form; rejecting and selecting musical ideas to achieve a musically satisfying composition; introducing some novel feature such as improvisation within a fixed composition. Progression also requires the teacher to be proactive in ensuring that pupils can acquire the skills and knowledge they need to carry out set tasks. Theoretical models linking musical expectations to different stages in child development provide a useful framework for considering progression when planning.

Any planned musical activity requires you to consider your own role as teacher observer and teacher facilitator. The monitoring of individual pupils over a number of lessons allows you not only to assess pupil learning in relation to intended outcomes but also to observe what other musical ideas, skills, creativity and originality are brought to the work.

Individual

There are times when individual activities may be appropriate, such as when listening to and appraising recorded music, or evaluating a composition or performance. Such opportunities allow a personal response to sound, a private moment to engage with feelings, or serve as an occasion for making an individual statement in the form of a composition or a performance. It is taken for granted that artistic creation is often an individual activity. Composers, painters, sculptors and writers often work alone. The GCSE music syllabus provides pupils with a number of opportunities for individual work, and you may think about encouraging pupils, particularly in Year 9, to undertake some composing and performing tasks on their own, as good preparation for these activities at GCSE level.

MANAGING A PLANNED LESSON

Good teacher organisation and preparation, with clear learning objectives and motivating teaching material, is essential if the lesson is to succeed.

The classroom is a busy place and as a student teacher you will need to have your teaching methodology written down and in front of you for reference. This the 'how' of your teaching, and should include:

- organisational strategies
- timing of different activities
- resources needed and how they are to be presented and made accessible.

When planning and structuring lessons you need to think about grouping pupils in a way suited to the activity and to your intended outcomes. Do you want them to sing and play an arrangement as a whole class, before dividing them into groups to arrange their own versions? Would this strategy be helpful, by giving them some starting ideas and you a point of reference when discussing their work with them?

Your planning also needs to take account of the setting in which pupils are working, as a whole group, in small groups, or individually.

Task 4.3 Managing observation of learning

During your school practice observation period focus on one or two groups of pupils over a period of two weeks. Make notes on the following:

- their understanding of the task
- the range of musical skills within a group
- how pupils talk about the set task and their music
- the resources used to support the learning
- request for teacher support and the kinds of questions asked
- changes made to their work and how these decisions are made
- examples of pupils helping pupils with skill learning, such as playing a particular rhythm accurately
- strategies adopted for practising their pieces, particularly sections which do not work
- pupils discussing ways of developing and extending their ideas
- pupils who need some technical help
- pupils not making any progress over the two weeks and others who could achieve much more
- difficulties around personalities, such as leadership disputes
- any interventions you made and your reasons for doing this.

Keep a record of these observations for discussion with your mentor and as the basis for an approach to your own planning and teaching.

THE NATIONAL CURRICULUM AND PLANNING

The Statutory Orders for Music (England and Wales) were first published in 1992, revised in 1995 and re-revised for implementation in September 2000 (see Chapter 3).

The Orders apply to all maintained schools, including foundation schools, in England and Wales. Independent schools are not required to teach the national curriculum but many refer to the document in order to structure their own planning and teaching. Teachers are required to devise schemes of work which set out the learning across a key stage.

The structure of the national curriculum for music is defined under the headings Programmes of Study(POS) and Attainment Target and Level Descriptions (see also Chapter 3).

The POS define the areas of learning for pupils which should be taught with reference to:

- controlling sounds
- creating and developing musical ideas
- responding to and reviewing own and others' work
- listening and applying knowledge and understanding
- breadth of study across the key stage.

Music curriculum design should ensure that by the end of KS3 all pupils have developed broad and balanced knowledge, skills and understanding in these areas. Teachers are also required to consider how they ensure that 'knowledge , skills and understanding are developed through the skills of performing, composing and appraising' (DfEE/QCA 1999b: 6). There is also an emphasis on 'breadth of study', which in music should include a wide range of musical styles from different times and places, and opportunities to listen to live and recorded music. You need to plan accordingly, making it clear on your lesson plan which programmes of study you will be covering. It is easy to overload your plan with too many programmes of study when you are teaching music in a more holistic way rather than through a compartmentalised approach. You need to tease out the POS which are most significant in relation to the learning objectives for any particular lesson.

PLANNING FOR EFFECTIVE TEACHING

All music departments have the freedom to devise their own schemes of work and lesson plans which reflect:

- teachers' own creative ideas and areas of musical expertise
- pupils' differing needs and interests
- the selection of suitable and appropriate published resource material,
- NC requirements while at the same time preserving autonomy.

The scheme of work devised within a music department is usually broken down into units. This is now an established way of organising the curriculum in secondary schools, and provides teachers with opportunities to ensure broad and balanced activities over a number of weeks. A Year 7 unit may last four or five weeks, covering a half term's work, whereas a unit devised for Year 9 may last a whole term. Longer projects allow pupils time to develop their own ideas and maximise their musical skills within the units, encouraging depth as well as breadth within the teaching. It might be argued that while the school curriculum follows its present structure, one which was 'essentially created by the nineteenth century, following some eighteenth century models, and retaining the medieval curriculum at its centre' (Hargreaves 1982: 155), it will always be a challenge to the music teacher to ensure deep and meaningful learning in such a creative and expressive art as music. Hargreaves believes that all pupils should benefit from more time being spent on the expressive arts, and that the arts should be viewed as essential to the core curriculum. This challenge still remains for music teachers, constrained as they are by time and resources: to avoid surface learning in favour of organising worthwhile musical experiences. As Bannon and Cox observe, 'Music teachers tend to see large numbers of classes across the whole range of age and ability for a small amount of time: many see between 400 and 600 pupils per week on this basis' (Bannon and Cox 1997: 259). How many teacher-initiated musical activities take place outside the constraints of the curriculum, supplementing and enhancing the range of musical experiences for motivated pupils? You may wish to discuss, with your mentor, ways of managing these two distinct strands of the same job.

PLANNING A UNIT OF WORK

A unit should have an overall aim. The aim does not detail the how and what of the teaching but, in as succinct way as possible, summarises the focus of the whole unit. The wording should be kept short and precise. The learning and assessment objectives for each of the lessons taught within the unit define the specific skills and knowledge areas to be undertaken by the pupils.

Here are some examples of suitably worded aims:

- to improvise and appraise 12 bar blues
- to explore musical contrasts and develop an awareness of the potential of graphic notation
- to develop a working knowledge of melodic line and harmonic accompaniment
- to develop composition based on features of the Javanese Gamelan tradition.
  (ACAC 1997)

Figure 4.1 shows an exemplar for a unit plan. The title, aim, relevant prior learning and overall resources are clearly stated. Devising such a 'cover sheet' allows you to create a unit title which may appeal to pupils, clearly define your overall aim, consider relevant prior learning experience to be drawn on and extended, and consider, in advance, the resources you need to gather in order to teach the unit.

You naturally bring your own subject knowledge and research to your unit planning, but you have to adapt and revise this in relation to the range of ability and prior musical experience within the year group you are going to teach. You need to ensure that you have researched areas with which you are not familiar, drawing on a range of published material and selecting and modifying what you think may work best with your pupils. You should also be aware of how musical learning may integrate with learning in other curriculum areas.

During the induction period in your teaching practice school you should observe your mentor teaching the departmental scheme of work. At this time you should begin to think about how you are going to plan for the different year groups that you are going to teach. Make sure you obtain a copy of the scheme of work before

Figure 4.1 Exemplar unit plan

UNIT PLAN

Unit Title: Shaping the Music

Duration of Unit: Four Weeks   *Class*:   7B

Aim: To explore musical contrasts and develop an awareness of the potential of graphic notation

Prior learning relevant to the unit

Before commencing this unit pupils should have experienced the following:

- recognising and identifying a range of tuned and untuned percussion instruments through listening
- handling and playing these instruments musically, exploring a range of playing techniques and sharing and talking about the sounds
- exploring the voice in unusual ways.

Resources:

- tuned and untuned percussion
- any additional instruments, such as strings, wind or keyboards
- graphic score
- recorded extract and pupil copies of extract taken from score.

(ACAC 1997)

---

you begin to work on your planning. Your unit plans should complement the already existing schemes of work within your school.

LESSON PLANNING

When considering your planning take into account the length of the lesson and the resources available to you. The following examples show how to write objectives into a lesson plan and are written in terms of what pupils ought to be able to do. This strategy directs and supports assessment criteria.

By the end of this lesson the pupils should be able to:

- improvise over a simple harmonic sequence
- recognise a changing ostinato within a piece of music
- arrange and perform a simple harmonic accompaniment to a song

Task 4.4 Finding out about schemes of work and discussing and refining your own planning

Discuss the music scheme of work with your mentor.

- Talk about some of the work you have seen that might influence your own planning.
- Find out how closely you need to keep to the scheme of work.
- Ask if you can bring your own ideas to your planning, and discuss some of the departmental resources you will wish to use or indeed others you may be able to bring to the lessons.
- Share your lesson ideas in order to test them out against experience.
- Offer your own musical skills as a resource.

During your observations, write down the musical areas pupils are studying in the different year groups, for example: ostinato, simple harmony, or musical styles such as blues, gamelan traditions and minimalism.

Observe and list different ways in which musical material and ideas are presented to pupils, for example:

- whole group activities
- small group composing/arranging
- individual appraising using written responses.

Keep a record of your findings to inform your own planning, teaching and classroom management.

- compose in the medieval style, using modes and drones
- listen to and appraise a range of blues extracts.

Design or use an already formatted template on which to write your lesson plans. Figure 4.2 (overleaf) is an example of such a template.

Care should be taken not to overload a lesson with too many objectives but to ensure that pupils are able to achieve those set. At the same time work should be interesting and challenging, thus allowing pupils to extend their knowledge, skills and interests. You also need to prepare extension ideas and further challenges before you teach the lesson.

Pupils should be made aware of the lesson objectives so that they are clear about your expectations, but you must also allow some flexibility for them to bring their own interpretations and ideas to their work. Skills of independent learning are useful in all walks of life and such flexibility encourages the development of personal autonomy in learning. To help pupils remember lesson objectives they can be written on the board before the beginning of the lesson. You may need to refer to such written expectations at various points during the lesson in an encouraging and constructive way.

Figure 4.2 Exemplar lesson plan

NORMAL LESSON PLAN

Unit Title: Working in Harmony   *Class*: Year 8

Date: 27 February   *Lesson*: 1 of 3

Duration of lesson: 1hr 10mins

Learning and Assessment Objectives:	POS
Pupils learn to sing a song and create their own arrangement of it using given chord symbols	1a, 2b, 5b

Time	Task	Assessment Focus	Resources
9.15	Whole class learn the song *Zion, Me Wan Go Home* Discussion of meaning of words, context and style		Teacher's copy of the song to hand
9.25	Whole class sings and follows written score of the song including melodic line, and chord symbols. Discussion about resources to be used for accompaniment		Pupils' copy of the song to be handed out
9.40	Working in groups, pupils create their own vocal or instrumental arrangement of the song	Small group arranging	A selection of tuned and untuned instruments
10.05	Groups perform and appraise work in progess		

Adapted from ACAC (1997)

The teacher has to ensure that pupils can access the tasks set which is another reason for assessing prior knowledge at the beginning of a unit. Providing a range of options from which pupils can make choices is a way of ensuring that all are able to participate.

Learning and assessment objectives should be linked to what the pupils are actually doing, whether they are singing or playing, composing or arranging, appraising or performing. It is through these activities and your responses to their achievements, that learning takes place. Lessons should be structured in such a way that activities are connected and allow for progression. For example, if you decide to start the lesson with a whole class 'warm-up' activity you need to ensure that the musical aims and content of this relate to the rest of the lesson and are not isolated from the main focus of the learning. Such activities can also have built into them a range of complexity, thus challenging pupils, allowing experimentation and encouraging them to reflect on and define their own achievements.

Music lessons vary in duration, but in most schools the average length of a lesson is about one hour. This time allocation will affect your planning, the number of activities you can organise and the objectives you can set. For example, short lessons which last only thirty to forty minutes may present difficulties with organising group work and allowing time to provide important feedback to pupils about their work and progress. Recording music on cassette may therefore be a good way of ensuring time for whole class discussion about work in progress or final outcomes in a subsequent lesson. A lesson lasting an hour or more can allow time for pupils to experiment with and develop musical ideas. The management of practical activities and resources also has to be taken into account when planning. The setting up of the classroom beforehand, with all resources to hand, is crucial in maximising the short time allocated to curriculum music in the majority of schools.

RESOURCES

The starting point for resources and materials are those contained in the department of your placement school. At first these will define what is possible in your classroom. Good quality resources need to be chosen in order to support the delivery of your learning objectives. In our experience it is relatively uncommon that any published set of resources fully serves the individual needs of your classes, groups and individuals. Clearly many published resources are important in saving music teachers vital time, yet the only reason for using them is because they are right for a particular set of circumstances.

It is also most important that you begin to develop your own materials and resources (for example, worksheets), and many of the tasks in this book allow you to do this. As you get to know your classes you will be able to tailor these resources to the specific needs of pupils in your classes.

Task 4.5 A review of published resources

Choose a published resource (this can be repeated for others) from your school or the library and carry out an audit using the following headings:

Title, Author, Publisher, Date

Intended age group, range and coverage

Format(s)

When to use, user friendly aspects

Problems, issues

Adaptability, any useful additions / changes

Verdict/usefulness

EVALUATING YOUR OWN TEACHING AND THE PUPILS' LEARNING

Adopting the reflective practitioner model encourages you to ask questions about your own effectiveness as a professional within the classroom. You need to know that pupils have left your classroom having learned something new, or having been changed in some way by the activity in which they have been engaged. Without naming pupils, you can usefully write up one or two short case studies after each lesson which analyse differing levels of response to the work. Evaluating your own teaching is an essential part of your training and of your ongoing professional development. As you become more proficient in the classroom your concerns and focus change and your evaluations should reflect this development. We now can offer some guidelines for the evaluation of your taught lessons

Evaluating the lesson: some questions to ask yourself about your own teaching and about pupils' responses

How well did pupils achieve the lesson objectives and what evidence can I provide about individual achievement?
Check understanding of the lesson objectives in discussion and observe individual pupil response as they undertake set tasks. Pupil achievements form the basis of their various assessments and you need to gather evidence in the form of cassette or video recordings of practical music-making alongside written work and scores.

How effective was the differentiated planning achieved by set task and by outcome?
You need to make clear your expectations, such as occurs when there are set task

outcomes. You should consider how you encourage and support pupils in activities such as composing, where outcomes vary in quality and reflect individual or group responses.

How did I further engage pupils who found the work easy and manage and support pupils who were not engaging in the lesson or found the work difficult?
You need to have considered these possibilities when planning your lesson but also need to develop your overall awareness within the classroom, knowing what each pupil is doing.

Were my instructions clear and my use of language appropriate?
If pupils are asking too many questions about what they are supposed to be doing or failing to get on task quickly, you need to consider the way in which you have introduced the work. You also need to be aware of pupils for whom English is an additional language or who may have special needs with the spoken and written word.

Evaluating the unit: some questions to ask yourself about the overall effectiveness of the unit

How well did your planning ensure a range of musical activity with continuity and progression for individual pupils?
Consider how you provided links and connections for the pupils from one lesson to another, and ensured differentiated and appropriate tasks.

How successful were you in employing a range of teaching strategies appropriate to the age, ability and interest of the pupils?
You may reflect on your role as teacher and facilitator and on your ability to frame questions and interpret pupil response. Pacing and timing of activities is also an important area to consider when evaluating your teaching.

Were printed teaching materials clear and did they appeal to the pupils?
Consider the range of questions, the clarity of any explanations, and illustrations and the overall success of the material in relation to the set task.

Were there any equal opportunity issues to consider in terms of distributing resources or issues concerning pupil attitudes towards others in whole class and small group work?
You may consider how proactive you were in your management of any inequality issues during the lesson and whether or not your strategies were effective.

What would you do differently planning the unit again?
Such consideration can lead to refining of ideas, reworking of future teaching materials, consideration of effective use of resources and useful ongoing discussion with your mentor and trainee colleagues about classroom management strategies.

Planning for teaching is a time-consuming activity, and you may change and

Task 4.6 Comparing responses of two different classes in the same year to the same unit

What was the range of ability, skills and interest within each class?

Did you adapt your teaching or material in any way for one or both of the classes?

Review your own relationship with each of the classes with reference to class management and teaching strategies.

Identify some of the external factors which may have affected the realisation of your teaching plan.

Write a short report (not more than one side of A4) comparing and contrasting the responses of the two classes.

rework your ideas and approaches as you prepare different units and lessons for same different groups. As your classroom management skills develop alongside knowledge of your pupils, so your own confidence grows, and you will begin to teach the material you have planned with a new flexibility. Plans are frameworks, and are inorganic until the moment you present the ideas and materials to the pupils. They can then be transformed and transcended as they become reality. It is at this moment that your planning comes alive!

A SUMMARY OF THE KEY ISSUES AFFECTING PLANNING

Planning should acknowledge:

- prior musical experience and knowledge
- the need to select relevant and motivating teaching materials
- the challenge of classroom management in the teaching of music
- the need for good organisation of whole class and small group work
- the benefits of effective employment of musical resources in the classroom
- the desirability of providing opportunities for homework and extension activities
- the need for awareness of equal opportunities: gender, culture and anti-racist teaching.

Teachers are constantly reviewing current practice. This may be done on an individual level by personal evaluation, but it is also good to share practice with your subject tutor, your course tutor and other student teachers. Finally, keeping up to date through professional and academic literature is an important aspect of your professional development and ensures that you engage with current good practice.

FURTHER READING

ACAC Curriculum and Assessment Authority for Wales (1997), *Music, Optional Test and Task Materials* developed by P. Adams, J. Coplan and K. Swanwick in consultation with the Curriculum and Assessment Authority for Wales, Cardiff: ACAC. These materials are exemplars of planning to teach music musically.

Kyriacou, C. (1991) *Essential Teaching Skills,* Cheltenham: Thornes.

—— (1998) *Effective Teaching in Schools*, Oxford: Blackwell. These books offer much excellent practical and generic advice on planning.

5   The management and organisation of music lessons

Chris Philpott

INTRODUCTION

This chapter discusses aspects of the management and organisation of pupils in the music classroom. There are many generic issues addressed in *Learning to Teach in the Secondary School* (Capel, Leask and Turner 1999), which do not need to be rehearsed here but to which you should refer. We now cover those aspects of management and organisation which are particularly pertinent to the teaching of music. Behaviour management is a concern to all student teachers and of particular concern in a practical subject such as music.

Behaviour management and the associated concepts of discipline and control have become popular topics in the media and we are often told that behaviour is poorer than it used to be. Given the added concerns of parents, it is understandable that students are worried about classroom management, especially in the early days of teaching practice. Indeed, there is a common assumption that one must control a class before one can teach it. This, we shall argue is a fallacy for it is through the effective teaching of the subject that pupils can be induced to behave well. Many of the causes of misbehaviour can be pre-empted if the music lesson is:

- well planned
- well prepared with, for example, stimulating resources
- interesting
- suitably differentiated
- musical.

We deal more fully with these issues elsewhere in this volume.

Student teachers bring with them a love for their subject and the passion and enthusiasm for communicating this is the most useful tool you possess when you first enter training. Trying to control a class *without* the subject is often more than the inexperienced teacher can handle. In the case of music it is clear that making music invites and requires its own discipline. However, deciding *not* to engage in practical work under the guise of 'getting them under control' can do more harm than good, for example, poor motivation of pupils which can lead to poor behaviour. You *can* engage your pupils in music to both control and motivate them! This decision can be a frightening leap of faith, and we are not suggesting that dealing with composing and performing activities is always easy, but this strategy will pay dividends if carefully planned and managed.

THE PRACTICE AND MANAGEMENT OF WORKING WITH THE WHOLE CLASS IN MUSIC

In this setting you are likely to use written work, discussions, class ensembles, singing, listening and combinations of these.

The classroom ensemble

We suggest that all of the skills required for the management and organisation of any musical rehearsal are equally applicable to whole-class music-making, whether instrumental or vocal (see also Chapter 7).

As with all rehearsals seating arrangements such that all players and singers can see and be seen are very important. Music classrooms which are physically flexible are easier places to solve these types of problems. For example, it might be possible to move desks out of the way to set up the class 'band'. Once tables are out of the way the class can be organised in a horseshoe shape (or concentric horseshoes) such that the communication so vital to conducting a rehearsal or performance can take place without bodies or equipment in the way. Even if there is nowhere to put tables they

---

OBJECTIVES

By the end of this chapter you should be able to:

- understand some strategies for the management and organisation of whole class work, i.e. class ensemble and singing
- develop some strategies for conducting classroom discussion
- understand the importance of the physical set up of the classroom in managing the music lesson
- understand the importance of musicianship in classroom management
- place behaviour management in the wider context of effective teaching
- understand some strategies for the management and organisation of group work
- understand how to promote a safe classroom.

can be arranged such that you minimise the rows and columns which might hamper effective communication. Space can, of course, be a problem in the music classroom and it is not always possible have ideal arrangements when there are pupils, teacher and much (often bulky) equipment to fit in. For this reason some heads of music have done away with tables all together. As teachers we need to strive for the best compromise in terms of space and effective communication with the 'band' (see Figure 5.1).

Figure 5.1 Arranging the classroom for ensemble

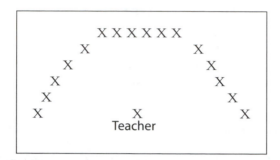

Task 5.1 Setting up the classroom

How do your mentors set out the class for whole class ensemble work? Draw some plans and share these with the rest of the college group. Which arrangement do feel is most appropriate for this type of work?

We will discuss the distribution of instruments later. Once these have been given out a serious concern with the class ensemble, band or orchestra is how to stop the pupils 'doodling' while others are rehearsing or talking. Given that this can be a problem for professional musicians we need to be philosophical about this when dealing with our pupils! Much of the solution lies in setting up clear expectations and constantly reinforcing these. For example, we might establish a rule of 'beaters down' while not playing or an agreed signal for 'stop playing', for example, the teacher puts a hand in the air. Reminding your pupils of these rules will establish a routine providing you are consistent in your application of them. Electronic instruments can be a particular problem unless the music room is fitted with a master switch!

Singing

Much of what has been said about the classroom ensemble can equally apply to singing with the whole-class. While singing can take place 'a capella', it is quite likely

Figure 5.2 Arranging the class for singing

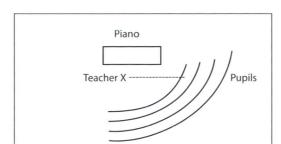

Task 5.2 Singing and
classroom management

How do your mentors organise their classes when singing? What do you feel
to be the best organisation of pupils when singing?

In singing and classroom ensemble work; what techniques do the teachers
use to rehearse these sessions? How is extraneous 'doodling' controlled? Do
teachers use published materials or arrange their own music for the class?

that pupils need some harmonic or melodic support when learning new songs
and when performing in public. This means that you must not be afraid to use
all available means to achieve success (especially if you are a non pianist) such
as using your own voice, instrument or even learning new skills, for example,
the guitar, keyboard harmony or ICT.

In these situations we often find ourselves teaching from the piano. Some
music teachers have perfected the technique of teaching 'over the piano' yet this
can present an unhelpful barrier to the inexperienced teacher who wishes to
fully communicate with the class. The electronic keyboard or guitar presents
less of a problem. It might be possible, however, to put the piano at an angle to
the group such your body language can come into play during the 'rehearsal'.
It is still desirable to do away with tables, for children often gain confidence
while singing in 'tight' groups. This strategy permits close contact and communication between pupil and teacher and mitigates against children being 'lost'
beyond the edges of the piano; the teacher can also sit down if she wishes! The
diagram in Figure 5.2 shows how this might be organised and can be used for
pupils sitting on chairs, the floor or when standing.

The national curriculum requires that we indulge in a wide variety of music-
making activities in class and singing can be one of the cheapest and most
gratifying ways to engage the programmes of study.

Written work, tests and worksheets

Whole class written work may support the practical topics in hand. Writing might involve research from books, reading and note taking from texts, writing reviews of performances or compositions or writing up 'neat' copies of notations. The management of such work is easier if explicitly related to practical sessions.

Whole class discussions

Whole class discussions happen most effectively when there is a set of shared expectations about the conduct of the activity. For example, pupils might be required to

- speak one at a time
- listen with respect to others.

In addition to basic ground rules there will need to be shared expectations for the conduct and nature of discussions. Pupils need to know how long the discussion will last, the purpose of the discussion and what are the desired outcomes. A summary at the end also adds clarity to the process. The seating arrangements for discussions should be considered in the same detail as for a rehearsal. The issues remain the same, that is, effective teacher - pupil and pupil - pupil communication. Finally, Kyriacou (1991) suggests that we need to make decisions about the extent to which we lead the discussion, for part of our role is to encourage and facilitate confident contributions by the pupils.

Task 5.3 Classroom discussion

What ground rules for discussion do teachers use? Try to transcribe part of a discussion and examine the strategies employed by your mentor and the responses made by pupils. How are seats arranged during discussions?

THE PRACTICE AND MANAGEMENT OF SMALL GROUP AND INDIVIDUAL PRACTICAL WORK

Which activities can be managed in groups?

The management of group work in particular can appear stressful, yet can also produce some of the most rewarding, fruitful and musical work. However, group work requires the most careful planning. Any of the activities encountered in whole-class work can take place in smaller groups, and indeed might be a logical extension of them, for example, rehearsing of parts for a performance or composition, based on ideas encountered in the whole-class setting. Singing, performing, rehearsal, listening, composing, notating and discussion are all possible activities in groups. Group and individual practical work can provide necessary variety and also the time and space for pupils to form meaningful relationships with their work.

Forming groups

The groups formed will depend upon the work in hand, for example, pairs, individuals, small groups or large groups will be appropriate in different situations. However, there are certain issues to be addressed. Is there an optimum group size? In some circumstances it is possible for pupils to get 'lost' during group work and thus achieve little. In particular, composition can be ineffective in very large groups (five is a possible maximum) unless the class is used to working in this way. One strategy for managing group composition is that of 'stepping up' into larger groups from smaller ones, for example individuals into pairs, and pairs into fours. This way all pupils get a chance to demonstrate what they know and understand and a chance to solve the problem in hand.

Another vexed issue is how groups are formed. This depends on the relationship you have with your class. Friendship groups are popular yet this may place personalities and abilities together, which can militate against the individual needs of all the pupils. Thus, forming groups needs to be carefully managed. A pupil left on his or her own can be a fraught experience and it might be possible to appeal to the better nature of other groups. However, this is not worth pursuing to the point of upset (on either side) and it might be appropriate for the pupil to work on their own in exceptional circumstances.

Transitions

By implication, group work involves pupils moving from one grouping to another and possibly from one place to another. The smoother the transition the greater the chance of effective work being carried out. Kyriacou suggests the following points to help with smooth transitions:

Box 5.1 Types of group organisation

Pupils can be grouped in a number of ways, as listed below and you might consider the advantages and disadvantages for the various tasks you set and classes you teach.

- friendship groups
- ability groups
- teacher organised groups
- mixed ability groups
- single sex groups
- mixed sex groups
- 'stepping up' groups in size.

- Try to avoid the need to repeat instructions or the need to clarify to the whole-class after or during the transition.
- Make sure all activities that logically fall prior to the move or change have been carried out.
- Be sensitive to the length of the preceding work, for more time may be needed in order for the next activity to be effective.
- Take care and effort to set up a suitable sequence of activities as well as the learning content.

(Kyriacou 1991)

Transitions must be planned and in particular the pupils need a clear understanding of what is required of them as they move from the whole-class to group work. Clarity of teacher explanation and expectation is vital in such work. Without this understanding, it is likely that some pupils will be off task and the quality of learning will be compromised.

Distribution of instruments and resources

Pupils in music lessons often move around with equipment, some of which is bulky and expensive. It is important that teachers establish the likely resources needed for any particular activity, and have thought about their distribution. The distribution of instruments can descend into an ongoing worry for the pupils about getting the 'right' equipment, and they can spend much time with a 'shopping' mentality at the instrument table or trolley. On the other hand, if you set pupils a problem to solve then having time to choose instruments is important. You have several options:

- 'Go and get your instruments' leading to 'the mad rush': even the politest of children can lose all sense of decency in these circumstances, but it can work with classes you know well.
- Place instruments required on the floor or on a table and ask pupils to come and get their equipment a group at a time or even one at a time.
- Early in the lesson ask pupils to make choices before they arrive at the instrument table; while this avoids the supermarket mentality it is important that they understand the sonic potential of the instruments available. This understanding should develop early in the pupils' lives at the secondary school.

In whatever way instrument distribution is achieved, choice appropriate to the task is essential and this needs forward planning by both you and your pupils.

Use of space

If there are practice rooms to use for group work then pupils should know where they are heading, especially in the unlikely event of each group having their own space. If there are no practice rooms can practical group work take place at all? Can group work take place in one music room? Clearly, in cases where individuals have headphones on keyboards this is not a problem, and yet this can be a lonely approach to composition if used exclusively. There may be occasions when you want your pupils to compose on acoustic instruments, in groups and you are forced to place all, or some of them, in the same room. This can be a stressful experience for pupil and teacher alike and you must be convinced of the usefulness of such an arrangement before proceeding. Group composition work *can* take place with all pupils in one room and on occasions it is the only way such work can be carried out (for example the peripatetic teachers are using the practice rooms!) There are noise implications, yet this can be controlled. Perhaps a bargain can be struck with pupils over acceptable noise and use of the instruments. It is also possible to set up control signals to call for silence or less noise, for example a single piano chord, a hand in the air. Another alternative is to 'split' the class and while some do practical group work, others can be involved in activities such as writing up graphic scores. Finally, many music teachers are creative in their use of space outside of the classroom, for example using corridors, other empty rooms, or the school hall. However, you must be careful not to upset other teachers or classes!

Intervention

There are various types of intervention in group work. Indeed, it must be stressed that we do have a duty to teach in these circumstances and pupils should not be always be left to their own devices. Thus, your generic teaching skills come to the fore when offering alternatives, suggesting ideas and practice drills, prompting and leading and so on. On occasions pupils lack ideas when placed in groups and you need to offer help once you are satisfied that their struggle is a fruitless one. In particular the need for intervention arises in the teaching of composition at all levels; it is important to be supportive in the creative process. Discussion with groups can be an important opportunity for appraisal and critical evaluation and it is here that the music teachers question and answer technique is important. The following questions are some examples.

- What happens in your music?
- What is the music like?
- How can we improve this idea?
- Have you tried this idea?
- What do we call this musical device?

These are all possible questions we have noted elsewhere.

Once groups are settled, try to make a brief early visit and then mix quick visits with longer stays for 'quality' time depending upon the groups' needs. This type of support is a little like spinning plates and you need to be alert to which groups need a 'spin' at any one time. This can be physically demanding work.

Coming back into the whole-class situation

The time spent by pupils on their practical group work is an important issue; in other words, when do we bring the class back together? This period varies depending on the age and ability of the pupils. Anecdotal evidence suggests that many younger pupils do some of their best work in the first five or ten minutes. It is important to give your pupils space and time to rehearse and finish work, yet also be sensitive to 'dead time' once the work has run its course. Vast patches of unused time can lead to behavioural problems. The options here are extension work or bringing pupils back together for appraisal. Some early Year 7 tasks might only require ten minutes worth of group work, providing expectations are made clear. Year 10 pupils might be left for an entire lesson having little contact with the rest of the group. However, we feel that it is good practice to have a plenary as a conclusion to the lesson, to celebrate or appraise work.

Bringing the groups together again needs careful management to avoid congestion and ruining an otherwise productive atmosphere. Once pupils are settled back in the whole-class situation they can be called to account for their work by:

- performing it
- rehearsing it
- appraising it
- appraising the work of others.

It is difficult to hear and appraise everyone at the end of a session; apart from anything else attention wanes if too much detailed appraisal goes on. However, you might feel under pressure to at least *listen* to all contributions with selective amounts of appraisal for each performance.

The recording (if needed)

The recording has a way of creating a disciplined atmosphere; pupils rarely wreck the work of their peers during recording. Again, agreed signals might indicate the difference between a 'run though' and the actual recording. The playing back of the recording is an opportunity for appraisal and pupils are usually excited and motivated by this. However, it must be said that it is easier to appraise live work due to the obvious flexibility of asking for playbacks and 'dissection'. The recording might be used for a more general review of the work, for example, in the style of a newspaper critique. If pupils are to record their work through notation they may need the instruments again if they are to be fully accurate.

A note on the use of keyboards

Keyboards are often used for paired and individual work in performance and composition. Providing these are set up on tables near to sockets and without leads trailing, then the management of this work can be less fraught especially if headphones are available. However, one of the most important uses of keyboards is their potential for exciting sounds within the group context, and along side acoustic instruments. This combination needs careful management when pupils and/or instruments are on the move. In particular you need to establish expectations about the safe transport of electronic equipment and where keyboard players can set up in practice rooms and/or areas of the music room.

Maximising effective work

By way of summary, for successful group work we suggest you consider the following points:

1   Make the work interesting, relevant and challenging.
2   Ensure that it is well matched to pupils' abilities and learning needs.
3   Try to relate the work to past experiences both within the lesson/scheme and in relation to previous lessons/schemes.
4   Have high expectations of achievement.
5   Be well organised.
6   Build in accountability through assessment/appraisal using both informal and formal methods.
7   Make sure the tasks are clear to pupils.
8   Do not leave pupils outside of the classroom for longer than is needed for the task to be completed.
9   Consider the use of worksheets to aid concentration on the task.

Task 5.4 Group and individual work

Focus on your placement school and the way group and individual work is carried out. Find out how teachers:

- form groups
- effect transitions
- distribute equipment
- use space
- intervene in pupil activities
- bring classes back together
- make recordings
- use keyboards.

Are there any differences in the strategies used between age groups? How do you account for any differences you find?

10   Try to cope with early finishers by giving extra relevant work, for example, notation.
11   KEEP THEM BUSY.

Finally, in a well-managed classroom pupils come to understand your expectations for work, behaviour and procedures. Effective group work often rides on the back of good teacher–pupil relationships, which can maximise a purposeful working atmosphere.

Health and safety issues

Essentially, careful planning, and organisation of whole-class and group practical work promotes safe practice in the music room. However, as pupils move around with instruments and use electronic hardware there are important considerations for the safe conduct of lessons. The guidelines above minimise threats to pupil safety, yet student teachers should be also be aware of and plan for the following situations:

- Some instruments are heavy and may need to be placed in practice rooms before the lesson (remember your own health and safety!) or carefully carried by pupils in an uncluttered environment; in some cases they should not be moved at all (see local guidelines).
- Some instruments are an awkward shape and again need to be transported in and out of the room without other pupils trying to make the same journey with less cumbersome equipment.
- Electronic leads and connections should be checked regularly for exposed and worn wires.
- Pupils need guidance on the careful transportation of electronic appliances, for wires and sockets can easily fray and/or become exposed, for example, do not swing 'power packs' around by the lead.
- When setting up electronic keyboards in rooms, leads should not be placed across door ways or placed under chair legs.
- Any permanent set ups for electronic equipment, for example, studios and laboratories should have wires safely and securely placed (pinned or taped?) in relation to the movement of classes.
- When using mouth blown instruments, for example, recorders, from one class to the next you need to take advice on effective disinfecting.

Task 5.5 Health and safety

Find the health and safety policy of the school and/or department. Use it to identify any other issues of health and safety which might impinge upon your music classroom.

It is likely that there is a school and departmental policy on health and safety in the classroom, and many of the more general school 'rules' are likely to be of use here such as no running indoors, consideration for others and so on.

SUMMARY

Most activities can be managed in whole-class, small group or at the individual level. Furthermore, there can be a free flow between the groupings and activities within any one lesson or scheme when using a variety of approaches to bring about musical learning. Can you suggest further examples of activities for individual, whole-class and group work listed in Table 5.1?

It is worth emphasising that the well-organised music lesson in which pupils are motivated to achieve is one in which behaviour problems are least likely to occur. In a sense the whole of this book works towards this end. While we cannot guarantee that pupils *will* behave in such lessons, we can guarantee that they will behave *much better* in a lesson which contains these features.

Table 5.1 Activities and groupings

Activities Groupings	Appraisal	Composition	Performance
Small groups	Discussing pieces in small groups. Worksheets. Notating compositions. When problem solving. Teacher Q + A work.	Group composition for example, on theme exploiting a concept or extra musical idea. Improvising on pre-determined guidelines or structure.	Preparing a performance, for example, a song or instrumental arrangement. Practising parts for whole class ensemble.
Individual	Written work. Notation. Worksheets.	Composing in a keyboard laboratory. Preparing (improvising) ideas to bring to a larger group.	Preparing a solo piece (instrumental or vocal). Working through 'graded' pieces to develop technical skills.
Whole class	Class discussion. Teacher Q + A. Appraisal of group/ class performance/ composition.	Whole class composition, for example, timbres into rondo structure. Improvisation around a 'theme' such as growth or on a raga.	Whole class singing (rehearsal and performance). Class ensemble/ orchestra.

In this chapter we have suggested that:

- Behaviour can be managed through *musical* lessons.
- Whole class music-making needs to follow the pattern of a good rehearsal.
- Group work which promotes creativity and problem-solving can still be carefully managed and organised.
- There needs to be clarity of expectations especially when conducting a practical lesson.
- Your musicianship is an important device in managing and organising the music classroom, as is the discipline of music itself.
- You need to carefully consider the use of space in music rooms and surrounding areas in order to maximise learning.
- Safety is always an important consideration during practical work and is an essential feature of planning.

FURTHER READING

Merrion, M. (1996) 'Classroom Management for Beginning Music Educators' in Spruce, G. (ed.), *Teaching Music*, London: Routledge. This chapter gives an overview of classroom management with some suggestions for preventative discipline.

Harris, R. and Hawkesly, E. (1989) *Composing in the Classroom*, Cambridge: Cambridge University Press. This book is full of excellent ideas for the conduct of group composition in the classroom. It covers both the management, teaching and learning of composition.

6 Strategies for teaching and learning in the music classroom

Approaches to listening, composing, performing and appraising

Chris Philpott

INTRODUCTION

When planning lessons you will need to formulate objectives, in other words what you expect pupils to learn by the end of the lesson or unit (knowledge 'about', 'know how' and knowledge 'of' music). You also need to prepare the resources and materials to structure learning through a planned sequence of activities. Equally important, however, are the strategies, approaches or tactics you use to bring about learning. Teaching strategies and activities are not the same thing. Activities are a description of what the pupils are going to do, for example 'today we are going to listen,

OBJECTIVES

By the end of this chapter you should:

- be aware of a range of strategies and approaches to bring about learning
- understand how teachers and pupils can behave musically and the importance of this for musical learning
- be able to develop strategies for learning from a variety starting points
- be aware of extra musical devices to support the abstract nature of musical learning.

appraise, compose or perform'. Strategies are the ways in which you bring about musical learning and these require a rich description of ends and means, for example, *the use of question and answer to elicit subjective responses from pupils such that we can introduce and develop musical vocabulary*. Teaching activities are the vehicles for teaching strategies. In this chapter we examine further teaching and learning strategies, in addition to those identified elsewhere, to help you develop your understanding of how to promote musical learning.

STRATEGIES FOR TEACHING AND LEARNING IN THE MUSIC CLASSROOM

Immersion as a basic principle of music education

One of the central tenets of this book is the importance of sound before symbol in musical learning. The implication of this is that pupils need to be immersed in music; immersed as an audience, as performers and as a composers as the basis for the learning of musical concepts, notations, technical skills and for building understanding relationships with music (knowledge 'of' music). The concept of immersion underpins the rest of this chapter. There is nothing new in this notion. Indeed, music educators such as Kodaly believed in the importance of children learning about musical concepts and processes through a thorough immersion in song at an intuitive level. On the basis of this immersion he felt that 'technical' and theoretical aspects of music could then be taught. There is much in the work of Kodaly which points to the need for *readiness* in children before they move on and that to bypass this process can lead to misunderstandings and poor learning.

An example of immersion can be applied to the popular approach of teaching music through the elements and associated musical concepts.

It is possible to pick out certain concepts and *immerse* pupils in them through listening, composing and performing. For example, for pupils to understand the concept of 3 time we can devise activities which include listening and appraising a piece in 3 time, simple notation (possibly graphic) in 3 time, performing simple pieces and echo clapping in 3 time and composing a 'waltz'.

Immersing pupils in particular musical concepts is important to the learning of technical names and notations. Central to this learning are the associated activities of listening and appraising.

Immersion and the centrality of listening

The music national curriculum suggests that it is good practice to integrate the process of musical learning, in other words, that arising out of performing there are inevitable implications for appraising and composing. Strategies need to take account of this integrative implication and it is poor practice to leave too many activities 'free standing'. The main force for integration in music is *listening* and

Task 6.1 Immersing pupils in musical concepts

How could you teach pupils one of the following musical concepts?

- Simple ABA form.
- The concept of the 'semitone'.
- The concept of 'swung' quavers in jazz.
- The concept of 'ostinato'.

Write an outline of a scheme or lesson plan for teaching one concept and present to a seminar group. Alternatively, plan, teach and evaluate the lesson yourself.

the associated act of *appraisal*. Mills' (1991) research supports the quality of learning which can arise from integration. She visited a school either side of an intensive programme of composition. On each occasion she asked the pupils to write down what they had noticed about *Mars* from *The Planets* by Holst. In almost every case the quantity and quality of the writing had improved; moving from blow by blow accounts of what happened to aspects of rhythm, mood and orchestration. The pupils had not listened to *Mars* in between times and nor did they expect the researcher to return. Mills considers whether the improvement was due to the development of their listening skills as composers, and suggests that listening while composing can be as much a learning experience as listening to a recording (Mills 1991). Mills' work shows the centrality of listening in music-making and receiving of all types. Indeed it is impossible to imagine music making of any type without listening and appraisal (although the latter might occur more at an intuitive level). Listening and appraisal are the common elements of being an audience, performer or composer and as such are the 'glue' for both immersion and integration. The problem for you as a music teacher is how to access your pupils under- standing when they are listening to music (their own or others). Strategies which can be used to draw out your pupils, musical understanding of pieces listened to include:

1   Listening and appraising 'professional' music in response to a project, for example, *after* composition or performance and not before. Some teachers feel that professional recordings can appear daunting to youngsters. Playing the music after the event can make them more receptive to professional recordings and pupils identify with composers who have tried to solve similar expressive problems.

2   Listening to contrasting versions, for example, covers, variations, movements, contrasting pupil compositions on a similar theme.

3   Listening to pieces of a very different character as stimuli for appraisal.

4   Listening and appraisal as instructional input, for example, form or the expressive qualities of certain instruments.

5   Listening and appraisal as self assessment and evaluation of pupils compositions and performances.
6   Matching pieces to other stimuli, such as pictures, paintings, sculptures or
poems in order to aid analysis.

Further ideas on this theme can also be found in Chapter 7.

One of the major tools at your disposal to access and develop pupils understanding of the music while listening is through questioning.

Learning through questioning when listening and appraising

Questioning, both 'on the hoof' and in planned worksheets, are important strategies
for any teacher when assessing and developing learning. Brown and Edmondson
(1984; quoted in Kyriacou 1991) have suggested the following reasons for using
questioning in class, to

- encourage thought and understanding of ideas and procedures
- check understanding, knowledge and skills
- gain attention and aid management
- review, revise, recall and reinforce
- teach the whole class through pupil answers
- give everyone a chance to answer
- use bright pupils to encourage others
- draw in shyer pupils
- probe after critical answers
- allow expression of feelings, views and empathy.

In addition, questions you ask can be categorised as *open* questions or *closed*
questions; *high order* questions or *low order* questions. An open question might be 'is
this a successful passage; why do you think this?', a closed question is 'when was
Count Basie born?' A high order question might ask a pupil for a description of the
structure and expressive gestures heard in the music, while a low order question
might ask which instrument played the opening fanfare? It is through their responses
to questioning that pupils can both develop their musical understanding and also
make it explicit. Question and answer is one of the most important strategies the
teacher has to access pupil understanding. We suggest that you now try Task 6.2 in
association with Box 6.1.

When questioning pupils, we are asking them to become music critics and so
learn how to back up their comments and judgements with knowledge and understanding. However, it is not necessary for a pupil to know the 'name' of something
in order to understand it. Pupils can sense that a piece gets louder and then dies away
without knowing the Italian terms for this. However, having an aural image is
perhaps a necessary precursor to naming (as in language development), in other

Task 6.2
Questioning

Make a list of questions which might be asked of pupils when they are listening to a piece of music, while they are performing and during / after they have composed. In each case write down examples of an open, closed, high order and low order question that could be used to promote learning in these activities.

Share these questions with the seminar group.

Box 6.1 Questions in the music classroom

In the music lesson, questioning by the teacher can be used to:

- Aid and focus attention. (What happens at the beginning of this music? What is the music like?)
- Discriminate between various elements. (How does the accompaniment contrast with the melody?)
- Focus on a particular strand in the music. (What are the brass doing in section B?)
- Identify, describe, specify. (Which musical device is used here?)
- Interpret and explain. (What effect does the composer achieve and how?)
- Analyse and synthesise. (In what ways do the group achieve contrast?)
- Speculate and hypothesise. (What would happen if we ...?)
- Evaluate. (Does this work? If so, why?)

---

words, sound before symbol! It could be argued that if pupils are not listening to music then they are not being immersed.

The strategies for learning which follow try to flesh out the notion of immersion in more specific and concrete terms. Again our concern is for the development of musicianship through practical engagement with musical activities. We begin by looking at strategies for learning when pupils perform as a class ensemble.

'Conducting' the class as a rehearsal: the class as an ensemble

We suggest that all of the skills required for conducting *any* musical rehearsal are equally applicable to whole-class music making, whether instrumental or vocal. The teacher's role here might be summed up as one of:

- *Directing:* bringing pupils in, stopping them, running over difficult bits, slowing down and so on.
- *Encouraging:* giving pupils confidence in their abilities.

- *Suggesting:* how things might go.
- *Questioning:* how things might go.
- *Facilitating:* challenging pupils and developing them.
- *Modelling:* demonstrating ourselves vocally or instrumentally.

Indeed, these are all features you can associate with a good rehearsal.

> **Task 6.3 Conducting a good rehearsal**
>
> Identify some features of a good and bad rehearsal? It may help you to remember conductors and teachers from your past, as well as contemporaries, and how they 'conducted' their rehearsals. Make some brief notes on the strategies they used.

'Conducting' a good rehearsal does not mean that you need to be a brilliant conductor, but at least have the ability to *conduct* an interesting, lively, well-paced session. We have all sat through rehearsals in which certain parts have been 'gone over' many times (often not improving that much) and wishing that the conductor could balance achievement with the motivation and engagement of the whole band. This balance is equally important in whole class music-making, for pupils feel better about themselves when they make progress, and do not want to sit inactive for long periods of time. Pupils feel that they have achieved something if they gain some further control over their voice or instrument when performing, in terms of accuracy, technical dexterity, dynamic range and variety and so on. They also feel a sense of achievement when they become aware of, and respond to, the structural and expressive potential of the music: when they develop musical understanding. The lesson/rehearsal needs to be conducted with clarity of gesture and language (technical and explanatory) which helps pupils to produce a performance of discipline, control and expressiveness.

To sustain achievement for all, you need to incorporate pupils who have outside instrumental tuition in your planning and have appropriate parts for all types of players. It is unlikely that published materials fully 'work' with the instrumental resources found in each class and at the very least they need to be adapted to your own particular needs. The ideal solution is to tailor the musical parts to the age and abilities of the pupils, through arranging your own music for classroom ensemble. In any case you need to prepare and know the material inside out if you are to sustain musical achievement.

Finally, much work with the classroom ensemble of necessity engages teachers in providing musical models for their pupils. Whether vocal or instrumental, these models need to be conducted with confidence and, most importantly, musically. The quality of these models is important as pupils use them as templates for their own understanding. We summarise the features of conducting a rehearsal in Box 6.2.

Box 6.2 Conducting a lesson or rehearsal (summary)

Conducting a rehearsal might involve the following:

- Conducting as in *moving* with the music, and conducting as in *taking* the lesson/rehearsal; however, student teachers do not need to be marvellous conductors as long as they can beat time clearly and put over something of the expressive qualities of the music in their actions.
- The lesson/rehearsal needs to conducted with clarity, such that all participants know the answers to the questions, When do I play? When do I stop? What do I do while the others are playing? What is expected of me?
- The lesson/rehearsal needs to have pace and include all pupils.
- The pupils need to feel that they have achieved something.
- The teacher needs to provide convincing musical models.
- Good eye contact should be kept with the class.

Task 6.4 Practising 'conducting' a rehearsal

Practice your conducting technique with the college group or school ensemble. Concentrate on clarity of gesture in 2, 3 and 4 time. A member of the group might be able to run a workshop here. Concentrate on bringing players in clearly at the beginning and keeping a clear and steady beat. Try different speeds and offer advice on technique and expression. Try to change the dynamics through your actions and try to reflect the expressive qualities of the music in your movements.

The classroom ensemble can recreate music which has been composed and also engage with improvisation. We now turn to strategies for learning through improvisation within the context of the class ensemble.

Learning through improvisation

One of the main tasks of the music teacher when encouraging first attempts at improvisation with pupils, is to clear away the technical barriers. Once pupils are more experienced it might then be appropriate to set more challenging problems. Completely free improvisation is, of course, impossible for there are always structures and ideas provided by the style, genre or from a pupils' informal learning in the 'culture'.

One way of approaching early attempts at melodic improvisation is to take away the problem of 'wrong notes', that is, where any note chosen will 'work'. This strategy does engage pupils with note selection and constructing melodic shape, yet also provides them with the safety net of knowing that all notes 'fit'. For example, in a blues in the key of D, melodic instruments can be set up for an F pentatonic (with Es and Bs taken off or marked with chalk) such that any improvisation 'works' with the blues chord sequence played by the teacher (see Figure 6.1).

Figure 6.1 The Blues in D

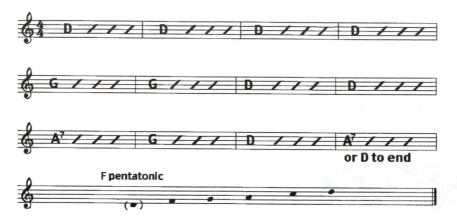

First attempts at improvisations can also be approached through two-bar question and answers, which at first can be practised with the teacher through clapping. Books such as Eddie Harvey's *Jazz in the Classroom* (1988) offer some useful advice on question and answer technique, and he encourages pupils to intuitively 'feel' the two-bar structure as opposed to reading it (see Figure 6.2).

Figure 6.2 Question and answer

Improvisation can also take place within the context of notated classroom ensemble pieces, for example, in the 'blues' shown in Figure 6.1, you could write a simple riff in the F pentatonic to be learned by the whole class (see Figure 6.3). This could be interleaved with improvisations in the form of twelve-bar breaks (which might involve three questions and answers) or a two-bar answer to the riff itself. Other 'white note' approaches can work in the same way and initially preclude the need for chromatic instruments (see other examples in Figure 6.4). Each of these can provide easy access to improvisation in the whole-class situation and also in groups.

A more advanced approach to improvisation (and thus more difficult) can be made by asking pupils to improvise using the blues scale and pay attention to the underlying chord structure.

Figure 6.3 Riff and break

Figure 6.4 Further ideas for improvisation

Mood: brilliant and confident

Other forms of improvisation can begin with extra musical themes or ideas, for example storm, machines, the arch, which might include some direction by the teacher or a pupil. Improvisation can take a musical concept as starting point such as 3 time. Improvisations can be set in a strict pulse or 'free' time depending upon the learning at stake. Much Indian music, for example, has both a 'free' section (called alap) and a more metrical section of improvisation over the 'tala' rhythm.

Above all it is important to give pupils the confidence to take part, for making up music on the spur of the moment can be a very daunting task. Clearing away as many of the technical barriers as possible is one way of addressing this problem. Much of what we have said about classroom ensemble is equally applicable to strategies for the teaching and learning of singing. However, there are specific points which need to be made about approaches to this particular activity.

Task 6.5 Developing and using improvisation

Student teachers need to build their own confidence in improvisation before trying it out with pupils in a large group. Take one of the ideas suggested above, such as using two-bar question and answer technique or an extra musical idea, and build up an improvisation on your instrument. Try this exercise with a partner or small group of musicians. Finally, try this with a small group of pupils by building their own confidence as suggested in the text.

Musical learning through the teaching of singing

Singing can be approached in many different ways and it a is cheap and flexible activity. The strategies which follow for the teaching of singing can be used to bring about musical learning of all types, although they are hardly exhaustive and should be supplemented by further research and the tapping of expertise within your group or school placement.

Warming up

In order to maximise the potential for musical learning it is important that pupils are warmed up both physically and psychologically before they sing. There are various techniques which are both useful and fun. Some do not involve using the voice, such as:

- stretching various body and facial muscles
- shaking and moving parts of the body
- yawning
- breathing exercises, for example, in and out to a set number of pulses.

Some techniques for warming up do use the voice, such as:

- vocal effects and different voices, such as speaking voice, shouting voice, whispering voice, growling, laughing, squeaking, sliding, wobbling (all of which could be conducted through echoing the teacher)
- rapping words, and sets of vowels/consonants
- exploring and singing simple melodic shapes to vowels and consonants, such as ee, ay, ah, oo, oh, mm, nn.
- using songs which are already known by the pupils.

These warm ups can of course be combined.

It is important to build a good relationship with the class which allows these 'warm ups' to take place in a positive and responsive atmosphere, yet this situation may take time to develop.

Task 6.6 Warm-ups for singing

Share with the seminar group any 'warm ups' that you know or have been used with you. Which of them use the voice? Which of them use other parts of the body? What is the purpose of each? Why have they been used?

Getting started and choosing songs

You cannot lead a song that you do not know properly, and thus preparation by learning the song is vital. Consider starting with songs that the pupils already know, and try to get accustomed to singing with the children before you sing *to* them. Also, build up a repertoire of songs which you know to 'work' and which can be drawn on when required.

The choice of song is important not least because you need to feel happy with the material you are using. The words need to be appropriate, interesting and able to be read by the class. For the pupils to develop musically they need to be challenged and yet presented with material that is largely within their capabilities. It is important to observe classes singing before taking them, such that their capabilities can be evaluated. If pupils have a limited experience of singing they might have a low and small vocal range and this needs to be taken into consideration. If there are problems with singing in tune then it might be that the song is not in a comfortable vocal range. Problems can also be caused by overestimating the extent of the pupils' vocal control, for example, songs with many leaps and jumps are difficult for inexperienced singers. However, pupils do need to be given opportunities to sing for, as Mills (1991) maintains, nobody ever learnt to sing in tune by not singing at all!

The national curriculum (and good sense) requires that we teach songs with a variety of musical content, form and style. Sometimes we can draw successfully on songs which are currently favourites (perhaps in the charts) yet caution here can avoid disappointment. For example, many pop songs are sung by soloists who include large amounts of embellishment, and this does not easily transfer into the whole class choir situation without some 'straightening out'. Sometimes this can be circumvented by the use of soloists for verses and whole class for the choruses, which tend to be less ornamented.

You should know which aspects of musical learning you are hoping to promote by singing, and how this relates to the lesson plan and scheme of work. You must ask yourself – why are we using this song and what do we hope the pupils will gain from it? However, singing for the sheer fun of it is also rewarding!

Teaching songs

The lyrics of songs can be learned by heart in the rehearsal process if they are simple enough and can be rapped as a preliminary to learning the melody. Alternatively large words can be printed on sheets (although this has the disadvantage of 'heads down'), or put on an OHT and projected onto a wall. With the advent of 'Internet Karaoke' web pages of lyrics can also be projected while downloading MIDI files as accompaniments. Notation may be used with the words, although it is important to be realistic here, in relation to the age and ability of the group and the reasons for learning the song.

We suggest that teaching the song should be carried out as musically as possible, that is, the learning should be conducted within the context of making music. The structure of the song is important and musical repetition in songs can be exploited to make learning more efficient. Mills (1991) suggests that we need to balance absorption and segmentation when learning a new song. The following suggestions might be used and are adapted from Mills.

1   A sung starting note is easier to copy than one played on an instrument.
2   Try to begin with a full teacher performance, asking the pupils to join in when and if they can; let them hear a full and musical model of the song (*absorption*).
3   Try to teach the song as a continuous piece of music, for example, through the echo singing of phrases such that even during this phase of *segmentation* we are continuing to behave musically,
4   Try not to be too disjointed in the teaching, with too much stopping during 'run throughs'; some mistakes correct themselves with familiarity, and over-rehearsing the difficult bits can be very disheartening. There is a limit to the amount of learning which can take place in one lesson.
5   Encourage breathing at the ends of natural phrases.
6   Inciting more volume can often cause shouting, while sensible breathing and good posture are the keys to a fuller sound; some children have naturally quiet singing voices.

Beginning with a deconstruction of the song can delay the 'musical' event beyond the pupils capacity to remain motivated or interested. The point is that we can encourage knowledge 'of' the music in parallel with 'know how' from the outset. Musical understanding is not only a result but *part* of the learning process.

While teachers need to know their songs and model them confidently, this does not mean that they need to be marvellous singers themselves. When supporting pupils' singing male teachers are often at an advantage as their voices can be heard above what are often trebles and maturing (broken) voices at key stage 3. However, where possible the male falsetto voice is also useful when modelling difficult treble melodies.

Some student teachers may not be first study pianists or indeed keyboard players. However, some harmonic support for singing is important. Harmonic support can be provided on a guitar or by using keyboard harmony. Given that songs can be selected which only use drones or very few chords, most musicians can build their skills to provide this type of support for pupils when they are singing. Having said this, we do not need to be able to play the piano or guitar to teach singing. Our most useful asset is the confident use of our own voice in a song which we know well.

Adding instrumental parts

Instrumental parts can be given to all pupils, although they need to be differentiated in relation to individual needs. Often the most effective accompaniments are simple, for example ostinati, repeated chord patterns, drones, rhythms or motifs taken from the melody itself. These parts can be notated if desired yet if simple they can be learned aurally. Indeed, such parts might aid motivation and further enjoyment of the song.

Notation

The more notation that pupils can read, the more music is open to them to play and perform. However, there is a three-fold dilemma in the secondary classroom:

1   the possibility of relatively sophisticated (intuitive) young musicians who cannot read traditional notation,
2   the pressure on time to introduce notation in a musical and meaningful way, and
3   pupils who *can* 'read'.

Performing in class does offer us opportunities to use songs and ensemble pieces to developing pupils' notational skills. As music is modelled to them in a singing lesson, so the eye can 'hook' onto written structures. If the song has been learned by ear and memory then notation can be introduced subsequently and the experience of linking ear to written symbols is all the more complete. Various strategies can be employed to make staff notation more accessible, such as writing in note names, or performing and notating well known tunes; again this gives the opportunity for eye and ear to link up. If you do not teach notation in 'musical' situations you risk the danger of emphasising a disjuncture between the pupils intuitive musical understanding and their ability to 'read'; in the past this has often caused alienation and demotivation in music lessons.

In summary, we emphasise the importance of teaching singing in 'real' musical circumstances, that is, as part of a process which prioritises performing, listening and even composing and improvisation.

Performing and recreating music is an important approach to immersion. Indeed, support for this can be found in the 'apprenticeship' model of musical learning given theoretical flesh by writers such as Plummeridge (1991) and Elliot (1995). Elliot suggests that the teacher needs to become a mentor, coach and model to the pupils as apprentice musical practitioners. This approach has many resonances with community-based models of musical learning, for example those

Task 6.7 Teaching a song

Learn a simple song or round by heart and teach it without the use of printed words or music to a small group of pupils or student teachers. Try to accompany this is in some way after you have taught it. Explain why you might use this song in a lesson or scheme; what is the potential for the learning of musical knowledge?

found in the English brass band movement and the Javanese gamelan. Musicianship is local or context-dependent, and what Elliot calls 'procedural knowledge', in other words, how to make music successfully, is developed by immersion in real musical practices in the classroom. The emphasis is on 'knowing how' to take part in music and this can be *caught* as well as *taught*. For Elliot performing is the main musical activity of our culture and this needs to be reflected in the classroom.

However, composition *is* a part of the national curriculum, and if listening is central to all music making, then composition has the power to integrate the elements of musical experience. Taking part in composition leads naturally to the integration of listening, appraising and performing opportunities. We now turn to some strategies in which composition is prominent as a unifying force for immersion and integration.

Musical features: an approach to tackling knowledge 'of' music

Swanwick (1988) argues that unless we plan for musical understanding and knowledge 'of' music, then we cannot expect it to happen except by accident. We have seen (1979) that he places knowledge 'of' music at the top of an objectives hierarchy for the classroom. He suggests that one route to ensuring genuine musical experience is through the use of *real musical ideas in specific musical contexts*, that is, what he calls *features*. The use of features is the guarantee of contact with music on its expressive level as opposed to 'concepts' which are isolated from musical experience. For example, the opening four notes of Beethoven's Fifth Symphony are an expressive feature, not a musical concept. Only by engaging with real music in context, Swanwick argues, can we hope to develop real musical understanding.

This approach might work in the following way. Taking the figure from the opening of Siegfried's 'Trauermusik' from *Gotterdamerung* by Wagner (see Figure 6.5), you can make it the basis for composition, improvisation, appraisal and performance. You could explore the expressive and structural potential of this 'feature' and possible transformations of it, by asking the question, what would happen if?

- What would happen if it is played it lightly like a whisper?
- What would happen if it is speeded it and made into a more nervous 'feature'?

Figure 6.5 A musical 'feature'

- You could experiment with playing the rhythm as an ostinato on a chord cluster, on a minor chord, on a major chord.
- You could use the rhythm as an accompaniment feature to a song such as the round *Old Abram Brown*.
- Pupils could compose death music of their own by adding episodes to the Wagnerian 'feature'.
- You could base a class improvisation around the same process.
- You could listen to the original music and talk or write about its expressive and structural qualities.
- What expressive features do other examples of funeral music have?

The point is that the primary emphasis is on forming relationships and 'playing' with the expressive qualities of the music (see also Chapter 2).

Task 6.8 Musical features

Extract some 'features' from a variety of different works. Choose one feature and suggest how you might use it to bring about knowledge 'of' the music. Design an integrated unit of work from this starting point. Present the scheme to the group or your mentor.

Swanwick is concerned that unless we engage directly with expressive and structural qualities of music then musical learning can become a barren and reductive experience. This is an important point although if you are committed to this principle then there are many different starting points for musical learning. We now turn our attention to strategies for learning based around 'expressive problems' in which we assume that knowledge 'of' music can potentially arise from any starting point.

Teaching and learning based around expressive problems

In this approach the expressive problem is seen as the essence of musical activity and a strategy for musical learning (see Boxes 6.3 and 6.4).

Box 6.3 What are expressive problems?

The composer confronts himself with expressive problems and must solve the problem of how the piece can be put together successfully. *The performer* needs to solve the problem of presenting the music coherently and address how the composer has solved a particular compositional problem. *The listener* is constantly interpreting how the composer- performer (they might be the same person) have solved expressive problems. There is always, at the very least, an intuitive appraisal and interpretation of particular solutions to particular expressive problems.

The expressive problems approach may emerge from almost any aspect of musical knowing; in short from any starting point. If the expressive problem is framed around the fundamental activities of music making, it is possible to turn even the driest and dustiest piece of 'knowledge' about into a meaningful musical experience. Any starting point may lead us into the realm of appraising and solving musical problems, as we search for a means to express ourselves in the context of the traditions and styles which surround us (see Box 6.4).

In this approach, starting points can be concepts, skills, features, factual knowledge, the elements or activities. All of these points can be turned round and viewed in terms of expressive problems, providing we have a commitment to immerse pupils in music and plan to cover the knowledge types in an integrated approach to the understanding of music. All music-making can be viewed in terms of problem-solving whether creative, recreative or in audience. All musical 'knowledge' can be used to set, solve or seek solutions to the problems posed in the context of becoming a better musician. By setting expressive problems from a variety of starting points we maintain direct contact with real music and maximise the chance of pupils engaging with musical meaning and building meaningful relationships with it.

Task 6.9 Using expressive problems to design a teaching activity

Take any starting point (e.g. a specific example of any knowledge type) and develop a range of strategies based on the expressive problems thrown up. Is it possible to cover all of the knowledge types? Design a scheme of work to show your thinking.

It is often the case that a particular expressive problem is set for a professional composer based on ideas which are not musical at all, for example the composer of film music. We now turn our attention to extra-musical ideas as important ways of stimulating learning and for the 'holding' musical learning which can, after all, be very abstract.

Box 6.4 Some examples of the expressive problems approach

Factual notes on the history of the blues (knowledge about)
How does the music reflect the history? How did/do blues performers/composers solve the problems of creating meaningful music in this context? What expressive features and structures are to be found in the blues which reflect its history? Can we perform a blues piece? How can we compose a blues piece?

Learning three notes on a recorder (know how)
How can we effectively accomplish this skill in order to perform with confidence? What tunes can we now play? What are the expressive possibilities of these notes? Can we compose with them? Can we recognise them in different orders?

Learning about the concept of the semitone (knowledge about)
What is a semitone? How are tones structured on the keyboard? How can we play chromatic notes effectively and with confidence? How have composers used them? What would happen if ...? How can we use them in our compositions? What expressive effects are possible?

Musical learning through extra-musical ideas

Music is by its very nature an abstract art in which meaning is notoriously difficult to pin down. It is common for us to attach feelings, emotions and ideas to the music we are listening to, and this is an important way in which we can hold our knowledge 'of' music. Extra-musical ideas are one way in which music can be *known* and also as a stimulus for learning. The following strategies might be employed when using extra musical ideas in the teaching and learning of music:

1   Many composers have been inspired by extra-musical themes; it has often been a part of their expressive problem. Examples include setting a 'programme' or an event to music (*Pastoral Symphony, Symphonie Fantastique* and so on), or when setting words with a story to music (Beatles songs). Some composers have been inspired to 'paint' a musical version of a picture (Mussorgsky in *Pictures at an Exhibition*). Given that this is the stuff of real composers, the use of extra-musical themes as an expressive problem for pupils is a perfectly valid way of working.

2   It is possible to use extra-musical ideas as ways of teaching and learning the expressive shape and structure of music. One of the reasons that music is significant for us is that its shapes and structures are congruent with other aspects of our life (see Chapter 7 on music and language). For example, the rise and fall of tension, ebb and flow, birth and death. The first movement of Shostakovich's Tenth symphony is in the shape of a huge arch as is (on a smaller scale) 'Bydlo' from Mussorgsky's *Pictures at an Exhibition*. We can use these extra musical ideas as props and supports to our understanding of

music. These props are important when we talk about music in appraisal and when we stimulate composition by our pupils.

3   Another approach is to develop a scheme around different pieces of music used in relation to the same extra musical theme. For example, music which has become associated with 'conflict'. We might use *Brothers in Arms* (Dire Straits), *Mars* (Holst), *Dance of the Young Knights* (Prokofiev), *Threnody for the Victims of Hiroshima* (Penderecki). We might ask, what modes of feeling are each operating in and how do the composers achieve these? Composition can then be inspired by a reading of the poem *Anthem for Doomed Youth* by Wilfred Owen or inspired by 'features' of the original pieces played.

While music can never definitively describe extra-musical ideas, these ideas clearly have an important role to play with professional musicians and thus inevitably for the music classroom. Always be sensitive to the ways in which musical ideas can be introduced and how pieces which explicitly relate to extra-musical ideas can be used.

Task 6.10 Extra-musical ideas

Make two lists:

- a list of pieces which have an explicit programme
- pieces (or parts of pieces) which have a 'likeness' for something external to music, for example an arch or other shapes.

Discuss with other members of the seminar group how these can be used to stimulate a scheme of work.

From extra-musical ideas there are many implications for composition. Much composition is conducted in groups and working in groups is an important strategy in musical learning. We now turn the benefits for learning of working in groups, the management and organisation of which has been dealt with in Chapter 5.

Learning from composing in groups

Given that a significant amount of composition is conducted in groups, we need to be clear about the benefits to musical learning from this form of organisation. In other words, we can use group work as a strategy for bringing about learning. Harris and Hawksley (1989) have identified the benefits to learning of group work, which can be categorised as 'musical' and 'non-musical learning'.

- Musical learning in groups: the development of the ability to explore and

solve musical problems, the development of musical creativity and imagination, development of skills of musical appraisal, ensemble skills, technical
skills, aural skills and so on.

- Non-musical learning in groups: the skills of corporate decision making, the
  ability to defer to other people, respect for others work, learning give and
  receive constructive criticism, working freely within a disciplined environment, development of general creativity and imagination, the development
  of confidence and so on.

Task 6.11 The benefits of group work for musical learning

Read carefully the 'benefits of group work' noted earlier.
  Observe some group work in school and try to identify any these benefits
for pupil learning.
  What other benefits can you identify?
  What are the drawbacks for musical learning of using group work?

Finally, in the light of all of these strategies and approaches for musical
learning we need to examine strategies for continuity and progression. We have
dealt with some of these issues elsewhere (see Chapter 2) but now turn to some
specific examples of how continuity and progression might be achieved.

Strategies for achieving continuity and progression in musical learning

The concept of *musical progression* implies that knowledge, skills and understanding develop over time, from year to year and from week to week. How, for
example can we build in continuity and progression around the concept of
variation? Lessons might be based around how composers have solved the
problem of variation (there will be many solutions), how the elements have
been employed and transformed, how we might employ successful variation
techniques in our own compositions and how to put these over most effectively
during performance. Continuity can then be achieved by formally revisiting the
notion of variation. Indeed, the music national curriculum requires that the
range, demand and quality of musical engagement is the key to progression. The
example in Box 6.5 (overleaf) suggests how continuity and progression might
be managed over time in relation to the concept of 'variation'.

Bruner (1966) has suggested that 'ideas' can be addressed with any age of
pupil, but that the nature of the engagement will change depending on their
developmental stage.

Box 6.5 An illustration of continuity and progression in the concept of 'variation'

Year 7
With some of your songs, ask what would happen if we . . . ? How can we make a single repetitive beat more interesting? Initiate compositions called 'variations on one note' (or a simple tune such as *Twinkle, Twinkle*). Listen to Charles Ives' *America* variations; appraise changes to the tune (the National Anthem!).

Year 8
Play a recording of variations on *Frere Jacques* (John Iveson). How is the tune changed? Sing the tune and ask, what would happen if . . . ? Begin to learn the tune on instruments, play as a class and compose variations which might be included in a class 'set'.

Year 9
Discuss the concept of cover versions while appraising various examples. Use motive, phrase or whole tune (provided or chosen by pupils) as basis for a composition or class performance.

Years 10 and 11
Listening, appraising, performing and composing more complex 'sets' of variations, such as Rachmaninov's *Paganini* variations.

SUMMARY

In this chapter we have explored a range of strategies for teaching and learning in music, in other words, the tactics which can be used when engaging pupils with listening, composing and performing. All of these strategies assume that pupils need to be immersed in music in order that they develop as musicians. The strategies covered are by no means exhaustive and are only a range of possibilities. It is part of your professional responsibility to constantly reflect on ways in which the pupils can be developed musically. Different teachers have different priorities and emphasise certain strategies at the expense of others, depending upon their philosophy of music education. However, most teachers are eclectic and employ a range of strategies depending on the job in hand. In this chapter we have assumed that you need to approach musical learning through practical engagement (immersion). However, the statutory requirements for music allow a good deal of interpretation, depending upon ones' own definition of musical understanding and how best to achieve the educated state.

In this chapter we have seen that:

- Teaching and learning strategies are not the same as activities.
- Teaching and learning strategies should aim to immerse pupils in music.

- There are a range of strategies which can be used depending upon the nature of the musical learning in hand.
- Behaving musically as a teacher and requiring your pupils to behave as musicians is an important source of musical learning.
- All starting points can be turned to musical ends providing that you pursue their expressive implications.
- You should not be afraid to use extra musical means to support the abstract nature of musical learning.
- Continuity and progression can be achieved by planning increasingly sophisticated engagement with music.

FURTHER READING

Harvey, E. (1988) *Jazz in the Classroom,* London: Boosey and Hawkes. This book offers many excellent ideas on how to develop your pupils ability to improvise.

Allen, P. (1998) *Singing Matters,* London: Heinemann. This set of curriculum resources provides many materials and ideas for a 'musical' approach to singing in the classroom.

7 Music, language and learning

Chris Philpott

INTRODUCTION

There are many possible points of contact between music, language and learning. These include:

- music and language as being mutually beneficial to each other
- music as having the same properties as spoken and written language
- music *as* a language
- music as a *type* of language
- music as a 'language' of various cultures.

Issues surrounding the links between language and music have played an important role in the development of music education in this century. For example, in what way is it possible for pupils and teachers to talk about music? In what ways can we show our understanding of a piece of music? How is the language we use about music related to musical understanding? What is the relationship between our intuitive or 'literary' use of language and the development of a specialist (technical) musical vocabulary? How are the written symbols of notation related to the essential nature of music?

In this chapter we address each of these issues and suggest that our beliefs about the essential nature of music are inextricably bound up with what we can say or write about it.

Initially we examine the possibility of an interdependence between music and language in human development.

MUSIC AND LANGUAGE AS MUTUALLY BENEFICIAL

At certain stages in human development it is difficult to distinguish between music and language and this is especially marked in young children. Barrett has written on the commonalties shared by music and language, noting that children's 'early language attempts often contain music characteristics' (Barrett 1990: 67) and that in:

> their most natural form – i.e. song and spoken word – music and language share the same vehicle for expression, the voice, with a consequent emphasis on the aural medium; indeed the child's first experiences of music and language are often linked
>
> (ibid.)

In these circumstances it would be odd if there were *no* links between linguistic and musical development, and they appear to be a reciprocal source and inspiration for learning. For example, SCAA (1997) have explicitly set out the ways in which music can help with language development at key stage 3. This document suggests that both music itself and the use of language *about* music can have a significant impact on the attainment targets of speaking and listening, reading and writing. If this is the case, then just how are music and language related?

MUSIC AS SHARING THE PROPERTIES OF LANGUAGE

Given the parallels between linguistic and musical development in the pupil's early years and the idea that they seem to stem from similar physiological and

---

Task 7.1 Music and literacy

Read the English national curriculum document and the QCA document *Music and the Use of Language* (1997, key stage 3) . What contribution can music make to basic skills in literacy?

psychological sources, some writers have speculated on the possibility of a direct comparison between music and language. Sloboda (1985), has suggested that there are many similarities:

- both are particular to humans
- both contain the potential for infinite combinations of possibilities
- both can be learned by listening to models
- their natural medium is through vocal and auditory sound processes
- both involve the use of notational systems
- the necessary skills must be received and absorbed before they can be used
- there is some universality of form across cultures
- they can be examined in terms of their phonetic, syntactical and semantic structure
- there is a parallel between Chomsky's theory of an underlying linguistic structure over which various transformations take place and Schenker's idea of a limited number of harmonic structures which provide a fundamental outline for tonal compositions.

Authors such as Cooke (1959) have attempted to take this a stage further and have described music as a 'language' of the emotions with its own 'vocabulary' and grammatical laws. Music, Cooke maintains, has precise public messages and composers can communicate, through a musical vocabulary, the emotions they feel themselves. This is often referred to as an 'expressionist' position and much of Cooke's vocabulary is based on inflections of 'major' and 'minor' in relation to pleasure and pain. However, it is because of the difficulty of developing a sustainable musical vocabulary that writers such as Sloboda (1985) and Bernstein (1976) have found many problems here. For example, it is not difficult to find contrary incidents of minor = pain, major = pleasure in western classical music. There are no easy dictionary definitions for musical ideas and it is for this reason that it is impossible to imagine them being somehow translatable from one 'language' into another.

Clearly, music finds it difficult to stand as a 'language' when faced with criteria derived from our spoken and written forms. Yet music means something to us, or else why would we listen to it. What is the nature of this meaning? A more fruitful area of enquiry might be to explore music as a 'type' of language.

MUSIC AS A TYPE OF LANGUAGE

If music cannot be like language itself then perhaps it might be better viewed as a 'type' of language. But what sort of language is it? The issues and problems can be appreciated by a comparison of the influential work of Langer and the national curriculum for music and their respective views on the nature of music as a 'type' of language.

Langer (1957) felt that music could not refer to specific emotions or ideas, but does present human 'feelingfulness' in symbolic form. Langer argues that music and the world of feelings share certain attributes. She suggests that the essence of both is movement, both physical and psychological, taking place in time and space. Feeling has form, for example, growth and decay, birth and death, ebb and flow, intensity and resolution, excitement and calm, struggle and fulfilment. Music shares these properties and can be seen as a tonal version of the felt life, where the rhythms of life are the basis of musical structures. The important point here is that there is an *intuitive* link between feeling and music; they share the same pattern and we can sense these when participating.

Task 7.2 Music as a type of language

Langer (1942) has described music in the following ways:

- it shows a composers knowledge of feeling
- it gives insight into the felt world
- it resembles certain patterns of human experience
- it reflects the morphology of feeling
- it reflects the life of feelings.

What is the difference between the views of Cooke and Langer? Can you see any implications for music education from each? Discuss your views with other members of your seminar group.

Indeed, Langer's views have been highly influential in music education over the last twenty-five years. For example, Swanwick's seminal book *A Basis for Music Education* (1979) draws heavily on her views. However, the implications of this work have been notoriously difficult to pin down in terms of curriculum content.

A different view on the nature of music as a type of language can be found in the national curriculum for music (1999b). The various working parties have chosen to interpret music as a 'type' of language through the 'elements' and the musical concepts which make them up (see Table 7.1 overleaf).

This approach, through the elements of music, is at the same time both controversial (is musical understanding really conceptual?) and useful (in terms of notating curriculum content). The ephemeral and elusive 'language' music is pinned down, if not to the satisfaction of all. While some musicians and teachers might argue that music is reduced here to a series of isolated conceptual 'facts', there is much

---

Task 7.3 The elements and musical concepts

Write a list of all the 'concepts' you can think of associated with the elements listed in Table 7.1. Try to break down the concepts into their smallest components. Collect as many examples as possible from other members of your group.

Table 7.1 The elements of music and some illustrative concepts

Element	Illustrative concepts
Pitch	Tonality, shape, harmony, modes etc.
Duration	Pulse, timing, metre, syncopation etc.
Dynamics	Volume, gradations etc.
Tempo	Speed, pace, gradations etc.
Timbre	Sound quality, combinations of instruments, articulation etc.
Texture	Musical layers etc.
Structure	Contrast, repetition, variation etc.

precedent for music being described in this way. Many planned music programmes in the past have regarded music as a 'type' of language articulated via the elements and the musical concepts contained within them for example, the *Manhattanville Music Curriculum Project* (1970), Davies (1993). The national curriculum regards the elements as underpinning musical processes which are universal and cross-cultural. This conceptual (technical) view of music as a 'type' of language can be contrasted with the more intuitive vision of Langer (1957) who argues that music is a tonal version of the shape of our feelings.

MUSIC AS A 'LANGUAGE' OF VARIOUS CULTURES

Much sociological and anthropological writing also approaches music as a 'type' of language. Music it is argued (see Shepherd *et al.*1977 and Small 1977) has the power to encode aspects of the society or culture from which it originates. Some examples are:

- Tonality, with its emphasis on dominant central key or note can be likened to the hierarchical power relations of western society.
- Early twentieth-century music, i.e. atonal, twelve tone music can be seen as encoding man's alienation from an increasingly 'ugly' society.
- The 'blues' has a strict repetitive structure yet freedom within which to improvise; the slaves were bound and yet needed a form to express themselves within this context.
- There are cultural delineations which structure our perception to certain types of music, such as heavy metal and opera.

Indeed, it has been suggested that music can only be really understood by members of the culture which produces it. However, much anthropological writing (such as Blacking 1976) argues for music as a universal 'language' that is eminently understandable cross-culturally.

USING LANGUAGE ABOUT MUSIC

The nature of music as a 'type' of language is inextricably linked with the things that pupils and teachers can say *about* music. As teachers we are charged with the development of our pupils and an inevitable consequence is that we talk with them about music. Our primary concern here is for the use of spoken and written language to promote *music*al learning. It is through language (although not exclusively) that we can talk about music and extend our learning. There are three important implications of this shift from music as a type of language to talking about music:

1   The themes of intuition (Langer 1957) and conceptual, technical analysis (NC) are both important to our understanding of the ways in which teachers and pupils can talk about music,
2   That we can bring important lessons from our knowledge of linguistic learning to our ideas on musical learning,
3   That these realisations can influence the way in which we plan and prepare for teaching and learning.

The more intuitive stance derived from Langer and the more technical one from the NC are not mutually exclusive. Indeed, much of this chapter explores the relationship between these two and the ways in which they are both part of musical experience, the musical learning process and the ways in which we can talk and write about music.

Your pupils can talk and write about music! It is quite natural for them to do so even though they may not have the technical vocabulary to describe what they hear. What is more just because your pupils cannot use a technical vocabulary does not mean that *they have not heard* the content of the music. Children intuitively understand the contrasting 'characters' in the Mussorgsky's 'Goldenberg and Schmuyle' (from *Pictures at an Exhibition*). They can hear and sense the 'build up' in the opening of Richard Strauss's *Also Sprach Zarathustra*. They know that heavy metal has drive and raw energy. You ignore these intuitive responses at your peril, for they are responses to music itself and represent genuine understanding. By the time pupils reach secondary school they have much intuitive understanding and varying amounts of 'technical' vocabulary to describe their experiences. You need to encourage children to 'describe' their intuitive experience as a starting point. How can you help pupils to describe their intuitive understandings? How can you help them to make their understandings explicit? How can you help them to access their own responses to music? At this stage you are not *necessarily* concerned with technical vocabulary, for analysis does not necessarily involve this. It is also important to realise that intuitive responses to music are not somehow 'lost' once we become technical or conceptual, but are always the primordial source of understanding, in other words, responding to *this* piece of music.

You can also help your pupils reveal and develop their understanding of music through your own use of language, and by asking them questions which *can* be answered. For example, what is the music like? What happens in the music? Such simple questions automatically direct pupils to their musical experiences and the *musical* reasons behind them. While the music may make them 'feel' in a certain

Task 7.4 Describing music

Choose a piece of music and try to describe what it is like without the use of technical jargon or musical vocabulary. What is the music like? What happens in the music? How does the music sound?

During an appraisal session at school or during micro teaching in college, try asking these questions to pupils or fellow students. Ask them to write down their responses, then discuss these with a partner or small group and feed back directly to the whole class.

way you can move pupils on to suggest why this has been the case, for example, 'what was it in the music that made you feel in this way?' Swanwick (1979) helpfully distinguishes between music meaning something 'for' us (our personal subjective response, likes, dislikes, conjured images, connotations and so on) and meaning 'to' us (the objective use of expressive gestures and structures in the music which have brought about this personal response). Music of a particular socio-historical context which might mean little 'for' us but plenty 'to' us, for example, avant-garde music or music of an unfamiliar culture. You can move from the response 'for' us, which is likely to be individual, 'to' the objective facts of the music which will be common to all of the pupils in your class. The ability to put technical, analytical 'names' to this experience will vary from pupil to pupil and from class to class. While 'naming' can undoubtedly enrich musical experience the 'names' do not form the life blood of the experience itself. Your pupils can use 'literary' language to describe their intuitive experience.

If pupils are not used to analysing music in this way or if you perceive they are having problems in being 'literary' about the music you might need to provide them with a possible vocabulary using adjective groups (see Box 7.1).

Beginning with intuitive experience in this way means that we do not need to forget what Langer (1957) calls the 'significant form' of music and the holistic experience of it. *We do not need to forget music as a 'type' of language in her sense of being a language of human feeling.*

While we are not yet explicitly concerned with the 'elements' (and associated technical vocabulary) your pupils will quite naturally talk about them when

Box 7.1 Worksheet idea 1: using adjective groups

It might be appropriate to prompt pupils by providing a series of adjectives or technical concepts to select from. For example, in Table 7.2 based on *Bohemian Rhapsody* the voice quality boxes might read – *harsh, smooth, powerful, aggressive, crying* and the volume box might contain – *loud all the time, soft all the time, sudden bursts of loudness and softness, gets gradually louder and softer* and so on. The adjective or concept groups need to take into account the actual piece of music (the same groups of words do not easily transfer) and the age, ability and vocabulary (technical and non-technical) of the pupils.

Task 7.5 Using adjective groups in worksheets

Choose a piece of music with distinct sections and provide a range of adjectives for pupils to choose from when describing the music. Try this out on a class or other student teachers.

describing their intuitive experience. Your pupils will write and talk about high and low, loud and soft, fast and slow; for these are natural analytical categories when describing the qualities of music. However, your pupils might just as easily also use 'literary' descriptions such as 'powerful', 'smooth', 'spikey' or 'grand'. Intuitive understating is a gateway to more technical analysis and, indeed, the introduction of musical vocabulary when pupils are ready to understand.

One way to unlock pupils' intuitive responses is to ask pupils to compare pieces of music. In Box 7.2 we suggest ways in which this can be achieved, then in Task 7.6 ask you to develop some classroom material.

Box 7.2 Worksheet idea 2: comparing pieces of music

This can be a very fruitful way of getting pupils to talk about music. The grid shown in worksheet 3 can also be adapted for this or other types of worksheet design. You will need to be clear why you are asking pupils to compare the music and the guidance for analysis will need to be significant to these pieces.

1   Pupils can be asked to compare two very contrasting pieces of music for example, a Bach chorale and a Chopin prelude.
2   They can be asked to compare pieces which are similar. 'Cover' versions of songs work well such as *Help* by the Beatles, Tina Turner and Bananarama, or variations on a theme for example the Lloyd Webber *Variations*.
3   They can be asked to compare similar pieces such as choruses from Handel's *Messiah*.

Task 7.6 Comparing music

Develop a worksheet which asks pupils to compare two pieces of music.

LANGUAGE AND THE SEQUENCE OF MUSICAL LEARNING

Given some of the links we have made between music and language, it is important to reflect on the sequence of learning of which we now have some understanding.

When we learn our spoken and written language there is a clear sequence in which we move from the sounds of the words to their meaning to the written form. The same might be said for music; that we must mentally hold a *sound* if a concept or notation is to mean anything to us. The point, in terms of the sequence of learning, is that sounds and musical meanings come before written symbols/concepts *(sound before symbol)*; indeed, some cultures never fully notate or analyse their music. We need to make links between pupils' intuitive and analytical understandings. For example, a pupil who is being taught about 3 time needs to be immersed in the sense and feel of pulse and 3 time before notation makes any sense.

LANGUAGE AND THE DEVELOPMENT OF A MUSICAL 'VOCABULARY'

As musicians it is easy to slip into the use of technical language (no matter how simple) and expect our pupils to understand this 'shortcut'. One way round this is to provide, wherever possible, musical models of the things we are talking about and also carefully audit and purge our language of jargon. Most musical phenomenon can be described using 'literary' non-technical language in much the same way that pupils can use literary language to describe their musical experience. In a sense we must, as teachers, try to remember how we first learnt and understood music if we are to help pupils move on themselves.

However, you have the duty as a teacher to introduce musical vocabulary, (we cannot wait for everything to be discovered) although only after careful preparation, taking due account of the sequence of musical learning and making sure there has been *significant* exposure to a sound correlate for what we are introducing (such as musical models of a 'drone'). Technical/conceptual understandings can grow out of our intuitive relationships with music, both of which contribute to analysis (see Figure 7.1).

The implications for you as a music teacher are that you need:

1   An ability to actively appraise music yourself; you must be good at what you are asking the children to do, that is, the analysis of musical works.
2   The skills to make judgements about whether music is suitable for educative purposes, and be able to pick out important features for new learning and reinforcing past learning.
3   The ability to break down your own appraisals into a form that can be readily understood by pupils, and be able to talk about music in such a way that the 'language' used is appropriate for age and ability of the pupils. (For example, you might refer to "rising and falling scalic patterns followed by a perfect cadence" and this *might* mean little to the pupils but they will be able to hear and talk about such an event. Pupils are able to hear music that rises and falls and comes to a solid ending which amounts to the same thing but without the technical language. However, once the

Figure 7.1 Intuition, analysis and technical vocabulary

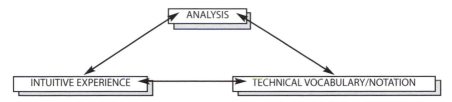

up and down patterns have been assimilated we might then talk of 'scales' as a development of critical vocabulary which can be reinforced at a later date.)

4   The awareness not to dismiss a particular response just because it did not use the 'right' word or seems wrong in some way; you need the sense to ask and understand why pupils have responded in a certain way.

5   The ability to ask questions which help pupils to develop musical vocabulary from their intuitive understandings; you need the ability to ask the right questions and set the right tasks such that the pupils are in a position to respond ('Which instrument plays the melody in the recapitulation?, might be rephrased as 'who plays the main tune when it comes back towards the end'?)

Based on our observations thus far we might recognise that the sequence of musical learning moves:

From musical experience to the elements and back to an enriched experience.

In developing a technical, musical vocabulary in our pupils you need to be aware that there are some confusions over the use of certain words and concepts which are common to pupils and teachers alike. Box 7.3 and Task 7.7 ask you to consider these, for an appreciation of such confusions is important to how you respond to the learning needs of individual pupils.

Finally, when eliciting responses from your pupils the worksheet is an important tool. It is possible to construct worksheets which offer pupils the opportunity to use both literary and technical vocabulary. Indeed, this will allow differentiated language be to used about the music and this can be done through a grid analysis. In Table 7.2 we have suggested a structure for a worksheet based around Queen's *Bohemian Rhapsody*, although this grid can be easily adapted to cover other pieces or several pieces for comparison.

Task 7.7 Confusions when using language about music

Have you any experiences of 'confusions' thus far in your experience? Discuss your examples with you mentors and other student teachers.

Box 7.3 Possible confusions when talking about the elements

Pitch
'High and low'. This needs care and clarification as some pupils think of these words as meaning high and low volume (and with good cause); also questions regarding pitch need to be targeted, for example, 'can you name a high pitched instrument in this piece?'. Asking 'what is the pitch of this music?' can often elicit the answer 'high and low'!

Dynamics
'Volume' or 'loud and soft'. This needs careful separation from language used to describe pitch (see earlier).

Texture
There are several current usages of this term such as 'thick' and 'thin' (the density of the orchestration); one tune as opposed to several at once (simple and complex; homophonic, polyphonic).

Timbre
The quality of the individual sound or collection of sounds (the latter can get muddled with certain definitions of texture).

Structure
The building bricks of music; how the music is put together; repetitions (same, variations) new ideas (contrasts).

Be sensitive to what children say or write about music for they may not necessarily be 'wrong' merely using their words in a particular way. You should also clarify what *you* mean by the use of certain words. Do not assume that all pupils, or indeed musicians, know what you are referring to.

PUPIL TALK

Clearly much of the talk which takes place in the music classroom is between the pupils themselves during group and paired work, and we should not underestimate the value and quality of this talk in the process of musical (and linguistic) learning. Auker (1991) makes the point that the most effective music teaching is that which allows pupils to make music. However, he also recognises the importance of language to musical learning especially the 'exploratory talk' which takes place between pupils themselves. Barrett emphasises that the quality of pupil talk has important consequences for the process of learning and suggests that:

> Talk arises spontaneously from the creative music experience. Talk occurs when the child selects and organises information in order to ensure its transmission with clarity and accuracy. The child must assume responsibility by initiating talk while working co-operatively on a music task, by sustaining talk and where necessary, by concluding talk.
>
> (Barrett 1990: 71)

Table 7.2 Worksheet idea 3: grid analysis of a piece of music

Bohemian Rhapsody by Queen (this piece falls naturally into five sections; the headings on the grid will need to be appropriate to the music being used and what you want pupils to listen out for).						
Section	*Instruments*	*Voice quality*	*Speed*	*What happens to the volume?*	*Mood/ atmosphere*	*Other comments, for example, special effects*
A B C D E						

Task 7.8 Grid analysis of a piece of music

Design a worksheet in grid form to appraise a piece of music for a year 7 group in which you cannot assume a great deal of technical vocabulary.

Try the same exercise with a year 11 group about to take their GCSE listening paper.

What different approaches did you take for each year group?

What were the differences in pupil response to the exercise?

Barrett feels that in such situations pupil talk is quite natural, especially when they are engaged in 'the musical challenge'. She is concerned that the quality of both musical and linguistic experience is served by such talk. She maintains that pupils use

- investigative language
- hypothetical language
- imaginative language
- descriptive language
- analytical language
- interpretative language
- comparative language
- reflective and evaluative language.

We suggest that you investigate pupil talk in the classroom, using the classification of Barrett to analyse your findings; see Task 7.9.

Your role as a teacher is one of facilitator by creating the conditions for pupil talk to take place. Auker believes that the quality of talking here is fundamental to the quality of the product, and maintains that:

> **Task 7.9 Listening to pupils talking**
>
> Listen to some pupils talking while they are composing or putting together a performance. Be sensitive to the effect that your presence will have on their talk. You might only pick up snatches of conversation from different groups. Use Barrett's categories of talk to analyse the language that you hear. Compare your observations with other student teachers in your group.

a better product will in fact emerge if we take seriously the role of language in the music lesson, because, lacking the musical vocabulary – it is through spoken language that children can begin to explore and share what they have to offer in terms of musical creativity.

(Auker 1991: 166)

How is it possible for you to facilitate pupil talk? One approach is to take the view that music education is musical criticism both for you as teacher, and your pupils.

MUSIC EDUCATION AS MUSICAL CRITICISM

The implication of much of what has been said so far is for music education as musical criticism with both the teacher and the pupil as music critic. Musical criticism does not necessarily involve us in making judgements about the value of a piece. The concepts of *good* and *bad* are not always useful constructs for the language of musical learning.

Swanwick (1991) finds that there are five dimensions or categories of musical criticism into which talk (pupil and teacher) falls. These categories are:

- control of sonorities (the tone and quality of sound itself)
- expressive characterisation (the character of the music)
- structural relationships (how the piece hangs together, evolves, uses contrasts and so on)
- personal evaluation
- historical and technical context.

Indeed, Swanwick maintains that there is no critical comment about music which does not fit into one or other of these categories, and that these categories fundamentally underpin our intuitive understanding of music.

SCAA (1997) argue for a similar set of categories in relation to the national curriculum:

- the musical elements
- musical resources

- how the musical elements and resources are used to communicate a mood or effect
- how the music reflects the context in which it is created
- how music stays the same or changes across time and place.

While the QCA categories have a rather more technical and conceptual basis, there are clear links with those in the Swanwick model. Engaging in music education as musical criticism for yourself is one of the first steps to encouraging your pupils to become music critics.

Task 7.10 Musical education as musical criticism

Take either the QCA or the Swanwick model of musical criticism.

Observe teachers discussing music with a class and try to keep a record of actual examples.

Try to place their comments (pupils and teachers) into the categories provided by the model.

Which categories does the talk of the music teachers and pupils fall into?

Repeat the exercise using published and departmental worksheets.

Discuss your findings with other colleagues in the group.

THE FORMS OF APPRAISAL

Much of this chapter has been about pupils appraising music through language such that they can make their understandings explicit, and you can take them on in their learning. The work of Flynn and Pratt (1995), suggests that 'getting at' the 'language' of music through language itself is a limited vision of appraisal. The implications of this work is that there are other ways or 'languages' through which we can access pupil understanding of music, such as through visual language, the language of movement, and other forms of notation. These are all important for there is nothing especially useful about the English language which means that it is potentially superior to other forms of appraisal, other than its convenience. The forms of appraisal allow pupils to make their intuitive understandings explicit in ways which are not limited to a 'musical vocabulary' or even literary description. We suggest that you try out this approach through Task 7.11.

ASSESSMENT

It is worth mentioning here the inevitable links between language, appraisal and assessment. Through pupils' appraisal of musical work, in both formal and informal

---

Task 7.11 Appraising music

Choose a piece of music that you know well and construct a sequence in which you ask pupils to appraise it through language, and at least two other forms of appraisal.

An example might be the opening of 'Confutatis' from the *Requiem* by Mozart. The initial ABAB is differentiated by, among other things, the use of male and female voices respectively. Pupils could be asked to draw a picture inspired by this music (what is it that the pictures and music share?). They could be asked to compose a piece inspired by the music or the picture they have drawn. They could be asked to move in response to the various sections.

---

situations, you can come to understand their learning and development. Pupils appraisals can become *one* of the foundations for your assessment. Your appraisals of pupils' work can also inform your assessment of them. In both formal and informal situations pupils' appraisals of music, their appraisal of themselves and your appraisal of their work can form the basis of assessment. In this sense there is a very close connection between assessment, appraisal and musical criticism. However, you should not rely only on pupils use of language in order to 'know' them and their work. *Performances and compositions stand freely as examples of pupils musical understanding without the need for words of description, analysis or explanation.*

NOTATION AS A 'UNIVERSAL LANGUAGE'

There are many arguments for the teaching of notation and the notion of a 'universal language' is often cited. While the case for notation is well documented, there are many attendant problems for you as a music teacher. For example, what is the relationship of notation to a musical idea? When should notation be taught? How should notation be taught? What forms might notation take? Given that notation is a part of the national curriculum we must address these questions.

We need to see the teaching of notation in relation to our discoveries about the nature of learning musical 'language'. It must be emphasised that notation is *not* musical language itself but *a* written form and is thus subject to the sequence of learning noted earlier. To ignore this connection is to court the possibility of your pupils failing to learn anything at all, and thus becoming demotivated and alienated from music lessons. In light of these observations we must ask ourselves what are the 'basics' in music education. We seem to develop our sense of words before we learn how to write them down, as we have noted earlier. The process of learning appears to be from sounds and meanings to written symbols, a principle which can also underpin musical learning.

One of the most challenging issues for the secondary school music teacher is to be sensitive to the nature of musical understandings at the age of eleven and beyond. Many pupils have been demotivated and alienated by a poor appreciation of their musical knowledge and the ways in which it has developed. By exploring the many and diverse links between music and language we can help our pupils towards meaningful and *musical* learning.

Task 7.12 Notation

How is notation taught in your school? What is the relationship of sound to symbol? What forms of notation are used/encouraged?

Devise a way of teaching the concepts of crotchets and quavers in a way which is faithful to the notion of sound before symbol.

SUMMARY

- We have suggested that music can be seen as a 'type' of language. We have an intuitive understanding of music which underpins a more analytical understanding, both of which are set in cultural and historical circumstances.
- When using language about music we must recognise these types of understanding. The process of learning is from intuitive experience to a more conceptual and technical understanding and back to an enriched musical experience.
- Much of the best musical learning follows this sequence.
- You need to develop the professional skills to bring about musical learning in the classroom through your own use of language, planning and development of materials.
- Music can help with the development of pupils' spoken and written language and vice versa.
- Pupils' musical understanding is not exclusively shown through talk or writing.
- Finally, there are important implications for music education and assessment as a form of musical criticism.

FURTHER READING

Auker, P. (1991) 'Pupil Talk, Musical Learning and Creativity', in *British Journal of Music Education* vol. 8, no. 2, Cambridge: Cambridge University Press

Barrett, M. (1990) 'Music and Language in Education', in *British Journal of Music Education* vol. 7, no. 1, Cambridge: Cambridge University Press. These two articles examine the role of talk and language about music in the mutual development of music and literacy skills.

Bernstein, L. (1976) *The Unanswered Question: Six Talks at Harvard*, Cambridge, Mass.: Harvard University Press. These lectures offer an analysis of music as a language and an interesting model for how musical meaning works.

Cooke, D. (1959) *The Language of Music*, Oxford: Oxford University Press

Langer, S. K. (1978) *Philosophy in a New Key*, Cambridge, Mass: Harvard University Press. These two classic texts examine the nature of music as a language of the emotions and as a 'type' of language for feeling respectively.

8 Addressing individual needs in the music classroom

Chris Philpott

INTRODUCTION

The individual needs of pupils in the music classroom can be understood in terms of:

- the *common* needs of all pupils, for example, an entitlement to music.
- the individual and *unique* needs of *all* pupils as learners regardless of gender or background.
- the *exceptional* shared needs of pupils who experience, for example, hearing impairment, autism, learning difficulties, and so on.

(adapted from O'Brien 1998)

OBJECTIVES

By the end of this chapter you should:

- understand the concept of inclusion in the music classroom
- understand the concept of differentiation, and how it can be achieved in the music classroom
- understand how common, unique and exceptional needs can be met through differentiation
- understand how a variety of teaching and learning strategies can be used to address individual needs
- understand how pupils with exceptional shared needs can gain access to musical achievement.

The individual needs of pupils are addressed when all pupils achieve their learning potential, and this chapter is about ways in which this can be brought about. In most cases the individual needs of pupils in all of the above categories can be met by careful planning and the *differentiation* of learning opportunities. Differentiation for individual needs might involve planning materials for the different abilities in your class. It might also involve planning for the use of specially adapted equipment as in the case of physical disability. Addressing individual needs is about *inclusion*, and this is achieved by providing all pupils with an entitlement to music education by making musical achievement accessible. Schools have a statutory requirement to address the individual needs of their pupils in relation to music, and there is no reason why they should not do this, despite the traditional frustrations of space and resources.

MEETING INDIVIDUAL NEEDS IN THE MUSIC CLASSROOM

Introduction

The national curriculum for music has a strong statement of inclusion (common to all subjects), which requires that effective learning opportunities are provided for *all* pupils.

> Schools have a responsibility to provide a broad and balanced curriculum for all pupils. The national curriculum is the starting point for planning a school curriculum that meets the specific needs of individuals and groups of pupils.
>
> (DFEE 1999b: 24)

The national curriculum document sets out three principles upon which inclusion should be based, and these are:

1   Setting suitable learning challenges.
2   Responding to pupils' diverse learning needs.
3   Overcoming potential barriers to learning and assessment for individuals and groups of pupils.

It can be argued that the *common* needs of pupils are addressed by the very existence of the national curriculum for music, which is an entitlement to music education, although music is and always has been in a position of fighting for time and resources. The *unique* needs of pupils as learners can be addressed through *setting suitable learning challenges* and by *responding to pupils' diverse learning needs*. Pupils' *exceptional shared needs* (commonly referred to as special educational needs) are addressed through *overcoming potential barriers to learning and assessment*. These principles have huge implications for your planning as a music teacher, when differentiating for the individual needs of your pupils.

Task 8.1 Exploring inclusion

What might the concept of inclusion mean for music education i.e. access for all pupils to musical achievement? How might inclusion be achieved? Share your reflections in a discussion with other student teachers.

Setting suitable learning challenges through differentiation

Setting suitable learning challenges is, of course, inextricably related to the nature of music and musical learning and we have spent much time on these issues elsewhere in this book. Bruner neatly sums up our position, when he suggests that in order to optimise learning opportunities we must consider:

- The conditions which must prevail for a pupil to be motivated to learn, for example, *when there is an appropriate problem to solve; the best learning occurs when there is a necessity to do so.*
- The structure of knowledge in each subject, in other words, *music education needs to be faithful to the essential nature of music itself.*
- The most effective sequence for knowledge to be presented to pupils; in other words, *what can we assume at various ages? What can we assume from our previous teaching? What do we know about the past experiences of the pupils? In what order should we present content?*
- How learning is reinforced; *Bruner suggests that extrinsic rewards are important yet learning will only continue if the rewards become intrinsic, when pupils are learning because they want to!*

(adapted from Bruner 1966)

In a sense the whole of this book is about individual needs and these can largely be met by adapting strategies suggested in the other chapters.

It is important that all pupils are given opportunities to experience success and fulfil their musical potential. Pupils need to be presented with content which is appropriate to their developmental levels and individual needs and this process is called differentiation. What is differentiation and how can it be achieved in the music classroom? It can mean a variety of things from structural differentiation through streaming and banding to individualised learning packages for pupils. For the purpose of this chapter we will assume that differentiation is a process in which you identify the most effective learning strategies for each learner. The aim of differentiation is that by accepting pupil differences you can bring about achievement, develop self esteem and sustain motivation for future learning, for *all* pupils. Indeed, this could mean teaching knowledge, skills and understandings from earlier key stages at the expense of programmes of study designed for the chronological age of the pupils. At key stage 3 you will find some pupils who need to work on the programmes of study from key stage 2 while others will need to work at levels more akin to key stage 4.

However, it would be wrong to think that differentiation is anything but good teaching. It is not something that can be bolted on, and Green suggests that, 'In addressing differentiation we are recognising and celebrating the range of different strategies that people use in order to learn, as well as the different rates at which they might learn' (Green 1998: 9). Indeed, it could be argued that differentiation is synonymous with good teaching. In the model proposed in Figure 8.1 you will see that it is a wide concept and much of your early practice will necessarily engage with differentiation, if only intuitively at first. Conscious planning for differentiation in your lessons can be thought in terms of the model shown in Figure 8.1.

Differentiation of content

Is it appropriate for all pupils to study the same content at the same time? The national curriculum is a basic entitlement yet does not suggest that all pupils are taught the same material at the same time. Differentiation by *content* can be a very sophisticated method of working yet has many associated problems of organisation and management. Clearly it is difficult to run differentiated content in the same class yet there is a sense in which music might lend itself to this approach, for example, through group composition and performance. Such practical work can lend itself to this approach and it certainly could flourish with GCSE or A level classes, which often involve smaller groups and opportunities for more individualised work.

Differentiation by resource

Differentiation by content has many implications for differentiated *resources* in terms of space, materials, recordings and so on. Given the wide variety of media at our disposal we are able to differentiate the resources given to various pupils for example, it might be appropriate for a group to listen to a piece in 'six-eight' after their composition has used this musical timing. It may be that some pupils need to be given opportunities to use ICT to support their work, for example, the use of the Internet or sequencing software.

Figure 8.1 Model of differentiation

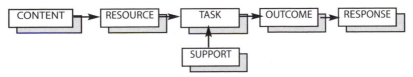

Source: Dickinson and Wright 1993

Differentiation by task

You can provide a variety of tasks which are matched to students aptitudes, abilities and interests. Differentiation by *task* can work particularly well in the case of musical 'literacy' (used here to mean reading and writing notations). 'Parts' for performance can be carefully crafted by the teacher to reflect the abilities in the group and yet with enough difficulty to consolidate and challenge pupils. Expectations for the notation of compositions can also be differentiated and various pupils can be asked to use graphic symbols, traditional notation or an appropriate mixture. Worksheets can also be constructed with differentiated questions which allow pupils of all levels to show what they understand and know. Differentiation by *task* for composition is rather more problematic especially if we are considering using grouping by ability. Given that much composition is undertaken in groups at key stage 3 we must ask ourselves whether we are we willing to sacrifice mixed-ability groupings where much social learning goes on? Are we willing to have particular groups 'labelled' by ability? Are we willing to sacrifice the learning which takes place when pupils 'play' with those who are more able (one of the major engines of musical development)? There is, however, a sense in which individual needs can become 'lost' in group work, for example, where some pupils do all the work and those who consistently underachieve work in the 'background'. Differentiating according to ability in composition needs to be given careful consideration. However, differentiating composition tasks is less of a problem where there is the possibility for individualised work with GCSE groups or in keyboard laboratories.

Differentiation by outcome

This is a common form of differentiation. However, if this is the sole form of differentiation it needs to be carefully monitored given that you have minimal input into the planning of the *outcomes*. Having said this, there is a sense in which music differentiates itself by engagement (Swanwick 1988). This is especially so in areas of problem-solving involving composing and listening, when pupils can engage with the music at their own particular level of musical development. This feature is an important aspect of our intuitive response to music and means that pupils of different abilities can work in the same groups on the same projects, even if their engagement is qualitatively different. There seems to be a common assumption that it is difficult to address individual needs in music because of the range of musical abilities arising through some pupils taking extra 'instrumental' lessons. On the contrary it seems that music can differentiate itself by engagement and this has been assumed by many models of musical learning around the world, such as the Balinese Gamelan and the British Brass Band System. In such 'set ups' it is assumed that musicians of varying abilities will and must play together in a mutually beneficial relationship (see also 'social learning' in Chapter 2).

Differentiation by support and response

It is likely that this form of differentiation is the most intuitively used by good teachers, particularly through individualised feedback. We can also plan for others to support and respond to the needs of pupils, for example, support staff, outside speakers, peripatetic staff and other pupils in the class. It is possible to use pupils of different skills and aptitudes to work with each other, and this is one way in which the learning of pupils of all abilities can be extended.

Differentiation by *support* and *response* are part of our stock in trade as skilful teachers such as when we tailor our response to the individual needs of pupils when they are appraising, composing or performing. Indeed, such differentiation underpins one of the themes of this book, that is, music education (teaching, learning and assessment) as musical criticism. We suggest that you identify the ways in which differentiation is used in your school (Task 8.2) and begin to apply to your own teaching.

Task 8.2 Forms of differentiation

Using the model (Figure 8.1) evaluate which forms of differentiation have you witnessed or used thus far. Map your observations against the headings used above. In what ways have the forms of differentiation manifested themselves? For each mode of differentiation imagine and note further examples for music which could be used.

Discuss the results of your mapping with your mentor and/or other student teachers.

Responding to pupils' diverse learning needs

Differentiation also embraces the need to adopt a wide variety of teaching styles both for the whole class and individuals such that:

- pupils are motivated by different approaches which sustain concentration through maintaining interest
- pupils' individual learning styles are taken into account

We have spent some time elsewhere exploring a variety of different approaches / strategies for the teaching of music (see Chapter 6). In your planning you need to consider targeting these teaching and learning strategies in relation to the learning needs of boys, girls, pupils with special educational needs, pupils with disabilities, pupils from all social and cultural backgrounds and pupils from different ethnic groups. Again the national curriculum for music has a strong statement of inclusion suggesting that we can target teaching strategies by:

Task 8.3 Planning for differentiation

Plan a scheme of work for a mixed ability group of twenty-five in Year 7 (5–6 lessons) on the topic of 'exploring vocal and instrumental timbre to produce musical contrast'. Five pupils have instrumental lessons (grades 1–3). Many of the rest are good 'intuitive' musicians. All pupils enjoy the lessons and can improvise and compose on classroom instruments with style and presence but are not 'readers'. One or two pupils have co-ordination problems but enjoy the subject. There is a wide range of ability in terms of reading and writing the English language. Relatively little musical vocabulary is held by any of the group but they all talk and write about music.

What differentiation strategies do you feel that you will need to plan for and engage with during the course of the lessons?

Notes to consider:

- All pupils should engage with listening, composing, (improvising) and performing.
- What planned differentiation is appropriate?
- Consider questions on worksheets. Can these be differentiated? Are the questions suitable for all pupils? Can they all have a go? What types of questions should you use: open, closed, technical, non-technical?
- Consider the issue of identifying differentiated parts for performance.
- How you can extend the most able pupils? How can they be used to 'teach' the others?
- What is the core experience of knowledge you want for all pupils by the end of the sequence of lessons?
- How can you reinforce the learning achieved by those who are less able?

Share your scheme with other students and your mentors.

- Creating effective learning by maintaining a secure environment in which all pupils feel valued, and by setting targets for learning which are attainable and which develop the self esteem of the pupils.
- Securing the motivation and concentration of pupils by building on interest and culture and accepting that pupils have a variety of learning styles.
- Providing equality of opportunity, ensuring that boys and girls are given the same opportunities and yet allowing for a variety of interpretations and outcomes.
- Adopting appropriate assessment procedures by using a variety of ways of coming to 'know' your pupils in response to a variety of learning styles.

We suggest you try to identify these conditions for learning in classes you teach or observe (see Task 8.4).

Task 8.4 Addressing individual learning needs

Using the strategies listed next, identify the attention given to individual learning needs in the music classes you observe. How do teachers make all pupils feel valued, how do they secure motivation and concentration, provide for equality of opportunity and use appropriate assessment strategies?

Prepare some notes for discussion with other student teachers, or your mentor.

In addressing individual learning needs, Green (1998) suggests that we need to be in tune with how our pupils learn, and that we must also bear in mind that there are many routes to musical success. We need to adopt an appropriate variety of teaching strategies to address these considerations, such as:

- talking, discussing, questioning, being questioned by pupils
- setting independent learning tasks
- didactic input
- practice/rehearsal
- learning music by ear
- learning music from notations
- improvising
- listening to and appraising music in a variety of ways
- problem-solving, creativity and so on.

This list mirrors the range of strategies introduced in other chapters of this book (see Chapters 6 and 7). Targeting these strategies will of course depend upon the individual child and class, and thus raises many implications for planning.

Variety is important in addressing the learning needs of all pupils in your classes. That is, by using a variety of teaching and learning styles within and across lessons you acknowledge that pupils learn in a variety of different ways. What is more, by

Task 8.5 Variety of teaching and learning strategies

Use Green's list of strategies to audit the range of teaching and learning strategies you have observed or used thus far. What other strategies can you add to the list?

To what extent have these strategies promoted musical learning in your classroom? How have they enhanced the musical learning of all the pupils in your classes?

Share your findings with other student teachers.

using a variety of teaching and learning styles you maintain the interests and motivation of your pupils. This is not variety for variety's sake, but the planned and targeted use of different strategies in relation to the learning needs of different pupils and the nature of the content in hand. If nothing else, variety is an attempt to prevent boredom, for the bored child will not learn.

Overcoming potential barriers to learning and assessment for individuals and groups of pupils

The national curriculum is clearly committed to inclusion and requires that we adapt our approach, where necessary, to give access to musical achievement and outlets for pupils to show us what they understand and can do. It is likely that we need to use unconventional and imaginative techniques in order to achieve this aim, especially when addressing pupils with *exceptional shared needs*.

There are widely held assumptions that music has an important role to play when addressing pupils special (exceptional) needs of *all* types. These assumptions include:

- Music challenging pupils of high intelligence and ability.
- Music therapy for those with physical disability.
- Music therapy for those with psychological disorders, for example, where music can become a cathartic, expressive experience and a tool to effect clinical cure.
- Musical development as transference into other areas of life/schooling, for example, music is said to stimulate the cortex and can bring about improved intellectual and physical performance, stimulate social development and bring about confidence in other subjects.
- Music having the power to develop self esteem.
- Music as having a role to play in language development; evidence seems to suggest that sung language can stimulate and develop the language centre of the brain, even though music and language are situated in different hemispheres for example, as observed in stroke victims.

In the general music classroom some pupils will have *exceptional learning* needs which cannot easily be met by planning alone, for example those with severe learning difficulties or physical disabilities. However, even in these cases pupils needs can *largely* be met by the differentiation of materials and tasks. Provision for such pupils might be associated with an intervention strategy such as providing specialist equipment or seeking external support as part of the strategy for meeting a statement of special educational needs. Strategies for addressing exceptional needs in the music classroom might include:

- Providing for pupils who need help with communication, language and literacy, for example, through the use of ICT, an emphasis on aural memory skills, music as means to self expression, large print and alternative symbols.

- Using all available senses and a variety of experiences to develop pupil understanding through the use of gesture and movement as a means of appraisal for pupils who have difficulty singing or speaking, and other forms of appraisal for pupils who have limited language skills (such as drawing).
- Planning for participation in all types of activities such as the use of beaters which can be played through head gear by pupils with a physical disability; the use of ICT to make and create music, through physical involvement with appropriate instruments for pupils with hearing impairment.
- Using music to help pupils manage their behaviour e.g. at key stage 4 to prepare for work by engaging pupils in the discipline of music and developing self esteem through achievable targets.
- Using music to help pupils manage their emotions and take part in learning by allowing music to be used as means of self expression; again building pupils' self esteem through achievement.

In such cases you need to plan for adequate time, classroom organisation and access to equipment such that *all* pupils can participate effectively. You also need to identify areas of the curriculum which may present particular problems for specific individuals. However, not all pupils who have disabilities necessarily have special educational needs.

Task 8.6 Special provision for pupils in the music classroom

What special provision have you noted in the music classroom? Make a list of the special provisions and the individual need being addressed. Share your findings in a discussion with other student teachers.

Re-read the national curriculum for music. Are there any aspects of the programmes of study which might be problematic for certain individuals to engage with? Are there certain special educational needs or disabilities which inhibit musical learning? In both cases make a list and state what adaptations could be made to afford all pupils access to musical achievement?

We shall now examine some specific strategies for dealing with specific exceptional shared needs within the music classroom.

Pupils with emotional and behavioural difficulties

Given that we have discussed the potential positive impact of music on exceptional needs, we should also consider that a pupil's special needs have the potential to hamper their musical development. For example, many pupils with emotional and behavioural difficulties (EBD), lack self discipline and skills of co-operation and concentration, which makes listening, performing and composing tasks formidable for both them and the teacher. Music-making in such instances can be vulnerable to disruption, especially in the hands of non-specialists with low confidence. Furthermore, some pupils with EBD can find the idea of self expression and creativity rather frightening.

The work of Packer (1987, 1996) has been important in developing strategies for the teaching of music with pupils who have emotional and behavioural difficulties in particular. Indeed, her research also suggests that music can have a positive influence on the many aspects of the lives of such pupils. In particular she has examined their behaviour while taking part in a music programme. She noted that many teachers at a special school avoided music for the reason that it was seen as a somewhat 'risky' pursuit with EBD pupils. Teachers were worried about their ability to control the pupils, or to channel them into any useful learning especially in practical activities. Packer asked teachers to grade pupil behaviour in their normal lessons on a three-point scale with 3 as acceptable and 1 as unacceptable. These grades acted as predictors of behaviour in a music programme which she then helped to introduce into the school. During the programme she asked teachers to grade pupil behaviour, this time on the basis of their work in the music lessons. In almost all cases the pupils were better behaved than the teachers expected. There may be many reasons behind this, for example, the novelty of the programme, but there is some evidence to suggest that the discipline of musical achievement can help to control the behaviour of pupils with EBD. Indeed, there is no reason why this should not apply to all pupils at school.

Packer offers the following advice when dealing with pupils who have EBD. She suggests that we:

1   Conform to a 'primary' model, for example, try to tie the work in with other extra musical ideas /areas of the curriculum. Also make the work active and fun!

2   Try to build in some familiarity. Try to avoid the completely novel because EBD pupils in particular are notoriously resistant to change. Link the work to past activities or themes.

3   The most important piece of advice is to *build in some instant success*. The difficulties of managing practical work can be addressed if the sweet smell of success is achieved early on. Given a background of consistent failure, academically and socially, such pupils do not have a large capacity for effort, endurance and optimism. They often give up at the smallest stumbling block.

4   Packer concludes by saying that once into music, the experience has the power to produce self-esteem and self-confidence.

5   Teachers should experiment with imaginative and unconventional methods which enable pupils to achieve through their abilities rather than be frustrated by them. This advice applies to special needs of all types.

We also believe that this advice is good for situations in many types of mainstream schooling, where some classes have up to 50 per cent (and beyond in some cases) of pupils who have a documented special educational need.

Dealing with exceptionally able pupils

The extra strand to music education (instrumental tuition), which is not replicated in other subjects in the curriculum, can often bring about development which uncovers an exceptionally able pupil. However, you should not assume that learning a musical instrument is the only way to identify such ability; it can arise during the work of the general music classroom.

Pratt and Stephens (1995) suggest that able pupils can be identified in one or more of the following ways

- they can imitate teacher models accurately on voice or instruments
- they can memorise music quickly
- they can read notations with ease
- they can sing accurately in tune and with natural expression
- they might show perfect or relative pitch
- they have a strong creative impulse
- they might have an unusual affinity to a musical instrument
- they have particular sensitivity to musical expression.

One response the authors suggest is to channel such pupils into appropriate extra curricular work which will challenge and develop them. Pratt and Stephens also suggest that teachers need to seek further advice, especially in case where they anticipate an exceptional talent. This advice might come from LEA advisors or other teachers such as peripatetics. The latter are particularly important if it is desirable to help the pupil begin learning a musical instrument. Of course, before this can happen parents need to be consulted in relation to obtaining an instrument, beginning lessons and carving out time for practice (it may be that music is not the only exceptional talent the pupil has!). In some cases it might be appropriate to pursue, with the parents, the idea of specialist tuition in a particular school.

Having said this, the general class music teacher must also differentiate for such pupils in their lessons, and this will need careful planning. The majority of pupils identified will not have an *exceptional* talent, and remain within the school as active participants both in and out of the classroom. Some possible strategies for differentiation for these pupils include:

- The use of challenging ICT software packages for composition and performance, such as sequencing and score writing.
- The use of outside support such as a peripatetic teacher, support teacher, other members of staff, older pupils, intellectual peers and so on, who have a variety of skills and knowledge.
- Setting high expectations and demanding work of quality.

- Developing a rich resource bank of challenging materials which provide a stimulating environment, such as a wide variety of CDs plus worksheets.
- Planning for extension activities, for example, challenging and high order questions.
- Discussing work at an appropriate level.
- Providing opportunities for guided independent study, research and problem solving.
- Giving them opportunities to work with those who are less able especially during composition and performance, for while we all learn from those who are more able than ourselves, we can also learn from working and guiding others who are less able.

It is, however, unlikely that an exceptionally able pupil is consistently at a higher developmental level than *all* pupils in *all* aspects of musical understanding. There is a danger that such pupils can become pushed too hard and that this is perceived by them to be unfair. On the other hand there is an increasing amount of anecdotal evidence to suggest that problems can occur when pupils underachieve. For example, when able pupils are not motivated or challenged then poor behaviour can result, and this can be a real barrier to further learning. Although addressing individual needs can require much hard work and energy from the music teacher, there are many dividends in relation to the pupils' engagement with the lesson and thus their motivation and interest to learn.

> **Task 8.7 Addressing exceptional learning needs**
>
> Have you observed / taken classes where it has been recognised that a pupil(s) have EBD or are exceptionally able? How have these pupils needs been taken into account in the planning?
>
> Make a list of any further indicators of exceptional ability in music, in addition to the list above.
>
> Make a list of differentiation strategies you have observed for pupils of exceptional ability.

Pupils with a physical, hearing or visual impairment

When planning for the needs of pupils with a physical impairment it might mean the adaptation of equipment to provide access to musical achievement. For example, beaters can be adapted with headsets for certain pupils. Also, hand chimes can be easier to play, for some, instead of hand–held beaters.

Hallam has suggested that 14 per cent of the population has a hearing impairment and yet only 10 per cent of these are totally deaf. Colour, vibration and sign can be used to allow pupils access to the expression and structure of music. Also, instrumentation with a strong vibration such as a bass xylophone or bass drum can be used such that pupils 'feel' the timbre and pulse of the music they are making.

Pupils with a visual impairment can work 'by ear', and are often good at it, memorising music and improvisation. These strategies will prove to be useful when working with such pupils. Problems with 'reading' can often be overcome to some extent by using large print and Braille music.

Dyslexia

A common special need is dyslexia. This dysfunction can be manifest in a difficulty with reading, writing, spelling and manipulating numbers which is not typical of a pupils general level of educational performance. Dyslexic pupils might exhibit:

- a slowness in processing what is heard
- problems with focusing visually
- confusion of left and right
- poor memory
- disorganisation in planning and sequencing.

Hallam (1998) suggests that teachers need to provide a safe and secure environment for such pupils, offer time and patience, praise all achievement, provide clear instructions and offer open-ended learning opportunities.

Task 8.8 Music and dyslexia

How might dyslexia manifest itself in the music classroom? What forms of achievement can music offer to such pupils? What planning would need to take place in order to ensure access to such achievement for such pupils?

The use of ICT

ICT offers one of the most important means of access to music for pupils with exceptional needs. Innovative ways of making music include:

- Touch panels which 'sound', connected to MIDI software; these panels can be sensitive to the pressure, speed and touch and represent a new way of accessing musical improvisation and composition for *all* pupils.
- Light beams which stimulate electronic sounds when interrupted in different ways by any part of the body; similarly these can be sensitive to the speed and type of movement.
- Software which utilise 'blocks' of sound/samples and take away many of the technical barriers of performance but still allow pupils to structure the samples into real compositions and arrangements.

All of these strategies have applications at many different levels of musical achievement, and represent important ways in which all pupils can access music-making, as ways of overcoming barriers and promoting inclusion.

SUMMARY

It would be wrong to think that there are *no* problems and barriers to a full access to music. Packer (1987) has identified that teachers at schools for EBD pupils are reluctant to introduce music into their classrooms mainly due to a perceived lack of training and confidence. Indeed, there are many issues and barriers associated with attitudes and economics as well as training. The challenge is to help pupils achieve musical experiences through their ability rather than being frustrated by their disabilities. To do this we need an openness to new ways of expressing music and its meaning, and in many cases our approach needs to be adapted to the individual. Laying on these opportunities is the business of teachers, although they require much support from outside agencies, further funding and the school.

Finally, there is a sense in which many of us have special needs in relation to music. In comparison to other societies we do not sustain the musical development of our children in comparison to say language development. We never stop talking at our children, yet we do not 'music' at our children in the same way as some other cultures. Thus, musical development can be rather patchy in comparison to language development. The result is that a pupil's innate 'musical ability' is not always fully exposed by the time they reach the secondary school and many will be musically under developed.

In this chapter we have seen that:

- There is a strong commitment to inclusion in the national curriculum which assumes access to musical achievement for all children.
- That inclusion can be achieved through differentiated learning opportunities.
- That in order to address individual needs a variety of teaching and learning strategies need to be used.
- That we need to be flexible and imaginative when planning for individual needs of all types.

FURTHER READING

Dickinson, C. and Wright, J. (1993) *Differentiation: A Practical Handbook of Classroom Strategies,* NCET. A useful overview of planning, management and organisation of differentiation.

O'Brien, T. (1998) *Promoting Positive Behaviour,* London: Fulton. Some of O'Brien's ideas for understanding and categorising individual needs have been adapted for this chapter.

Packer, Y. (1987) *Musical Activities for Children with Behavioural Problems,* London: Disabled Living Foundation.

—— (1996) 'Music with emotionally disturbed children' in Spruce, G. (ed.), *Teaching Music,* London: Routledge. These publications are an invaluable source for understanding the nature of EBD pupils and the positive strategies you can employ to work with them in the music classroom.

9 Music-related ICT in education

Bill Crow

Figure 9.1 Roland Fiddy cartoon © Roland Fiddy 1991

INTRODUCTION

Take a look at this cartoon. What does it suggest? The electronic keyboard appears to play unaided (possibly the boy has simply pressed the 'demo' button) and there is an absence of conventional musical 'performance'. What sort of music might be playing? Although the boy is dressed like an orchestral conductor, might we assume that the music is some sort of electronic-sounding pop pastiche? The small captive audience, placed in their front room as opposed to the concert hall, display varying degrees of emotion: indulgence, boredom, fear. It appears that technology has 'taken over', replacing human performance with machine-generated fakery.

However, looked at in another way, the cartoon might tell a different story. What if the boy had recorded his own musical ideas and choices into the keyboard before the performance? What if he was conducting with a sense of rhythm and responding to the music's expressive character with appropriate gestures? Or what if this was the first time his parents had ever seen him interacting with music in a positive way?

As a student teacher you need to reflect carefully about the relationship between electronic technologies and the essence of musical experience. You also need to consider how Information and Communications Technology (ICT) can effectively support pupils' musical learning as well as enhance your own teaching and future professional development.

The national curriculum for music states that:

> Pupils should be given opportunities to apply and develop their ICT capability through the use of ICT tools to support their learning in all subjects.
>
> (DFEE 1999b: 34)

For music at key stage 3 this statement implies creating, manipulating and refining sounds, and developing an understanding of the use of ICT within particular styles, contexts and traditions.

As student teachers you should become conversant with the *Initial Teacher Training National Curriculum for ICT in Subject Teaching* (1998). This document outlines the standards required of newly qualified teachers in the area of ICT literacy. It states:

> ICT is more than just another teaching tool. Its potential for improving the quality and standards of pupils' education is significant. Equally, its potential is considerable for supporting teachers, both in their every day classroom role – and in their continuing training and development.
>
> (DfEE 1998: 17)

This conception of what constitutes ICT is broad, including *common ICT tools* – computers, the Internet, CD-ROM and related software – and *traditional forms of ICT* – television and radio, video cameras and other equipment. To this list we need to add *music-related ICT* (the main focus of this chapter) which can include everything from electronic keyboards through to sophisticated digital systems which record and process sound.

Another important aspect of the ICT curriculum is that every teacher should be equipped with the knowledge, skills and understanding to 'make sound decisions about *when, when not* and *how* to use ICT effectively in teaching particular subjects' (ibid.). 'When not' to use ICT is, of course, of prime significance to all teachers. But music teachers in particular need to consider its role. After all, music is a practical subject that involves physical interactions and expressive responses. Music-related ICT should, wherever possible, *integrate* with classroom activities to support and enhance genuine musical experience. It should not replace acoustic activities or undermine and limit creative response.

Unfortunately evidence suggests that the use of music ICT in schools is still inadequate. An OFSTED (1995) report on music across all phases identified key stage 3 as an area with some serious weaknesses. The reasons for these weaknesses included: out-of-date or inadequate resources, lack of in-service training, teachers' perceptions and difficulties with resource allocation and management.

Nevertheless, these difficulties can and should be overcome. Music technology offers many benefits to both the pupil and teacher. Not least of these is the attraction of the technology itself. Pupils who do not possess traditional musical skills (possibly similar to our cartoon conductor), can now access the world of music in ways previously denied them. Pupils who do have traditional skills can further explore and enhance their musicianship while deepening their musical understanding.

ATTITUDE

> Should we not fear this domestication of sound, this magic that anyone can bring from a disc at will? Will it not bring to waste the mysterious force of an art which one might have thought indestructible.
>
> (Claude Debussy on the gramophone)

On occasions you still might hear musicians (and music teachers) express negative or antagonistic opinions about the way that technology interacts – some might say 'interferes' – with music and the musical experience. Other musicians can see the

OBJECTIVES

By the end of this chapter you should:

- Have reviewed your own and your placement school's attitude to music and technology.
- Have been prompted to profile your own competence in music-related ICT.
- Have noted the music-related ICT resources that are available in your placement school.
- Be aware of the range and breadth of new technology that might have relevance to the music classroom.
- Be aware of some of the ways that integrating ICT in the classroom can promote musical learning.
- Be aware of some of the skills that you and your pupils will need to access music-related ICT.
- Be aware of how ICT can support your own teaching in the classroom.
- Be aware of the potential problems of using ICT in the classroom, including issues of classroom management and health and safety.
- Have embarked upon projects which incorporate ICT into your lesson planning and evaluation, including your own classroom presentation.
- Have set targets for your future professional development in ICT.

benefits. Whatever your views you should be aware of the broad cultural debate that makes assumptions about technology and artistic expression. Even within popular music – a genre which has been shaped by technology – there are critics who applaud live authentic 'rock' performance while rubbishing studio based 'pop' production.

Attitudes to technology, artistic expression and education

The tasks in this section are designed for you and your colleagues – in groups or in pairs – to explore your own perceptions regarding *technology and artistic expression*. Try to consider your views both as *a musician* and as *a teacher*.

Figure 9.2 Music technology brainstorm

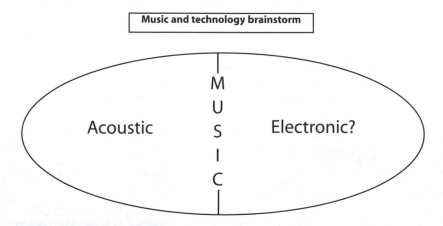

Task 9.1 Attitudes to music technology

Consider 'acoustic' music in relation to 'electronic' music. Use Figure 9.2 as the basis of a brainstorm for associated words. Now group your responses into the following areas

- musical style
- 'high' and 'low' cultural stereotypes
- the role of the performer
- authenticity

Fill in Table 9.2 – it is started for you – ascribing positive attributes to the 'Arts' column and negative attributes to the 'Technology' column. What sort of picture emerges?

Now consider some of the positive applications of technology in relation to the arts and education. In your early visits to your first placement school, try to get the views of pupils and teachers regarding the use of music-related ICT in the classroom. You might consider some of the following questions:

Of pupils:

- Do you enjoy using electronic keyboards/the computer to make music?
- Do you like some music technology more than others?
- What do you learn when you use music technology?
- What are the most common problems with music technology?

Of teachers:

- When do you find it most appropriate to incorporate music technology in the support of pupils' musical learning?
- What is the pupils' response to music technology?
- Do you use the technology to support your own teaching?
- What are the most common problems with music technology?

Write a short reflection on your findings.

Table 9.1 Attitude inventory

The arts	*Technology*
Wo(man)	Machine
Human	Mechanical
Expressive	
Unique	
Spiritual	
Natural	
Unpredicatable	
Indefinable	
Honest	
Immortal	
Inspired	

PLANNING YOUR OWN PERSONAL DEVELOPMENT IN MUSIC ICT

The ITT national curriculum for ICT in subject teaching requires that providers should audit trainees' knowledge, understanding and skills in ICT at the beginning of their course. This audit covers *the common ICT tools* such as word processing, e-mail, presentation software and data handling. In addition to computer based ICT there are the more *traditional forms of ICT*, for example, television, video, overhead projectors and sound recorders which also need to be considered.

You also need to audit your competence in those areas of *music-related ICT* that directly affect your work in the classroom, and this section should provide you with some appropriate starting points and suggestions. Remember that this is one strand in you professional development that continues throughout you career. If you are new to certain technologies make a start at an appropriate level. Always consider 'why' you might need to use music ICT to achieve your aims.

You will find in Appendix A a step by step guide to your own professional developments in ICT. This can be used, along with the chapter, as a basis for auditing your music-related ICT capability and setting targets for development during the training year and beyond.

APPLYING ICT IN THE MUSIC CLASSROOM

What is music-related ICT?

The definition of music ICT is very broad, including everything from the humble cassette tape recorder to sophisticated digital technologies which manipulate sound through computer systems. In planning your own use of ICT in the classroom you should be aware that anything which *records, stores and communicates musical information* falls into the category of ICT.

What follows is an attempt to outline, albeit briefly, some of the ways you should begin to consider using ICT in the music classroom. It is arranged into the following categories:

General presentation, recording and monitoring This section deals with the common and traditional ICT tools you would use to present materials and monitor pupils' work in the classroom.

Using electronic keyboards This section deals with the type of keyboard most commonly found in music classrooms. It typically offers a range of sounds, musical styles, auto accompaniments, basic recording facilities and in-built amplification.

The MIDI Computer in the music classroom This section deals with the computer and MIDI. MIDI stands for 'musical instrument digital interface' and is the link that conveys musical information between electronic musical devices and a computer. It can capture, edit and playback performances. Computers in this context can act as *sequencers* – capturing creative ideas, sophisticated *auto-accompaniment devices* or as *score writers*. They do not deal with acoustic sounds.

Creative sound: recording, processing, sampling, synthesis   This section deals with aspects of advanced sound recording and creation. Unlike MIDI it mainly deals in acoustic sounds and their manipulation. However, there are certain crossovers with these technologies – for example, sampling and synthesis – that should become apparent below.

Using CD ROM and the Internet   This section deals with computer based technologies which can present music related information in new and exciting ways.

Some general considerations

Your credibility as a teacher is affected by the sort of sounds these technologies make. As with their acoustic equivalents the cost of the instrument affects the tonal characteristics and quality of the sound. However, with careful evaluation and preparation even cheap equipment can sound effective.

Sound quality

Always consider the quality of the sound your pupils are hearing. Playing back recordings through the highest quality equipment or boosting sounds with additional amplification should be considered essential. *Where* the pupils are seated, the number of pupils and the size of the room should also feature in your planning. Attention should be paid to the timbral characteristics of electronic instruments and other devices along with the possibility of enhancing their sounds with additional effects.

Rehearsal

Never *assume* that a piece of technology is going to work. Always rehearse your interaction with the machine and check that the equipment is working before the pupils arrive in the classroom. Do not allow anyone to tinker with equipment once it is set up. Have plan 'B' ready if the system refuses to work.

Resource management and monitoring

Always plan how resources will be set-up, moved and accessed. If pupils are working on headphones, or in another area, you need to consider how to monitor and assess the work in progress. The placement of power sockets and issues of health and safety also have a bearing on the musical process. How the pupils are seated, sight lines, access to power sources and management of noise levels all affect your classroom interaction with the pupils. Devise, share and reinforce rules for the handling and use music technology equipment.

Storage and organisation

Where you store recorded information needs some consideration. Files on a computer can easily get lost unless you and your pupils label and store the information effectively. Careful file and folder management, along with the ability to search and find files easily, makes working with music related ICT more efficient.

The size of files is also an issue with audio files consuming large amounts of storage space. Moreover, the way a file is saved can affect future work. Audio recording often 'sets' a musical response at a particular point while MIDI files always remain editable. In some music-related ICT, such as electronic keyboards, the memories are easily wiped between one class and the next. Here you need to consider what other mediums might record pupil achievement and allow for future work to continue

General presentation and monitoring

Playing back recordings

One of the things a student teacher does early on in their teaching practice is to playback some sort of recording to the pupils. This should be easy: just put the tape or CD in the machine and press 'play'. However, in many instances this simple act can lead to stressful failure and loss of standing with the pupils. Where is the extract on the tape? Is the hi-fi system set to play the relevant media (cassette, CD, and so on)? What about volume and sound quality? Is the recording of sufficiently good quality to maintain interest?

You know that careful preparation and rehearsal is essential even in at the ' oh, anybody can do that' end of the ICT spectrum, and that even the cassette tape – in general still the most common media – can be difficult to handle. The newer digital technologies of CD, DCC and mini disc allow more accurate access, remote control and better sound quality.

Task 9.2 Playing back recordings

Try playing back a number of taped extracts on an alien hi-fi system (not your own). Try repeating extracts and 'fast forward' skipping. Fade in and out. Now insert an extract on CD. Draw up a list of dos and do nots with regard to playback of listening material.

Assist another class teacher by offering technical assistance with playback material.

Focusing and supporting, listening and appraising

Even with the slickest playback technique in the world you find that the pupils' attention wanders if the musical extract is *poorly recorded*, *overlong* or the listening task *unfocused*. To this end you need to devise listening and appraising tasks which engage the pupils in *active response*.

Active response can be enhanced by graphical or visual support. Here an attractive worksheet or a colourful overhead transparency (OHT) might focus listening. Video can also be used to support aural attention. Remember that today's pupils possess a great deal of tele-visual understanding. Harnessing this to focus listening can be a powerful support. As with listening, you should consider the quality of the visual experience, for example: sight lines, effective classroom blackout, quality and clarity of image.

Task 9.3 Supporting, listening and appraising

Devise an original listening and appraising activity, for example, record a selection of focused excerpts and support these by a worksheet and OHT. In planning your activity consider the 'before' – setting up the activity, framing, necessary information and response vocabulary; the 'during' – the activity that the pupils engage upon while listening; and the 'after' – the response outcomes, musical framing and linkage to other activities.

Record a video extract that you might use to support listening and appraising. Consider playback strategies: such as with/without sound, with/without vision, mismatching sound and vision, and so on.

Monitoring and assessment

You need to give some consideration to the *type* of system you use to record pupils' musical responses, coursework and performance outcomes. 'Fixed stereo systems' – which usually record through a microphone onto a stereo machine – and 'portable' systems – usually with a built-in microphone – both have their advantages and disadvantages. For instance, the former might offer the quality required for GCSE performance coursework while the latter might be more suited to the 'snapshot' recording of a pupil's work in progress – especially if the pupils are placed in a variety of locations. Video recorders should also be considered in this area, especially if there are interesting performance elements linked to the musical response. Multi-track recorders (dealt with later on in the chapter) can sometimes play a role in this sort of work but are probably more suited to small group creative work.

When making a recording try to consider other issues like extraneous noise pollution room reverberation and, in the case of video, lighting. If the recording is for assessment purposes make sure you include recorded details regarding the performers and their musical role.

Task 9.4 Recording

Make a recording of some of your colleagues playing live. Use a fixed recording system and/or a portable system. Evaluate the results.

Assist another class teacher by offering technical assistance with recording pupils' work.

As a pupil resource

Recording and playback technology can, of course, be placed in the hands of the pupils. The popularity of 'karaoke' machines has demonstrated how much people enjoy 'singing along' with musical backing tracks. This interaction with recordings can be extended into the classroom in a number of ways (see Task 9.5). Recording can often lend authenticity to the musical process while setting goals and targets for the pupils. The focus of 'recording' and 'sound quality' can be used as a spur to the effective listening and appraisal of peers. Similarly, video recording and playback can play a part in capturing creativity and performance.

Task 9.5 Pupils using playback

Consider the following statement:

Placed in the hands of the pupils, recording and playback technology can support pupils working individually, in pairs or as a group (see Table 9.2).

Using the headings in Table 9.2, make a list of practical activity scenarios that pupils could engage in.

In the first instance assume unlimited resources (for example, every group has a tape recorder and sufficient headphones). Then tailor the scenario to the reality of your classroom situation.

Table 9.2 Pupils using playback

Performance	Creativity	Autonomous discovery
by providing rhythmic and harmonic frameworks which support pupil performance	by providing aural stimulus, creative starting points, or examples of expected outcome	by providing aural/video texts for appraisal

Using electronic keyboards

Most music classrooms have a selection of electronic keyboards which allow pupils access to a hands-on instrumental experience. As always resource implications can hamper the effective use of these instruments but ideally classrooms should offer enough keyboards to allow individual or pair work, with and without headphones. The use of headphones is appropriate over short periods to support pupils' practice and/or discovery. However, the overuse of headphones should be avoided. Keyboards should play a part in ensemble groupings, mixing with vocal and acoustic instruments where possible. They can also play a discrete musical role in carefully voiced and balanced keyboard ensembles. Additional resource implications regarding the use of keyboards should include power packs, headphones, headphone splitters, power sources and trailing leads.

Task 9.6 Electronic keyboards

Assist a classroom teacher by setting up a classroom for a session which makes use of electronic keyboards. Try to ensure that all the equipment is in working order. Make a note of equipment failure and how this could be minimised in the future.

Work with a pupil on a keyboard task set by another classroom teacher. Try to record the pupils' responses to this task, and write a short report to discuss with the classroom teacher.

Developing skills on the electronic keyboard

When working with keyboards you should plan to *teach* the ICT skills which enable the pupils' musicianship. This plan should include teaching and learning strategies which cover:

- *Basic control:* setting up, volume, balance, and so on.
- *Making musical choices*: what timbre? What musical style? What speed? And so on.
- *Keyboard control:* the correct fingers to use, the geography of the keyboard, how to play single fingered chords, and so on.
- *Recording and storing*: memory features and possibilities.

As a teacher this means that you have to offer support and *aide memoires* – visual and musical – that allow the pupils to access the musical possibilities inherent in the keyboard. 'Pictures' of keyboards with hand placement, mini manuals which describe 'how to' and practical activities that develop technique alongside musicianship are just some examples. With so many choices available you need to consider giving directions which *limit choice* while enabling creativity and performance.

You also need to consider the role of the various support functions in relation to the development of musical skills and understanding. For example, single finger chord accompaniments offer multi-layered harmonic support for the novice. However, they don't tell us anything about chord construction or the instrumental function – rhythm, bass, harmony – of the various parts.

Task 9.7 Exploring electronic keyboards

Spend some time, on your own, with one of your placement school's keyboards. Explore the following:

- musical characteristics, such as number of sounds and styles, touch sensitivity, key size, range, and so on.
- technical functions, for example, single finger chord type, split function, auto accompaniment features.
- memory features, for example, can the keyboards record melody, accompaniment, or both? can they layer melodies or sequence accompaniments?
- sound quality, e.g. how realistic are the sounds? do some succeed more than others?
- other features, such as transpose function, auto harmony, sound editing, memory storage (disc drive).
- keep a record of your explorations for future use. Once you feel familiar with the keyboard, write a short 'how to' manual for pupils: for example, how to choose a voice or a style, how to play single finger chords.

Managing electronic keyboards in class

Pupils often 'muck about' on keyboards. The famous 'demo' button is an easy 'non-musical' choice for the pupil who is off-task. Sound effects (animal noises, car horns, and so on) can readily amuse and distract. Pupils, in the freedom of their own headphones, can often wander into uncharted technological territories (transposing the keyboard or disabling the volume).

Of course, there is nothing wrong with musical exploration, but as a teacher you need to be in control of that discovery. Ensure that the pupils have a clear set of guidelines regarding appropriate use of the keyboards in your classroom. When pupils are using headphones make sure that the time is structured and focused. If pupils are working in pairs consider what complementary musical activity each player can engage in. Clear musical goals and time limits need to be set and frequent monitoring has to be undertaken to ensure that pupils stay on task.

Whole class work can also be undertaken with keyboards. Here, while monitoring becomes easier, controlling noise level becomes more difficult. Sometimes having a 'central' power switch that turns the whole class 'off' can be a 'final' solution. However, other classroom control strategies should be tried before this. Conductor type signals and routines for quiet are possible here. Pupils can also 'fold their arms', 'sit away' from the keyboard or 'switch off'. Whatever the problems it should not deter from developing whole class approaches.

Task 9.8 Managing electronic keyboards

In your observations take note of how other music teachers manage the use of keyboards in class. Discuss these uses with other student teachers.

Draw up your own list of 'dos' and 'do nots' in relation to the use of keyboards in class.

Ways of using keyboards in class

Keyboards can be used to support you as a teacher as well as developing the pupils' musical skills and understanding. Try to conceive of lessons which *integrate* keyboards with vocal and acoustic approaches.

However, when used to support your classroom presentation, electronic keyboards can provide realistic musical backings which, when programmed into the memory, offer hands-free teaching. You can incorporate electronic keyboard support into your lesson presentations by pre-programming one of the following:

- a keyboard percussion backing to support rhythm work: copy clapping, call and response, word rhythms, raps
- a looped chord sequence to support vocal and instrumental 'round the class' improvisations
- a stored song accompaniment to support whole class singing
- a listening and appraising activity which utilise the timbres and styles of the keyboard.

Remember that, when using keyboards to support whole class activities, you should consider additional amplification.

It is also most important that pupils are guided into using electronic keyboards for musical purposes. To further their musical understanding, pupils might engage with electronic keyboards to:

- explore timbre
- explore musical style
- play tunes which also teach keyboard skills

- make up original tunes using rhythmic structure and defined scales
- play single finger chord sequences
- improvise over chord sequences
- layer melodic strands into memory banks.

Task 9.9 Electronic keyboards and musical understanding

Devise a short scheme of work (three weeks) which incorporates some of the suggested keyboard activities as well as acoustic activities. Try to include whole class, pair work and individual ways of working in your approach.

THE MIDI COMPUTER IN THE MUSIC CLASSROOM

Your placement school will have a number of areas where pupils and teachers can access computers. Most staff room areas have a computer which provides general word processing facilities. 'Computer suites' allow large numbers of pupils to develop ICT skills. School libraries often contain computer facilities. However, making music on these computers is often limited due a lack of additional musical equipment. A computer in the music department typically includes:

- a piano-style MIDI keyboard to play sounds into the computer
- a MIDI sound module or card to enable musical sounds to be accessed
- stereo speakers to hear the playback
- connecting devices and cables.

In addition there will probably be a printer, a CD ROM drive and possible links to the Internet and other recording equipment.

What sort of MIDI computer?

You need to develop a growing awareness of the type of hardware and software which is available to you. The size and speed of the computer, along with the features offered by its software, define how appropriate it is for subject-related objectives. You also need to know if the systems that pupils are using at home – for instance to complete homework- are compatible with your school's systems. Acquaint yourself with the 'type' of computer and software that your placement music department uses. This information may appear daunting at first but will certainly impact upon the way that you plan to use ICT to support pupil learning.

1   What platform is used (the most common platforms are IBM compatible/ PC, Apple Macintosh and Acorn)?

2   What is its processor power or speed (for example Pentium, G3, megahertz rating)?

3   What is its memory and storage capacity (expressed in megabytes and gigabytes)?

4   What other options are available (for example, CD-ROM, Internet access)?

Software and sounds

There are three main types of software which make use of MIDI information:

- *Sequencers* mimic a multi-track recording environment with performances being captured in layers and then played back. They make much use of graphic environments to represent the music (Cubase, Logic, Cakewalk, and others).
- *Score writing or notation packages* are concerned with the display of traditional notation. They assume the final product is printed on paper (Sibelius, Finale, etc.).
- *Auto accompaniment packages* usually interpret 'typed in' chord sequences. From this they generate accompaniments in a chosen style (Band in the Box).

While software packages often mix and match these types – with sequencers having scoring facilities and notation packages capable of sequencing – they are quite distinct in their handling of musical information.

With so much music software being developed it is worth getting clear in your own mind the educational benefits of such applications. Applications come in various guises, offering cut down 'beginner' versions through to full-blown 'professional' packages. Increasingly MIDI sequencers are being combined with digital audio (see later) to create *virtual studio environments*. You should weigh up the focus and features offered by such software, and match it to your own and your pupils' needs.

The sounds you access through your MIDI software are also a consideration. These sounds might come from a *sound card* inside the computer, an external *sound module* or a *keyboard with onboard sounds*. You need to become familiar with the range and quality of the sounds offered. In particular you need to be aware of the General MIDI standard for voices, which offers a set of 128 voices. Published support materials and downloaded MIDI files from the Internet nearly always use this standard. You also need to teach the pupils about the range and character of the voices offered by General MIDI.

Where is the computer?

The music computer is a complex set of expensive resources which does not take kindly to being moved and reassembled. Hence, in some departments the computer is locked away in a dedicated room separate from the general classroom. Unfortunately this can limit access. More importantly it means that the computer cannot make an appearance in the classroom. Placing the computer and its peripherals on a mobile trolley can often solve these problems of security and access while allowing its use in a number of learning contexts.

As you gain more competence you should try to use the computer in the classroom to support your own presentation. Table 9.3, shown later offers a range of roles that you might consider in this respect. Small groups of pupils may also use it – as part of a learning carousel – inside and outside the classroom. Whole class visual access to the computer screen is problematic. Overhead devices which project the computer screen are a possibility but are still comparatively rare in schools (they are very expensive). However, graphical representations of the screen can be shown on standard OHPs or presented in worksheet form. 'Screen dumps' of computer screen are relatively easy to achieve and import into other software packages.

Task 9.10 Solving the problems of using a computer in the classroom

Consider the problems associated with using the music computer in the classroom. How might you solve them?

What benefits do you perceive a music computer in the classroom might offer to the development of teaching and learning?

Share your reflections with other student teachers or your mentor.

Developing skills

The skills required to set up a music computer, load the software and begin to use the programmes effectively are greater than those required of electronic keyboards. More can go wrong and the learning curve in certain software packages can be steep. If you are a novice you might like to engage in some of the tasks outlined in Task 9.11.

Using the computer in the classroom

There are many ways in which you might use MIDI software and a music computer in the classroom. Table 9.3 (overleaf) outlines some generic ways in which it might support pupil learning in the classroom. Do not assume however that you *must* use a computer to achieve these ends. A backing track recording on tape, a looped chord sequence in the electronic keyboard's memory or a plain old-fashioned piano accompaniment will often do. In fact you should look to frame pupils' performance and creativity in as many contexts as possible. The flexibility which the computer offers (varying textures, transposing, adjusting tempo, and so on) might be particularly appropriate in a certain setting but only if you are competent in handling the technology.

Task 9.11 Using a computer

Some suggestions for developing skills:

- Observe a small group of pupils or classroom teacher interacting with a computer. Make a note of the following: setting up procedures, ways of working, solutions to common problems, routines like saving work and shutting down.
- Set up the computer on your own. Turn everything on in the correct order, load the software, check that MIDI is working and that sound is working 'in and out' of the computer.
- Load a music file and practice playing it back from different points.
- Record some simple teaching support materials (chord sequence, rhythm track, listening and appraising exercise) and save your work. Plan to incorporate it into a lesson.
- Begin a 'troubleshooting' guide for common problems and oversights.

Creative sound: recording, processing, sampling, synthesis

Recording and manipulating 'real' sounds as a source for musical creativity has a long and distinguished history. It goes back to the creative use of tape and microphones by the European avant-garde after the Second World War and it played a large part in the rock revolutions of the 1960s. These technological musical revolutions happened without a keyboard or computer in sight (although nowadays these technologies are closely linked to sound manipulation).

What is 'creative sound' technology?

There are a number of creative sound technologies – old, new and developing – which more or less start from the *microphone*. The sounds are generally recorded into a *multi-track recorder* or a *sampler*.

Multi-track recorders layer recorded acoustic sounds into tape or digital based *stand-alone* machines. Computers can also emulate the multi-track environment (often in tandem with MIDI).

Samplers generally record and manipulate shorter acoustic sounds, from single notes to short phrases. Many technologies use samples to recreate the sound of real instruments (for example, digital pianos). Others capture real performance elements for 'looping' into longer pieces. CDs of sampled material are widely available and technologies which manipulate samples in real time are becoming increasingly evident.

Once the sound has been recorded (and sometimes during the recording) the *sound processor* – often called the special effects (Sfx) unit – comes into play. This can

Table 9.3 Possible ways of using a MIDI computer in the classroom

Supportive musical backings

Example	Scenario	Teaching benefits
Improvisation Example: a 'round the class' rhythm and pitch improvisation over an idiomatic backing track	Whole class	This can provide controlled rhythmic and pitch support for the pupils, authentic stylistic musical accompaniment and 'hands free' direction.
Performance support Example: a 'classroom orchestra'	Whole class	This can provide supported part rehearsal, tempo and dynamic control, flexible repetition of sections, 'on the fly' rearranging of parts, printout of parts.
Song accompaniment Singing a pop song to an authentic backing	Whole class Individual Pair work Group work	This can provide all of the above plus flexible transposition control. Many pop songs are available on MIDI file.

Creative additions and starting points

Example	Scenario	Teaching benefits
Re-voicing musical texture For example, re-score a well known orchestral excerpt	Individual Pair work Group work	Here you can tailor work to differentiated need (including extension activities) by providing realistic starting points.
Adding parts to existing textures, For example, improvising a melodic idea over a given chord sequence		This sort of work can provide a wide range of musical contexts, idioms and cultures for pupils to explore.
Copying musical texture For example, playing in an existing piece from grid or conventional notation		It can develop pupil autonomy in learning while capturing achievement.
Rearranging structures and textures For example, assembling blocks of music into longer, more complex pieces		At its best it should link idiom and style to practical activity while deepening musical understanding within accessible contexts.

Interactive analysis

Example	Scenario	Teaching benefits
Unpicking textures, for example using mutes to explore melody, countermelody and accompaniment	Individual Pair work Group work Whole class	This sort of listening and appraising activity can deepen pupil understanding through interactive engagement.
Following the form, for example on-screen text to guide structural analysis		For the teacher it can provide a flexible 'play back' musical source for this sort of work.
Guided discovery, for example using grid and score edit pages to explore the elements of music		As before it can set tasks which go beyond the expectations of key stage level while developing strategies which promote resource based learning and ICT skills.
Aural tests, for example present hidden melodies for analysis and notation		

process the sound by adding reverberation, echo and a host of other effects to the basic recorded sound. Moreover the sound can be *edited* and *mixed* in the same way that MIDI information can. How flexible these editing features are depends on the equipment.

The *synthesiser* is one form of creative sound technology which does not rely on the microphone. It can, however, design, create and play back *new* sounds. Synthesisers are often contained in 'professional' keyboards but can also be emulated by computer software.

Task 9.12 Creative sound technology 1

Reflect upon the following questions with other student teachers:

- What advantages might multi-track recorders have over MIDI?
- Under what conditions might you use multi-track recorders?
- How might you use ready-made samples to support a pupil's work?
- Discuss the range of musical styles and genres which pupils might explore through sound processing.
- What would pupils learn by designing and creating sounds on a synthesiser?

Using Creative Sound ICT in classroom and extra curricular setting

As a student teacher engaging with such a range of equipment you need to make decisions about what is an appropriate use in any given classroom situation. For example, a multi-track recorder may benefit GCSE composition work but be an inappropriate medium for recording a GCSE performance.

As with other areas of ICT you should try to incorporate aspects of creative sound into you own classroom presentation. The use of a microphone, amplifier or mixing console can bring a degree of authenticity to your presentations. Moreover, their presence acts as a kudos-enhancing prop that suggests serious and professional intent to your pupils. With this in mind you might like to consider the following;

- present a pop song for class singing using a microphone with reverb
- devise a creative stimulus which makes use of sound effects and/or ambient sound
- include considerations of sound processing, placement and quality in your planning and analysis of listening and appraising.

In addition to the classroom, schools often use aspects of these technologies – microphones, mixing desk, sound processing, and amplifiers – in 'live' extra-curricular contexts such as school concerts and musicals.

Task 9.13 Creative sound technology 2

Spend some time with a microphone, amplifier and some sort of effects unit. Practice amplifying your own voice: say a poem, sing a song, experiment with non-musical sounds.

List the issues for teaching that arise from your experiments. Write a short troubleshooting guide on amplifying and adding effects to voices.

Planning for creative sound

Pupils like to *hear* their own voice. Creative audio offers them this facility by placing their voice in any number of different settings and contexts. In effect their vocal sounds – processed, layered or looped – become the building blocks of their creativity. When considering *vocal work* in this area you should try to develop a broad definition of the term. Raps, percussive pops and clicks, scat, exclamations, instrumental imitations and tonal and non-tonal singing should all be considered. Word sources such as poetry and stories along with dramatic contexts offer framing for such work. Visual media – for example, paintings and video – can offer further stimulus. In addition to vocal work these technologies can offer the instrumentalist the ability to sectionalise, layer and manipulate his/her own musical performance. Sampling offers the pupil without instrumental skills the opportunity to structure a variety of musical elements into an expressive whole. You might consider the effective structuring of drum loops (basic beat, variation, fills, exclamations, and so on) within the context of a rap performance.

Task 9.14 Planning for creative sound

Investigate a music department's current schemes of work with a view to incorporating a broad range of vocal responses linked to Creative sound ICT.
  Devise some practical classroom tasks.

Using CD-ROM and the Internet

With CD-ROM and the Internet you need not be limited to the computer systems available in the music classroom. You can explore these areas using the school's computer suite. This may, for instance, allow every pupil access to a computer. However, bear in mind that the computer suite won't have the additional (and sometimes necessary) resources available in the music classroom which enable you to integrate, broaden and enhance the ICT experience.

What is CD-ROM?

The CD-ROM (compact disc read only memory) is an easy to use medium which stores and links large amounts of information (easy, that is, if your computer has a CD-ROM drive and the ability to play back sound). Attractive point and click interfaces move the learner through collections of text, pictures, sound, animation and video. Because CD-ROMs store such large quantities of information 'search' tools are often available. These allow the user to go directly to a category, word or phrase. The information, when located, can easily be moved to other software packages – for instance, portions of text can be transferred to a word processor.

The learning characteristics of CD-ROM

The way information is handled on CD-ROMs is very similar to that of the Internet's 'World Wide Web'. 'Hyperlinks' are made between pieces of information, which allow a number of 'connections' to be made. This means that the learning, unlike many books, is non-sequential. Without guidance the pupil may navigate through the information in a random way. Unless the process is structured 'getting lost' or being unable to access the relevant information may lead to frustration, 'search' exhaustion and loss of motivation. What pupils 'do' with the information, once retrieved, also needs to be considered. Simply cutting and pasting facts into a word processor does not deepen understanding or enhance learning. As a teacher you need to be able to assess how the interaction with ICT is reflected in the pupils' learning.

Of course, handled carefully, and tailored to your pupil learning needs, CD-ROMs can enhance and complement a pupil's musical experience.

Types of CD-ROM

CD-ROMs fall into a number of categories, some of which are outlined in Table 9.4.

Using music related CD-ROM in teaching and learning

CD-ROM can, of course, support you as a teacher. Worksheets and overhead transparencies can benefit from the graphics offered therein while sound clips can be transferred onto another medium (such as music cassette) to support listening and appraising in the classroom. You may even use the medium 'live' with small groups of pupils or with whole class groupings if your school possesses a computer overhead projector.

You should also consider how pupils access a CD-ROM to support their own learning. The CD-ROM might be part of a learning carousel of classroom activities where the pupils engage in autonomous learning. Children engaged in this sort of

Table 9.4 Types of CD-ROM

Category	Example	Information available
General encyclopaedia	'Encarta'	Includes 'basic' musical information alongside other encyclopaedic entries
Music encyclopaedia	'Musical Instruments'	Surveys of musical instruments, musical styles and historical perspectives
Music analysis	'Stravinsky'	'About' composers or an analysis of single works
Interactive music making	'Rock, Rap and Roll'	These can range from encouraging creative response through to more tutorial types of interaction

Task 9.15 Evaluating a CD-ROM

Evaluate a music-related CD-ROM you have access to and write a report for your colleagues. You might like to consider the following criteria:

- Ease of use: is it too easy or too complicated to use?
- Depth of information: suitable for KS3 or 'A' level?
- Age relevance: is the tone too young or too adult?
- Musical relevance: does it develop musical understanding, skills, knowledge?
- Learning flexibility: can it be tailored to the needs of the pupils?
- Learning progression: does it require some fore-knowledge, like the ability to read music, or is it for beginners?

work should be encouraged to feedback their 'discoveries' to the rest of the class. Of course, any pupil interaction with a CD-ROM must be pre-planned and guided by you. You need to create task sheets that guide a group of pupils through a specific area of a CD-ROM and should include:

- specific activities (find out about)
- key words for searching
- listening and appraising activities supported with response vocabularies (musical elements, style, expressive response)
- interactive responses.

Be sure to include a timed structure for each task, roles for each member of the group and technical instructions on accessing the CD-ROM.

What is the Internet?

The Internet is a vast international network of computer terminals linked together by a common communications protocol. Estimates suggest that there are now over 57 million users in the world. The numbers are set to grow, as is the amount of information available. The government sees the Internet as playing a major role in supporting learning and teaching in the new millennium, and all schools should now be on-line.

Accessing the Internet

The information and resources available on the Internet can be accessed by anyone who has a computer linked to a modem, 'browser' software and an account with an Internet service provider (ISP). Nearly all the information is presented through the graphics and text-based medium of the World Wide Web (WWW) although other methods exist. This presents information in a very similar way to a CD-ROM. The other major use of the Internet is the provision for communication through electronic mail (e-mail). E-mail is now a major communications medium.

What is on the Internet?

Great claims are being made for the Internet and its power to disseminate information and the government is committed to developing a dedicated educational focus using the National Grid for Learning (NGfL). Table 9.5 outlines some of the areas that might be relevant to you as a prospective music teacher.

Using the Internet

As a teacher the Internet may help you plan in areas where your knowledge is rudimentary. It may also expand your knowledge. Sites devoted to the detail of music teaching – the major exam boards, BECTa, music education sites and so on – can allow you to clarify detail and enhance your ideas.

MIDI files are another major resource on the Internet. These files – which are a way of transferring music files between all software platforms – play back on any computer sequencer package connected to a General MIDI sound source. Many sites feature MIDI versions of classical pieces, TV and film themes, pop, rock and jazz

Table 9.5 Using the Internet

Category	Example
Communications	Electronic mail (e-mail)
	Discussion groups
	Computer conferencing
Resources	Sounds, such as audio and midi files
(which can be downloaded onto your	Scores and printed music
classroom computer)	Information, for example about musical genres
	Documentation, for example OFSTED reports
	Software, for example updates and shareware
	Product information
Shopping	Books, CDs, and so on
Electronic publishing	Many schools have their own web pages

pieces. Once downloaded the files can be tailored to you own and your pupils needs: transposed, rearranged, re-voiced and so on.

There are also an increasing number of formats for real audio files which do not take vast amounts of time to download (such as MP3 files), and potentially represent access to a vast body of CD-quality sound. Needless to say there are huge issues of copyright, although there exist many legal sites.

You should, however, be aware that the Internet is an uncontrolled, and hence unedited, resource area. The quality of the material must be carefully assessed before being passed on to the pupil. Downloaded information may be poorly programmed, factually wrong or unfairly biased.

Task 9.16 Using the Internet

Compile a list of the ways in which the Internet might support you as a teacher both in terms of your professional development and your curriculum planning and presentation.

Access the Internet and visit a music-related site. Download a MIDI file and attempt to play it back on a sequencer or the 'media player' on the computer. Keep a record of how to complete this task.

The Internet as a pupil resource

One of the ways pupils might use the Internet is through 'guided discovery'. Because of the vastness of the WWW, pupils will need to develop skills to allow them to search effectively for material. Many *search engines* are available to help them. But thinking of a 'key' word or phrase can be difficult for some pupils. Refining your pupils' vocabulary through careful support can enhance their musical learning as well as their ICT skills. As with CD-ROMs you need to structure the pupils' use of the Internet. Careful preparation and worksheet support are necessary.

As more and more schools offer pupils e-mail access you should consider ways in which this resource might support classroom work. Some schools have set up partnerships (occasionally on a European or international basis), where compositions and other types of information/conversations are exchanged.

Task 9.17 The Internet as a pupil resource

Devise a homework activity which makes use of the Internet. Plan the Internet activity in advance and support it with instructions. Make provision for pupils who don't have Internet access at home.

Think of ways in which you might use e-mail to communicate with pupils. What might be the advantages and disadvantages of using such a resource?

RESOURCE AND CLASSROOM MANAGEMENT IN RELATION TO MUSIC ICT

Managing resources

One of the biggest considerations in music ICT is the effective management of resources. When planning to use music-related ICT in the classroom you might need to check out the following:

- Are there enough resources?
- Is the equipment, including peripherals, working?
- Can the equipment be stored safely such that it will not become damaged?
- Can the environment effectively support the equipment?
- Is the equipment safe to use?
- How will I save and store the pupils' work?

No doubt you have come across problems and issues in relation to resources in your own school placement. As mentioned earlier you need to consider in your planning how you will respond when equipment fails. Supporting materials which do not require ICT, alternative activities or a 'lesson plan B' should figure in your thinking.

Task 9.18 Managing resources

Discuss the following with your colleagues and music teachers in your school:

- How might you best avoid resource problems?
- What support strategies might help you manage your resources?
- List some practical responses to equipment failure.
- After your discussions draw up a troubleshooting list which will enable you to look out for common problems.

Classroom management issues

Of course, even with the best preparation in the world, things can go wrong. When they do you may find you have classroom management problems to deal with. Like all other areas in the music lesson you need to teach rules which develop the correct attitudes to the handling and use of equipment. Similarly, you need to set expectations for how pupils will respond when equipment fails. Forewarned is forearmed and so here is a list of some of the common forms of inappropriate pupil behaviour in relation to music ICT resources.

Handling equipment:

- Unsanctioned movement of equipment.
- Lack of respect for the equipment.
- Peripherals (headphones, splitters, power leads) being 'misplaced' – deliberately or inadvertently.
- Pupils assuming they can 'fix' malfunctioning equipment.
- Pupils arguing over whom gets to use the best or latest equipment.

Playing equipment:

- Playing the keyboards at inappropriate times (for example, when the teacher is talking).
- Choosing inappropriate voices (for example, sound effects as opposed to pitched voices in melodic work).
- Setting off the demo.
- Inappropriate exploration (messing about) when on headphones.
- Playing too loud.

There are also general issues of management to which you should pay attention. These include:

- Getting attention when pupils are using headphones.
- Monitoring headphone work.
- Getting attention due to poor sight lines caused by equipment placement.
- Trying to occupy the class while dealing with equipment failure.
- Finding strategies to occupy the class while you record others.

Task 9.19 Classroom management and ICT

Draw up a set of classroom rules which deal with the handling and musical use of music ICT equipment

---

SUMMARY OF KEY POINTS

In this unit we have tried to introduce you to a range of ICT that has relevance to you and your pupils in the music classroom. It is important that you begin to use ICT as soon as you feel competent to do so and at a level which takes account of classroom pressure. It is equally important that you integrate ICT with other, more traditional, forms of music-making and that you reflect upon both when and how to use ICT in any particular teaching and learning context. You also need to consider carefully the management and resource implications of using ICT in a classroom context.

As a developing teacher you need to continually review your competence in the three ICT areas – common ICT tools, traditional forms of ICT and music-related ICT – in the light of new developments and the learning needs of your pupils.

In time ICT will become an integrated part of a range of musically exciting learning contexts for your pupils. In addition it can promote your own professional development, enhance your presentation strategies and improve your overall professional efficiency.

FURTHER READING AND SOME SUPPORTIVE RESOURCES

Various (1997) *The Music IT Pack*, Coventry: BECTa. This is a set of choosing and using guides that provides an overview of how music related ICT can enhance learning. It provides specific advice regarding resources and their application along with a glossary of commonly used terms. It also includes an evaluative guide to the use of CD-ROMs in music education.

Various (1998) *Music Technology in Action*, Coventry: BECTa. These are a set of teacher resource materials which complement the music IT pack. They provide a training guide for teachers backed up by practical examples of classroom application and cover electronic keyboards, MIDI sequencing, sound processing and recording and CD-ROM. The pack includes support files on CD-ROM and a training video.

Websites

www.becta.org.uk/index.html   Welcome to BECTa. This is a music ICT in education support site and the home page of the British Educational Communications and Technology Agency (formally NCET). BECTa's remit is to ensure that technology supports the DfEE's drive to raise educational standards, and in particular to provide the professional expertise the DfEE requires to support the future development of the National Grid for Learning (NGfL). There are lots of music education related articles here

www.mri.ac.uk/cd.html   Music Research Institute – Creative Dream. This is a research site. Here you will find details on the Creative dream, a three-year music education research project which seeks to find evidence of good practice in composing in the classroom with a particular focus on the use of keyboards.

www.teach-tta.gov.uk/index.htm   Teacher Training Agency. This is a general education research site. Here you will find current initiatives in the field of education. In particular you will find information on current training initiatives concerning ICT in our schools. The purpose of the Teacher Training Agency (TTA) is 'to raise standards in schools by improving the quality of teacher training, teaching and school leadership, and by raising the status and esteem of the teaching profession'.

www.musicwing.com/   MusicWing gateway. This is a general music teaching support site with a particular focus on music technology. It is run by Andy Murray who has worked on the BECTa support materials and produced the MIDI support work for Heinemann's Music Matters 2.

www.prs.net/midi.html   Classical Midi Archives

midiworld.com/mw_mflib.htm   MIDI Files at MIDIWORLD.

These are two examples of MIDI file sites. Here you can download files in a variety of styles. There are many other music-related ICT sites.

www.mp3.com   MP3 Files. This is the classic MP3 site which contains hundreds of these audio files which are manageable in terms of size and time for downloading.

Note: these sites may move. If the address does not work try a search using the site name.

10 Assessment in the music classroom

Pauline Adams

The word 'assess' is derived from the Latin *ad* + *sedere*, meaning to 'sit down together'.

(Ross *et al.* 1993: xi)

INTRODUCTION

> Assessment of pupils' learning and achievement cannot be viewed as separate or more significant than other aspects of educational activity. For those teaching the arts there has been long standing controversy about the feasibility and even the desirability of assessing progress in the creative arts. Opponents of the idea cannot see a way of evaluating development which intimately involves human feelings and emotions; proponents contend that the effectiveness of all forms of educational provision should be subject to regular assessment.
>
> (DES 1985: 18)

Current political emphasis demands that pupils' achievements are recorded in order to monitor the effectiveness of schools, and to raise standards. The Office for Standards in Education (OFSTED) is responsible for inspecting and reporting to the Department for Education and Employment (DfEE), and for disseminating good practice observed during school inspections. Documentation provided by schools for inspection includes assessment procedures, and written records of pupil achievement. Recorded assessment is also used for reporting purposes to outside agencies, such as parents, governors and taxpayers. It can therefore be argued that if music is to maintain a high profile within a school, assessment of and reporting on the progress of pupils is not only desirable but necessary.

The last thirty years has seen a transformation in the ways in which music is approached within the classroom. The focus on encouraging creativity, and the fostering of the notion of pupils developing a personal relationship with musicmaking, has presented music teachers with particular challenges in devising assessment models. When attempting to set clear and well defined criteria for summative judgements, much of what is important in the creative process may be lost, and it is easy to fall into the trap of trivialising the nature of the work being assessed.

The introduction of the GCSE examination in music made it imperative for teachers to consider ways in which they could assess performance and, in particular, the more difficult area of composition. The inception of a national curriculum for music and of the OFSTED inspectorate has to some extent focused the debate on the ways in which music can be both informally and formally assessed and recorded, in a way that meets inspection requirements. For example, do 'teachers assess pupils' work thoroughly and constructively, and use assessments to inform teaching?' (OFSTED 1995: 74). It is interesting to note that a government guide to good teaching in the arts (OFSTED 1998), focuses on continuity and progression within the curriculum but makes no reference to procedures or models for assessment. Indeed, the report cites many good examples of classroom practice, but does not inform us how OFSTED inspectors interpret assessment requirements in music or to what extent 'good teaching' incorporates assessment into practice.

The ongoing creative arts assessment debate will continue to rumble on – 'objective' versus 'subjective', 'cognition and reason' versus 'the realm of the creative imagination and the aesthetic' – and rightly so. It is the uniqueness of the arts which is often used to argue the case for their inclusion within the curriculum. Spruce suggests that what 'the arts require is an assessment model that has legitimacy in a whole-education context and also serves the specific needs of the curriculum area' (Spruce 1996: 171). The 'specific needs' aspect of assessment is the ongoing challenge to all those involved in music education.

OBJECTIVES

By the end of this unit you should:

- have gained an awareness of the challenges and possibilities when assessing pupils' music making
- be aware of complex issues which affect the assessment of music
- be familiar with the range of strategies you can employ for monitoring, recording and reporting pupils' work in progress.

THE NATIONAL CURRICULUM AND ASSESSMENT

The revised national curriculum orders of 1995 required all subjects at key stages 1, 2 and 3, excepting music, art and physical education, to be assessed against eight-level descriptions arranged in order of increasing difficulty from 1–8. An additional description above level 8 defined exceptional performance.

The requirement for music, art and physical education assessment was based only on end of key stage descriptions, setting out standards of performance expected by the majority of the pupils at the end of each key stage. Descriptions of exceptional performance were provided for music and art at the end of key stage 3. In 1996 SCAA (Schools Curriculum Assessment Authority) and ACAC (Curriculum and Assessment Authority in Wales) published teacher guidelines to exemplify standards which were intended to promote consistency in teacher assessment at the end of key stage 3. The features of progression, for each key stage, were divided into four levels: working towards, achieving, working beyond, and exceptional.

The assessment proposals as now implemented in the revised curriculum orders for 2000 include an eight-level scale for art, music and physical education moving to a common method of setting out standards for pupils' performances across all curriculum subjects. These eight levels are to be applied across the age range 5-14.

The eight-level statements are derived from the attainment target which sets out the 'knowledge, skills and understanding the pupils of different abilities and maturities are expected to have by the end of each key stage' (DfEE/QCA 1999b: 36). The national curriculum document also sets out the range of levels expected by the end of each key stage:

- key stage 1   levels 1–3
- key stage 2   levels 2–5
- key stage 3   levels 3–7

and expected average attainment levels for the majority of pupils at the end of each key stage:

- end of key stage 1   at age 7   level 2
- end of key stage 2   at age 11   level 4
- end of key stage 3   at age 14   level 5/6

See also Chapter 2 for a further discussion of these levels.

The NC guidelines suggest that when teachers are deciding on the level of attainment at the end of each key stage, 'each description should be considered alongside descriptions for adjacent levels' (ibid.).

Schools are expected to translate these descriptions in accordance with whole school assessment policy and to adapt the new legislation within their existing assessment frameworks. Indeed, many music teachers have already invested much time in finding appropriate wording for both subject specific and individual unit assessment criteria, and have devised ways of managing ongoing assessment within the classroom. For many music teachers gathering assessment evidence to make judgements about such criteria is particularly challenging, not least because music is timetabled only once a week in the majority of schools.

ASSESSING CREATIVITY

Good teachers want their pupils to achieve success through their own efforts and devise effective methods of teaching to ensure that pupils are able to achieve the knowledge and skills they need to pass set tests and examinations. A syllabus can be taught, targets can be met and, through quantifiable results, achievement and levels of success can be measured. However, such an approach to assessing music can be problematic and, as Swanwick warns we

> must avoid a reductionist attitude, imagining that we build up musical experience from rudimentary atoms: that, for example, we first perceive intervals or single tones and that musical lines or textures are assembled in our minds only after analysis of the component parts has taken place.
>
> (Swanwick 1988: 139)

Durrant and Welch relate their concerns to the more recent requirements for statutory assessments and the possible unreliability of teacher judgements. They are concerned that the 'assessment of composing, performing or tasks related to listening activities is not just about 'correct notes' or accurate reproduction of factual information, but is also about musical attainment having an affective as well as a cognitive facet' (Durrant and Welch 1995: 122).

For some music educators and artists the process of creating a composition or performance is as important as the finished product. If music is to be taught in line with current good practice (and statutory requirements), then the personal act of creating has to be seen as important. Time needs to be given for pupils to do more than 'scratch the surface'. One or two areas of work explored in depth, where pupils are given time to analyse, practise and refine their music, leads to more personal satisfaction and achievement than constant change of activity. Cognitive functioning and development and the acquisition of skills cannot be isolated or seen as separate from the 'affective' mode, which recognises feeling and expression as important to the learning process. Pupils can ultimately feel frustrated if they are not given the opportunities for real musical engagement.

It is at the point of completion that a piece of art, whether it be music, sculpture or poetry, moves from being subjective to objective, as it takes on new owners, and a different critical audience. Personal involvement in the process of creating an art object may be seen to end at the moment the work goes public. Letting go of our work, giving it away by sharing it with an audience to make of it what they will, allows us to move on to something new.

Any group of pupils working creatively with music generate a number of ideas, some of which they will try out, then either use or discard. Some ideas are dismissed at the discussion stage, or may be too difficult to execute in the time given. The ideas of more dominant members within a group task may be adopted, while other ideas are not even vocalised. As Fryer has identified it is sometimes difficult to see what counts as the creative element to pupils' work.

There is disagreement about whether an idea *per se* can count as creative or whether there has to be some tangible product. On the one hand there is an argument that it is difficult to gauge the level of creativity when there is no tangible product. On the other hand, it is hard to argue that good ideas and plans are not admissible, simply because they have not been translated into reality

(Fryer 1996: 18).

Pupils in the classroom are functioning in a number of ways and on a number of levels within different activities. They may be applying new-found knowledge of a technical skill, evaluating and revising an arrangement through discussion, reflecting on the effectiveness of a composition, or making a cognitive leap through social interaction. Teachers need to consider ways in which pupils learn, and be able to recognise, through keen observation, changes in pupil behaviour when engaging in musical activity. Such teacher awareness relies on a range of assessment procedures, so that the value of all that pupils do is acknowledged. Qualitative assessment, reflecting the creative processes and musical behaviour of pupils, has no place in the mechanistic, 'tick- box' systems imposed on some other curriculum subjects.

METHODS OF ASSESSMENT: CONSTRUCTING A FRAMEWORK FOR ASSESSING MUSIC IN THE CLASSROOM

Pupil development and achievement depends on the interactive process between teacher and learner. It is closely linked to the teacher's own subject knowledge, teaching skills and to the learning context. In chapters 3 and 4 of this book we emphasised the importance of thorough and appropriate planning in order to promote quality musical experiences. Assessment is an integral part of this planning. Indeed, many authors view assessment as an everyday activity: 'Assessment makes it possible for us to live – it guides all our actions. Assessing in everyday situations is often informal, intuitive' (Swanwick 1999: 71). The teacher is constantly making such informal and intuitive judgements in the classroom and along with the pupils, behaves like a music critic. Loane believes that 'when a music teacher discusses with pupils their composition or performance, this is a process of assessment' (Loane 1982: 242). Such views allow opportunities for deeper consideration when approaching assessment, and encourages teachers to look closely and with a critical eye at all assessment models presented, including those of statutory bodies.

TYPES OF ASSESSMENT

As a beginner teacher it is essential that you become familiar with existing assessment models and to consider how you are going to begin to monitor and gather evidence of pupils' achievements in your lessons. When planning for teaching, you need to think about assessment opportunities which are feasible and manageable during the different activities.

It is important to all of us when learning something new or working with novel ideas, to gain some feedback about development and progress. Sharing our work and talking through the processes with another person can help us to move on in some way, either by confirming our progress or by allowing us to rethink, or to gain greater accuracy in executing our ideas. We can be spurred on becoming focussed where we were floundering, or gain some important knowledge we need in order to proceed further.

Formative assessment

The main purpose of this form of assessment is to:

- gain insights into the way pupils respond to and interupt given material
- allow discussion between pupils and teachers about further development and learning
- provide informed feedback to the pupils about their learning and their work; feedback which is diagnostic and relevant to the individual as well as encouraging and positive
- review teaching styles and approaches and consider the effectiveness of differentiated work in relation to individual pupils.

This form of informal monitoring provides the teacher with an ongoing record of pupils' progress. It allows the teacher to answer key questions such as 'What new insights have pupils brought to their music making during this lesson or unit of work?' Care should be taken, however, not to over-monitor, as pupils need space and time to experiment, make mistakes, practise and refine their work. The teacher needs to make informed judgements as to how and when to intervene.

A well planned and organised lesson in which pupils are motivated and on-task enables the teacher to spend time observing, listening and interacting with the whole class, with groups and with individuals. The more sensitive the teacher's interpretation of pupils' responses to their work and learning, the deeper the insight into the way pupils interact with musical ideas.

You need to be quite clear about what you wish to monitor and assess but you must also be prepared to listen to your pupils, to their ideas and questions. If you do not listen you may miss the point. A general impression of what is happening is not enough. You should also monitor your own responses to pupils' musical behaviour, ideas and questions. For example:

- Are you dismissive if pupils' ideas do not correspond with your own?
- Do you ignore pupils who give a 'wrong' answer and praise those pupils who answer as you anticipate?
- Do you find yourself fascinated if a pupil brings an unusual perspective to interpreting a set task?

- How do you discuss and interact with your pupils' work?
- How do you respond to pupils whose expression and realisation is rooted in a different cultural context from your own?

As you circulate around the classroom, engaging in formative assessment, you need to define clearly what you are observing and looking for. To get you started here is a list of things to look for:

- To what extent has the task been understood and how quickly do the pupils embark on the work set?
- When a pupil is clearly off–task or reluctant to participate, what diagnostic and remedial strategies do you employ ?
- How do the pupils share the task within the group?
- What are the differing levels of involvement of individuals in relation to the task?
- How do pupils overcome difficulties and challenges, and what do they do when they are unsure how to proceed?
- What do the pupils talk about, and is it related to the task?
- What kinds of questions do they ask?
- What effect does teacher interaction with a group have upon consequent work?

We suggest you try Tasks 10.1 and 10.2 using the questions above and some of your own.

Task 10.1 Interacting with processes 1

Imagine you have set pupils a group investigative task, to try out a number of playing techniques in order to produce different sounds from a range of untuned percussion. What might you choose to observe as you circulate around the different groups? What kinds of questions might you ask in order to invite pupils to share their process with you? If they have completed the task what might you suggest they do next?

Imagine you have asked pupils to arrange a song you have taught to them as a whole class. In groups, they have reached the stage of refining and rehearsing their song for a performance which is to be assessed. As you move from group to group what are you looking for in terms of performance; list the criteria you would use to check progress.

How might you choose to intervene when a group is off-task, or satisfied with what is clearly going to be an under-rehearsed and poor performance?

Discuss your monitoring and formative assessment procedures with your mentor.

Share your early experiences of assessment with student teachers in other subject areas.

From your observations of group activities, and during whole-group shared sessions when pupils might perform their work in progress, or finished compositions, you can give pupils useful and appropriate feedback about their music. Feedback is best given as close to the event as possible in order for it to be most effective. During oral feedback you might start by focusing on positive aspects of the work, but you should not avoid constructive criticism, which may help pupils to further improve or refine their musical ideas. Such support may help pupils to overcome difficulties and more fully realise their potential.

Formative assessment allows you not only to monitor pupils' learning, but also to evaluate the effectiveness of your own planning and teaching. This is indeed one unique aspect of teaching. Not only are you responsible for providing learning opportunities and experiences for pupils, but you also have, in the form of immediate feedback, a learning opportunity for yourself. You are freely given material on which you can reflect in order to consolidate and revise your own classroom practice.

Task 10.2 Interacting with processes 2

Using a small tape recorder, record important snippets of pupils' conversation and discussion, both among themselves and with you. In a quiet moment listen to your recordings and analyse the conversations. Think about whether or not your intervention could have been more effective at various points. Listen to your own responses. Would you wish to change, rephrase or add anything?

How important was this task in helping you to think about ways in which you can informally assess your pupils' understanding and progress?

Remember to ask permission from mentors and pupils before you carry out this task.

Summative assessment

This form of assessment is used to record the overall achievement of a pupil in relation to a required standard as set out in defined criteria. This is known as criterion referenced assessment and is used to measure pupil performance against an explicit determined standard. The national curriculum (1999) sets out the criteria for all subjects, including music. The challenge for the music educator, however, is to avoid a reductionist approach and to ensure that the quality of pupils' music-making is fully defined and recognised in all its complexity. It is important not to view levels or grades as 'absolute indicators of capability' (Fryer 1996: 19), but as part of the continuum of learning. Pupils may view grades as indicative of failure and can become disheartened by what appears to be a finite and dismissive signal.

The 1996 Exemplification of Standards (SCAA and ACAC 1996) and the new NC curriculum levels (1999) attempt to define a progressive model against which to summatively assess pupils' achievements. However, Swanwick views some of the statements as problematic especially where 'more of' is equated with higher achievement in music.

> There is an unfortunate attempt to illuminate the concept of progression with such phrases as 'more complex structures', 'more complex aspects of musical knowledge' and 'greater musicality' Such language is imprecise and spuriously quantitative to form the basis of a viable assessment model
>
> (Swanwick 1999: 77)

Swanwick further suggests that a simple line of music played with an understanding of phrasing, and within the technical capability of the player, can demonstrate a high quality musical experience without any great complexity.

In composition, simple ideas can create desired effects by the economic use of musical ideas. Some of the music of Arvo Part demonstrates such an approach. The sleeve notes accompanying the choral composition *Seven Magnificat Antiphons* describe the work as 'most piercingly beautiful' and the pieces 'also show that simplicity of language in no way precludes a wide expressive range'. Part, when talking about his own music, comments on his titinnabuli style, 'I work with very few elements – just one or two voices. I build with primitive materials – with the triad, with one specific tonality'.

When making judgements about the personal and creative acts of pupils, and the enthusiasm and commitment they bring to the transformation of their own ideas, it is important not to fall into the trap of viewing music as a collection of hierarchically arranged skills to be aspired to in ascending order.

As you become familiar with different models of and approaches to assessment, you need to consider the approach you might adopt when defining achievement in music. The wording you use is critical when writing your subject-specific criteria. Are pupils working to a linear framework where they gradually travel along a prescribed route, or are they allowed to move freely between different musical layers? The account in Box 10.1 exemplifies the way all musicians connect and interact with their particular sound worlds.

Box 10.1 A musical journey

The cellist Stephen Isserlis arrived at Beverley Minster during the late morning to rehearse for an evening concert. He took his cello out of its case and, after tuning, spent about twenty minutes playing long bows on open strings. Perhaps part of this exercise involved gaining a familiarity with the acoustic of the building. Changes in tone and texture could be heard and there was a sense of exploration within the playing. The single notes gradually changed to scalic patterns played at various tempi, followed by phrases and passages as recognised in particular compositions by Bach and Brahms. The pianist arrived and there was a straight run through the first movement of the Brahms *Cello Sonata in F major*.

Swanwick in many of his publications (1988, 1994, 1999) has been at pains to devise qualitative criteria for musical development/achievement as opposed to the 'more of' criteria found in statutory documents. Looking at his eight layers of qualitative criteria for assessing the work of pupils, we can observe that Isserlis was interacting at different moments within all the different layers (see Box 10.1). Such a cumulative model allows for movement within the layers and conveys an integrated approach to learning. Isserlis was initially exploring the sonorities of the 'cello, controlling and changing tone colour by using particular bowing techniques. The emerging scalic patterns were played staccato, then legato with slurs, and gradually transformed into recognisable musical phrases. Evidence of the stylistic awareness needed to play Bach and Brahms revealed the personal commitment to gaining insight into the music of these composers. Such encounters and observations should lead us to consider carefully the way in which we construct assessment models for judging our pupils, ensuring that revisiting layers and adding new ones is part of an organic process, and integral to musical development.

The analysis of children's compositions by Swanwick and Tillman (1986), formed the basis of their eight–layer developmental model, which has also been extended to include assessment criteria for performing, and appraising (see Box 10.2).

Box 10.2 The Swanwick and Tillman model of musical development

Materials

Level 1 recognises (*explores*) sonorities, for example, loudness levels, wide pitch differences, well-defined changes of tone colour and texture.
Level 2 identifies (*controls*) specific instrumental and vocal sounds – such as types of instrument, ensemble or tone colour.

Expression

Level 3 (*communicates*) expressive character in music – atmosphere and gesture – or can interpret in words, visual images or movement.
Level 4 analyses (*produces*) expressive effects by attention to timbre, pitch, duration, pace, loudness, texture and silence.

Form

Level 5 perceives (*demonstrates*) structural relationships – what is unusual or unexpected, whether changes are gradual or sudden.
Level 6 can place (*makes*) music within a particular stylistic context and shows awareness of idiomatic devices and stylistic processes.

Value

Level 7 reveals evidence of personal commitment through sustained engagement with particular pieces, performers or composers.
Level 8 systematically develops critical and analytical ideas about music.

Task 10.3 Assessing the recorded work of your pupils

Choose two groups of pupils in a Year 9 class you have taught who have completed the same unit of work, and video record their final performance of group compositions or arrangements. Arrange a time when you can view or listen to the recordings with your mentor. Make sure you have your unit plan, lesson plans and assessment criteria for both the performance and composing tasks so that you can discuss fully with your mentor, all aspects of your teaching as well as your final assessment judgements.

Select the criteria on which to base your own assessment (for example, NC, school, Swanwick).

Your discussion with your mentor will focus on:

- the wording of the criteria and different levels
- the basis on which you have judged the work of the pupils.

Ipsative assessment

This form of assessment informs the pupil how they have performed in relation to their own previous efforts, and promotes independent learning. It is most effective when pupils are involved in monitoring their own progress and setting their own criteria.

As well as bearing the responsibility of organising and monitoring whole-class activity, the teacher needs to have an interest in the development of each pupil. Student teachers benefit from having the opportunity to share feedback on both positive and negative aspects of their own taught lessons, and it is within this context that the significance of individual pupil activity begins to emerge. Those moments when musical behaviour changes in some significant or even dramatic way are the most treasured.

There may be a sudden transformation as a pupil discovers a new technique which allows them to access music in a novel way. For example, a particular pupil was asked to learn to play a simple melody by Handel on the electric keyboard, using the correct fingering. The melody was chosen because of its technical suitability for a beginner keyboard player, and because it fitted in with the baroque focus of the unit of work. The student teacher ensured that the task was achievable, enabling the pupil to play with an accurate fingering technique for the first time, thus encouraging musical phrasing – an impossibility when playing the keyboard with one finger. The pupil gained two new and valuable musical experiences. The first, some technical facility on the keyboard which gave him a real sense of playing the instrument 'properly' and second, the skill to be able to interact in a musical way with the material provided and play a melody with fluency and phrasing. The pupil was fully aware of the progress he had made and was keen to further develop his keyboard skills.

In this case study, musical potential had been realised and the pupil became interested in and aware of his own progress. It is at this point that the pupil may be asked how he or she would like to proceed, having some stake of ownership in negotiated task setting, with achievable goals and opportunities for self assessment. For this pupil, adding block chords to the melody became important and was personally viewed as representing further progress.

Written self-evaluations by pupils can also provide the teacher with evidence of their awareness of their own learning processes. Metacognition, the development of awareness of one's own learning and understanding, is encouraged when teachers give opportunities for self assessment, both oral and written. Some educators would argue for such subjectivity to be central to assessment in the arts, for example; 'We are proposing that teachers and pupils should indeed sit down together in regular shared acts of assessment through talk' (Ross *et al.* 1993: 6).

Pupil self-assessment

Part of the formative assessment process may include pupil self-assessment. In music, this is often approached as a group effort, such as keeping a written weekly review of work, or by peer assessment where pupils perform their music and others make critical comments. This is not intended as a self-grading system for pupils but as a record of their perceptions of tasks, opportunities for comment on processes and progress, and self-recognition of their achievements in music.

The use of a pro forma for keeping records can perform a number of useful functions, such as keeping track of the different activities, what instruments have been played and by whom, evaluation by learners and teacher, comments on current progress, and agreed areas for further development. Although such a written record may appear too time consuming, it can in fact save time and ensure that individuals and groups are quickly on-task at the beginnings of lessons. Most importantly, pupils are encouraged to acknowledge ownership of their own learning.

Music in both creation and performance offers opportunities for critical appraisal through informal peer group assessment and evaluation. While pupils share work in progress and in final performances they can be encouraged to use constructive criticism in exploring the processes and challenges of both making music and of working in a group. Rowntree (1977: 147) suggests that 'peer evaluation is more productive as a source of insights for the teacher and as a means of involving students more actively in the learning process'. It is this aspect of self-appraisal that develops the critical awareness required for improving and developing individual musicianship.

There are, however, dangers when setting up such procedures. Both the self-appraisal pro forma and pupil appraisal of the music of their peers can become mundane and pointless exercises if the teacher does not have clear ideas about the ways in which these methods can enhance learning. The questions about the work have to be varied and change as pupils' knowledge, skills and understanding develop.

Task 10.4 Pupil self-assessment

After reading the last section design a pro forma for pupils' self-assessment. Remember to provide space for pupils to chart their involvement in the process and the also learning which they perceive to have taken place.

CONCLUSION: MANAGING ASSESSMENT IN THE CLASSROOM

It is clear that you need to collect evidence for musical achievement as a result of your teaching. In addition there is a statutory requirement to make judgements about a pupil in relation to the NC 'levels' and report these to parents at the end of key stage 3 (see Chapter 2 and chapters on examinations). However, apart from this requirement the ways in which evidence is collected, the criteria used for judgements and the reporting of these are a matter for individual music departments. There is great scope for different styles and approaches to assessment providing the evidence exists to make the statutory judgement at the end of KS 3. Some music departments choose to design assessment systems which are closely related to the statutory requirements, while others develop their own systems and use the evidence produced to make judgements against NC criteria at the appropriate time.

Most important for you, as a student teacher, is to collect a wide range of evidence of musical achievement such that the nuances of musical learning can be 'captured'. Rowntree (1977) exhorts us to 'know' our pupils and to get to know them in many different ways. Here are some practical suggestions for collecting evidence of musical achievement:

- A mark book of attendance, grades, marks, comments, homework completed.
- Tapes (audio or video) of compositions and performances.
- Self-assessments made by pupils.
- Pupils' written work for example, worksheets, scores and so on.
- 'Jottings' on significant features of pupils work such as verbal responses, contributions to the process of a composition, your comments to them (for example, keep a folder for each class using A4 sheets, three pupils per side and make one or two additions to the jottings per lesson which soon build up).
- Can you think of any other ways to collect evidence?

If collecting assessment evidence is seen as part of an ongoing daily routine, progressively the burden is reduced. This evidence can then be used to make judgements against any criteria you may wish or are required to use.

SUMMARY

During your training year there is much ground to be covered and it is inevitable that classroom management, planning and teaching take priority during the early stages of your school practice. Your limited period in school allows you some insight into pupils' musical behaviour within different year groups, but does not give you time to observe long-term progression. You do need, however, to become familiar with a range of assessment procedures at key stage 3, and where possible at GCSE and A level, both in the classroom and at the final grading stages required by the examination boards.

In this chapter we have seen that:

- Assessment is closely related to planning and teaching and that assessment opportunities need to be built into unit and lesson preparation.
- You need to assess what you have actually asked pupils to do and learn.
- There are many challenges to assessing music and that the qualitative aspects of arts assessment need to be central to the assessment process.
- Assessment occurs through an ongoing interaction between teacher and learner (formative assessment).
- Assessment is supported through the recognition of pupils as independent learners, by monitoring their own personal musical development and, by discussion with the teacher, agreeing new areas of learning (ipsative assessment and pupil self-assessment).
- Judgements (summative assessment) needs to be based on sound musical principles and from carefully worded criteria.
- A wide variety of evidence needs to be collected in order to make these judgements about pupils' performance.

FURTHER READING

Spruce, G. (1996) 'Assessment in the arts: issues of objectivity' in Spruce, G. (ed.), *Teaching Music*, London: Routledge. This chapter offers an excellent overview of the critical issues in relation to assessment in music education.

Swanwick, K. (1999) *Teaching Music Musically*, London: Routledge. This book is concerned with teaching and assessing music in ways which are true to the nature of music itself.

11 Public examinations 1

The General Certificate of Secondary Education (GCSE) in music

Chris Philpott with Chris Carden-Price

INTRODUCTION

The history of the development of school examinations in music is to a large extent the history of general school music. Indeed, even as we write the whole music curriculum and attendant examination syllabi are undergoing a thorough overhaul representing further important developments. This chapter does not deal with examinations for instrumentalists, except where they are specifically related to general music examinations.

OBJECTIVES

By the end of this chapter you should understand:

- how school music examinations, syllabi and assessment procedures have developed over time
- the issues which have driven changes in school examinations in music
- the nature and structure of the GCSE
- some approaches to the teaching of GCSE
- the assessment of listening
- the assessment of performing
- the assessment of composing
- other courses in music and the arts for the 14–16 age group.

Box 11.1 Some definitions

Examination   the assessment procedures used to assess pupils' knowledge skills and understanding of the syllabus after taking part in the course.

Syllabus   the knowledge, skills and understanding which must be covered in a course.

The course   the specific programme which has been devised to bring about the knowledge, skills and understandings laid down in the syllabus.

A BRIEF GUIDE TO THE DEVELOPMENT OF SCHOOL EXAMINATIONS IN MUSIC

In 1925 Sir William Hadow and Arthur Somervell drew up a draft music syllabus for the school certificate of the day (the equivalent of a collection of our GCSEs). They recommended that the syllabus contained sight singing, aural tests, elementary harmony and form, an outline of the music history, that is, western art music, and the study of set works. This vision for the music examination syllabus had a big influence over the next fifty years or so. Those of you who took the General Certificate of Education (O and A levels) will remember the aural tests of rhythm and pitch, the classical and baroque harmony papers and the coverage of western art music from 1500 to the present day. Although examinations do not necessarily dictate the way in which a subject is taught it is often the case that they do. The academic elements of these courses tended to be taught in ways which were congruent with their assessment, for example, the teaching of factual knowledge about history and the teaching of skills needed to write a two part exercise or notate a melody. Paynter has argued that, 'Examinations evaluate educational processes; they also *create* educational processes. The implications of any form of assessment are inescapable, for whatever system we adopt it must influence curriculum design and content and teaching method' (Paynter 1982: 17).

School music examination syllabi before the 1970s were dogged with the paradox that music is a practical – creative subject and yet tended to be taught and examined in an intensely academic way. There were also other issues, for example:

- The examinations tended to be exclusive, in as much as they were used as measures of a candidates suitability for higher education.
- Few pupils felt they had any stake in these courses and the examination groups were often very small.
- The 'backwash' into the pre examination syllabi (5–14) seemed to make music one of the least popular subjects in the curriculum (see Ross 1975).

In response to these issues a period of some turbulence has taken place in music education from around 1965 to the present day. Many changes have taken place and a simplified range of these can be seen in Table 11.1. These changes can be placed in the context of wider educational debates surrounding the relative merits of progressivism, traditionalism and reconstructivism (see Chapter 1).

Many of the issues which have surrounded (and still surround) music education can be seen in the developments shown in Table 11.1. These issues include:

- The relationship of academic studies to the practice of music itself for example, the relationship between notation and composition/performance.
- The role of world music, pop, jazz and folk in a general music education.
- The role of the examination itself, for example, as a record of achievement or preparation for the profession.
- Progression from NC to GCSE to A level.
- The notion that all children have the potential to compose.
- The role of music technology as access or barrier to music.
- The validity of different assessment strategies.
- The relative importance of discrete arts subjects or collaborative arts.

It must be said that the changes which brought about the GCSE examination were the most profound, given that they have also influenced the national curriculum and now A and AS levels. The GCSE examination was in many ways the manifestation of the work of writers in the field of music education (for example, Swanwick, Paynter), who had for some time been formulating a rationale for an inclusive music curriculum based upon the musical practices of listening, composing and performing. Many writers in the past had believed in these principles but had rarely been able to formulate a distinctive practical vision which informed the work of music teachers. The new course was radical and its legacy still has many implications for the debate over the music curriculum and its assessment at all levels.

THE NATURE AND STRUCTURE OF THE GCSE

While there has been some minor adjustment to the GCSE syllabus, the principle pillars of listening (appraising), composing and performing have remained remarkably intact. While a GCSE course is required to address these three activities in an integrated fashion, they are still examined separately (although there are plans for a more 'synoptic' approach). The 'classic' structure of the GCSE examination can be seen in Table 11.2. We then go on to explore a typical syllabus for each component.

Listening

The syllabus for the listening content is typically the most detailed, and pupils need to apply their knowledge to real musical examples in the examination. Table 11.3 shows a sample of the content which might need to be covered by units of work and which needs to be learned in order to tackle the listening examination at the highest levels.

Table 11.1 Some developments in music examinations and general school music

	5–14	14–16	16–18
1960s	Traditional model influenced by the assumptions of Hadow, such as singing, appreciation, theory, history.	The introduction of the Certificate of Secondary Education; a 'syllabus for all'. These syllabi ranged from watered down O levels to the inclusion of pop music and composition. These courses ran alongside the traditional O level.	Traditional model, for example, aural harmony, history.
1970s	Schools Council project 'Music in the Secondary School Curriculum' espouses creativity and self expression through composition. Traditional values still have a big influence, however, over many general music classes.	Development of CSE, for example, teachers can now design their own syllabus in relation to pupil needs. Academic–non-academic split occurs, such as career and non-career musicians	As for 1960s
1980s	In 1988 the national curriculum for music is published espousing the values of the GCSE, in other words, music for all as a practical and creative subject.	In 1986 a guide for the new GCSE music is published; one common syllabus for all pupils based on listening, composing and performing; some assessment is by course work and practical examination. Some history and aural is retained but always related to actual musical examples chosen from a wide range of musical styles and traditions.	Some diversification and and choices such as papers on specialist periods of history/harmony. Minor papers for performance appear.

| 1990s | Further development from the 1980s with the addition of music technology as an important means of access to musical achievement. | GCSE syllabi are more explicitly linked with national curriculum criteria. Some boards offer minor options, such as additional performance and music technology. Addition of Expressive Arts GCSE and GNVQ; music as one artform in a practical portfolio of course work. Music technology courses. | Further diversification of papers to include composition, music technology, performance, Twentieth Century harmony. Introduction of Performing arts A level and GNVQ with new forms of practical assessment. Traditional elements still exist. Introduction of AS level (half an A level) |
| 2000 | Further refinement and unification with GCSE and A level. | Further refinement and unification with NC and A level. Expressive arts, performing arts at GCSE and GNVQ. | Explicit links made with NC and GCSE syllabi content (listening, performing, composing) and assessment techniques. Performing arts courses, music technology courses (A level and GNVQ). |

Table 11.2 The 'classic' structure of the GCSE music examination

Listening	Performing	Composing
Usually 40 per cent of the examination.	Usually 30 per cent of the examination.	Usually 30 per cent of the examination.
Usually involves a formal listening test of recorded examples and a series of questions.	Can involve an external examiner or recorded work examined by local moderators.	Usually involves a portfolio of course work but can mean a terminal commission; assessed by the teacher, local moderator or external examiners.
Might involve some delineation in relation to style and genre to be studied.	Combination (or all) of solo performing, performing in an ensemble, rehearsing and directing an ensemble, improvisation; can involve a terminal performance of unseen music.	A score is not usually compulsory but a 'commentary' is.
Might involve a set work.		
Weighting reflects a traditional leaning towards aural tests and historical analysis.	Those who have instrumental lessons are at an advantage here.	Most controversial part of the examination (especially the assessment)

Note: There are some examinations which allow for options, typically using around 10% of the marks taken from the listening weighting, e.g. music technology, set work, performance on another instrument or voice, commissioned composition. These options allow some specialisation within the three elements.

While the content of Table 11.3 is easily written down, it can represent a very reductive vision of musical experience. The syllabus runs the risk of being taught in small units which deal with each of the 'concepts' and thus becomes contrary to the sprit of the examination syllabus. One thing for certain is that learning barren facts devoid of musical experience does not prepare students for the GCSE examination. In the listening paper pupils understanding is tested not by recall of knowledge 'about' but recognition in the context of real musical examples.

Performing and composing

It is also clear that through composing and performing, listening skills can also be developed, such as perceptual and reasoning skills and the use of technical vocabulary. The teacher has a big role to play here in formatively developing listening skills during composing and performing activities, for example, analysis and appraisal with the whole class, groups and individuals. However, by contrast with the listening requirements there are relatively few formal requirements for the syllabus

Table 11.3 Exemplification of GCSE listening syllabus content

Listening content	Examples of understanding and skills
Pitch	chromatic, whole tone, major, minor, cadence, modulation
Duration	triplet, dotted rhythm, syncopation, phrase, simple and common metre, irregular metre
Tempo	adagio, presto, accelerando, rallentando, rubato
Dynamics	common descriptions, crescendo, diminuendo, subito
Articulation	legato, staccato, tremolo
Timbre	vocal sounds, vocal combinations, instrumental families, instrumental combinations/ensembles, instruments of traditions, changing sounds for example muting
Texture	homophonic, polyphonic, solo, unison, contrapuntal
Structure	motive, decoration, sequence, binary, ternary, rondo, variation, sonata, symphony, concerto
Genre/conventions	opera, musical, fanfare, march, oratorio, cantata, ballet, programme music
Traditions/style	western European, popular culture, jazz, folk, Indian, Gamelan, African, Latin American, Caribbean, progression in styles over time
Notation	stave, pitch names, clef, key signature, note values, dynamic names and signs
Musical vocabulary	the technical names to describe the musical 'concepts' above
Perceptual skills	transferring sound into symbol, identifying when the above characteristics are being used, relating these to style /tradition and genre
Reasoning skills	expressing, with reasons, opinions about music, comparing how the elements have been used by different composers, relating music to context, commenting on the detail of performance

Notes: The terms used in this table represent the vocabulary which might be used in the terminal examination and the range of words pupils might need to use in their responses.
  Credit is also given for intuitive understandings of these characteristics, for example describing music without the use of a technical vocabulary, notating pitch graphically and so on.
  It should be noted that there is a distinct continuity of content between the national curriculum for music and the GCSE syllabus in relation to the 'elements', musical traditions and skills.

Task 11.1 The GCSE listening syllabus

Find the current GCSE syllabus used by your department and compare the listening components of Table 11.3 with the requirements of that syllabus.

Compare the listening requirements for the GCSE with the national curriculum for music. What are the similarities and differences?

What evidence of progression is there from the NC to GCSE in relation to the listening content?

Share your observations with other student teachers or music colleagues.

in relation to composing and performing, although it is assumed that the course develops the pupils' ability in these activities. Teachers have a good deal of flexibility in designing a course which leads pupils to the final examination. In Boxes 11.2 and 11.3 we give a list of the possible contents a GCSE course might need to be covered in relation to performing and composing.

While listening, performing and composing are examined separately, the GCSE syllabi espouse an integrated approach to the teaching of the course which leads to the final examination. We now explore some approaches to teaching GCSE with integration in mind.

APPROACHES TO THE TEACHING OF GCSE

All of the strategies and issues related to planning, use of language, learning, management, assessment and so on, apply equally to the teaching of 14–16 year olds who are involved in the GCSE examination course. Given the explicit links which

Box 11.2 The content of the performing course

The content of the 'performing' course develops to pupils' skills in:

- technical control
- using appropriate musical expression
- interpretation
- the clarity and accuracy of rhythm and pitch
- the use of appropriate tempo
- the effective use of dynamics
- fluency of performance
- sensitive balance of phrasing
- stylistic awareness
- sense of ensemble
- use of notations.

Box 11.3 The content of the composing course

The content of the 'composing' course develops pupils':

- ability to develop musical ideas
- ability to use music elements and resources within a given or chosen brief
- ability to exploit and control the medium
- ability to create structural interest (unity, variety, balance shape, design and organisation)
- consistency of style
- appropriate use of melody, harmony, texture, tempo, rhythm, dynamics, timbre
- or in experimental work density, duration, nuance, location
- use of notations.

---

have now been made between good practice at both key Stage 3 and 4 we should not be surprised by this. For example, the design of units which integrate listening, appraising, composing and performing are common to good practice in both phases.

Coverage and integration

Coverage of the 'content' of the listening syllabus is important. However, there is also the need to design a course which allows pupils to develop individually in relation to performing and composing. Units of work designed for Years 10 and 11 need to be carefully mapped such that this balancing act is achieved, that is between individual choice, creativity and development and the needs of the 'content' in the listening paper. Coverage is most easily mapped when engaging in whole-class teaching. Individual and group work is less easy to map in relation to coverage. Individuals need to work on particular performing skills and develop their own personal composition portfolio and this is necessarily an important part of learning for GCSE. The development of a personal musical identity needs to be balanced with the syllabus requirements.

The tensions between coverage and integration, the individual and the group are not insurmountable if given careful planning. They can, and should, be held together by a constant spirit of musical criticism (see also Swanwick 1988, 1994):

- within groups
- between groups
- between individuals
- between teachers, groups and individuals.

The development of musical vocabulary, relating sounds to symbols, expressing opinions about music, relating music to context can all be developed through a thorough and ongoing analytical dialogue which is built into the culture of the GCSE music classroom. Such an approach ought to be a part of every lesson, for example, in the form of sharing work as a means to developing the understanding of all pupils. Musical criticism (appraisal) is the glue which holds together an integrated approach to musical learning (see also Chapter 6). Figure 11.1 illustrates a basic model for an integrative approach.

The implications of the integrated model in Figure 11.1 suggest that:

- we can begin in any segment
- we can move between segments within and from lesson to lesson
- appraisal is the 'glue' which links the segments
- listening is thus central to each segment.

Task 11.2 Integration of units of work for GCSE

Develop an integrated scheme/lesson of your own for pupils in Year 10. Include specific examples of the listening, composing and performing activities you set your pupils and identify opportunities for appraisal (musical criticism). Share your ideas with other student teachers.

Differentiation, continuity and progression

One of the main criticisms of the GCSE course has been that it does not prepare pupils for A level. These two courses have, indeed, been quite different in approach and expectation although the most recent developments make more explicit links (see Chapter 12). While a significant number of pupils who study A level music specifically use their qualification as part of a future career, the sprit of the GCSE is *music for all* based upon a normal exposure to classroom music at key stage 3. The dichotomy between courses for careers and courses for all, which has dogged music education for many years, is manifest here. It is expected that the curriculum beyond 2000 will address these issues by forging more coherence between the two examination courses.

However, we feel that music teachers of the old millennium (and we include ourselves) have not fully addressed the individual needs of their pupils at key stage 4. If there is a problem with progression to A level then we ought to be exploiting opportunities for differentiation at GCSE, in other words preparing suitable pupils for A level during these years. For example, it is likely that pupils who wish to progress to A level show a big commitment to music at GCSE and are often performers on an instrument or voice to a reasonably high standard. If we are honest then it can be accepted that certain parts of the GCSE will pose few problems to such pupils, for example, the performing papers are being covered in

Figure 11.1 A model for the integration of musical learning

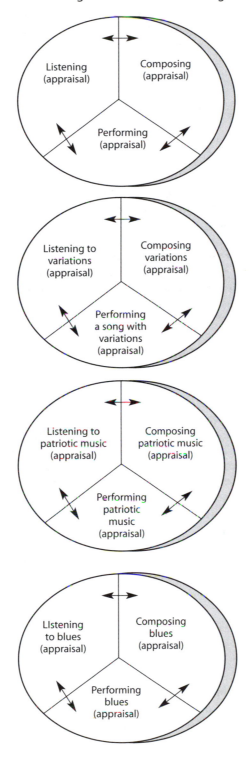

large part though external lessons and groups (the politics of such an advantage is another issue!). There are, it would seem, ample opportunities to introduce such pupils to Advanced level work. It could be that 'musical' pupils have not been extended in the GCSE years because teachers have not taken a longer view. Strategies for differentiation and extension might include:

- requiring pupils to notate compositions in detail
- using ICT to arrange, manipulate and notate arrangements and compositions
- differentiated listening questions during appraisal
- differentiated development of musical vocabulary
- differentiated performing and composing tasks
- individualised learning and research, such as use of the Internet, projects on harmony and so on.

This is not to suggest that advanced work should not be carried out musically (see Chapter 12). In any case, it is likely that GCSE work becomes more individualised as the course progresses to the final examination, and collation of the course work portfolio.

ASSESSING THE GCSE

Assessment in music and arts education is problematic and GCSE assessment highlights many of these issues. The controversies are most apparent in the assessment of performing and composition and relate specifically to the *criteria* to be used when making *judgements*, and the *evidence* upon which these judgements should be based. This is a difficult area for arts education and the GCSE has been bold in developing criteria despite these difficulties. We examine some typical forms of GCSE assessment here and briefly consider one or two problems.

Assessing listening

This is the least problematic area of assessment and is normally associated with a tape provided by the examination board. Pupils are typically played music from a variety of traditions and are asked to

- identify musical characteristics
- relate the music to its context
- show awareness of progress in traditions
- compare pieces
- express opinions with reasons
- use an extensive musical vocabulary
- use and understand staff notation.

Long questions can often be accompanied by a skeleton score and these come closest to the 'old' O level aural paper. The music can be played anything between five and ten times, although all music is played at least twice. There are parts of the questions which cover all levels of musical understanding, yet the long questions are more likely to include staff notation. In *Short questions* there are also differentiated parts aimed at all pupils; the aim is to test recognition and musical vocabulary and not factual knowledge. The types of questions given as examples in Table 11.4 (overleaf) appear under headings taken from the 'elements', yet there is much in the way of transfer from one heading to another. When you have looked at Table 11.4, use it to address Task 11.3.

Task 11.3 Assessing listening at GCSE level

Design two GCSE questions on pieces of your choice.

A short question with between three and six parts (remember to include questions which all pupils can attempt). A long question which requires pupils to follow a short score (melody only, perhaps incomplete) with between eight and twelve questions. Try out your questions on other student teachers or on a GCSE class for practice/ revision. Find past listening papers and explore further the types of questions which have been used.

The listening paper is marked externally yet the mark scheme does appear on the examination paper. However, it has taken some time for teachers to 'tune in' to the marking schemes. For example, some problems have existed around the pupils' use of language in some of the questions requiring a freer response. The examination boards recognise that the test is one of aural perception and yet have reasonably high demands on the use of technical musical vocabulary if the top marks are to be achieved. Given the breadth of the 'content' it is difficult for teachers to ensure that their pupils are using the 'correct' language to describe an extract in order to achieve the top grades. Credit *is* given for the use of non-technical or literary language but there has been some confusion over what might constitute an adequate description. Add to this the range of music which might possibly be used in the examination and it is not difficult to see the origin of teachers unease. While this problem has been alleviated by better acquaintance with the examination and more precise definitions from the boards, the issue is still problematic.

Assessing performing

In a sense musicians are used to the assessment of performance; the Associated Board graded examinations and various music 'competitions' are a testament to this. The GCSE boards had the problem of constructing valid criteria which could be made public to teachers and pupils alike. Some of the problems included:

Table 11.4 Sample questions from the GCSE listening paper

Pitch	Tick the statement which best describes the tonality of this extract (begins in major then moves to minor, begins in minor then moves to major, begins in major and stays in major and so on). Insert the missing accidentals. Complete the melody in bars. Which shape best matches the tune (selection of graphics)?
Texture	Is this music homophonic or polyphonic? Give a reason for your answer. How does the texture change in this extract? Describe the texture in this extract.
Structure	Underline the plan which best represents this music. How does the composer create contrast in this music? Which musical form is suggested by the opening of this extract? What form is this music in? Complete the pattern of this music which starts AAB …
Traditions	From which period does this music come? Underline the period when you think the music was written. Describe four ways in which African music has influenced this music. Underline the country of origin of this music. Give two reasons for your answer. Underline the style which bets describes this music (blues, swing, rock, reggae).
Duration	Which of the following rhythmic patterns can you hear at the opening? Add a time signature. Complete the rhythm in bars. Describe the rhythm in bar 11 (dotted, syncopated, etc.)
Tempo	How does the tempo change in this extract? Place an X where the music slows down. Which term best describes the tempo of this music, e.g. allegro, adagio? Insert the following instructions, e.g. rit., a tempo.
Dynamics	Indicate the dynamics in the boxes provided. True or false: the choir would be marked *ff* at the beginning? How is contrast achieved through the dynamics?

Articulation	Add phrase marks to the melody.
	Insert marks for staccato on the score.
	Which term best describes this music e.g. staccato, legato?
Timbre	Name the instruments/family of instruments playing.
	From which country do these instruments originate?
	Underline the type of voice singing.
Comparisons	Describe four ways in which the first version is different from the second.
	What has happened to the style and instrumentation in version B?
Opinions	How does the music build to a climax? How is this achieved?
	What atmosphere or mood is created by the composer?
	Describe three ways in which the composer achieves this.

- What constitutes a good or poor performance.
- How is it possible to construct a system of assessment which takes into account the difficulty of the piece?
- How is it possible to construct a system which allows simple pieces that are played well (musically) a chance to score highly?
- How is it possible to differentiate between the difficult piece played poorly and the easy piece played well? should credit be given for attempting a difficult piece?
- Do pupils who pay for instrumental lessons outside of the course have an unfair advantage in this section of the examination?

For all of the performing options, that is, solo performance, performance in an ensemble, rehearsing/directing an ensemble, the examiner (whether external or internal) needs to make judgements on the difficulty of the music being played and the standard at which it is being played. The boards have gone to great lengths to help examiners and teachers make these judgements.

The difficulty of the piece is often judged in relation to exemplars provided by the boards which might typically show an easy piece for the trumpet, an elementary piece, an intermediate piece and a difficult piece for the trumpet. For argument's sake these might correspond to grades 1–4 of the Associated Board instrumental examination standards.

The standard of the performance is judged against criteria for the level of perform-ance in relation to technical and aesthetic elements, such as impact, control and so on. An example of typical criteria is given below adapted from WJEC (1998).

Level 5: A thoroughly convincing, accurate and distinctive performance.
Level 4: Accurate playing with a good sense of performance, conveying the character

and mood of the music and responding to expression marks dynamics and phrasing.

Level 3: Reasonably accurate, secure and convincing and moving forward at a reasonable pace. Generally conveying the character and mood of the music but with a few errors in pitch and/or rhythm in evidence.

Level 2: Accurate at times and fairly secure but a faltering performance with lapses destroying the overall fluency. Some attempt to convey the mood of the music.

Level 1: Shows some attempt, but generally weak and hesitant.

Judging the mark can be made by plotting the level of the performance against the level of difficulty (Table 11.5). Thus a pupil who achieves a level 4 in performing an intermediate piece will achieve sixteen marks. Another method is for the mark given for the standard of performance to be multiplied by the difficulty of the piece and an overall grade achieved. Either way the system takes account of the difficulty of the piece and the standard of performance.

Issues arise from this style of assessing performance, which include:

1   Are the criteria valid descriptions of performance?
2   Is it possible to describe aesthetic impact?
3   How do you feel about the 'perfect' performance at foundation level receiving a maximum of half marks (only two marks more than a 'higher' piece played relatively poorly)?
4   Are those who have additional instrumental lessons at an unfair advantage in this system?

Swanwick is concerned that marking schemes such as those in Table 11.5 are obsessed with quantitative differences between the levels of difficulties and technical virtuosity. He remarks, 'This is not totally satisfactory and may make too much of relative virtuosity, as well as luring performers into water technically too deep for the good of their musical development' (Swanwick1994: 106). However, Swanwick also recognises that devising such criteria is problematic, 'The problem is to define

Table 11.5 A typical marking grid for GCSE performance

Difficulty Level	Easy (1)	Elementary (2)	Intermediate (3)	Hard (4)
6	12	18	24	30
5	10	15	20	25
4	8	12	16	20
3	6	9	12	15
2	4	6	8	10
1	2	3	4	5

this quality in a way that provides reasonably explicit grounds for judgement and at the same time remains true to music; issues of reliability and validity' (Swanwick 1994: 107).

These types of grids are constructed for the assessment of all types of performing. As music teachers we need to use them, although we must also play a part in the ongoing development of criteria which are both useful and musical.

Task 11.4 Assessing performance at GCSE level

Collect the GCSE performing criteria from your school.

Informally assess some GCSE performances as and when they occur during lessons (observed or taught), or ask other student teachers to play on second and third instruments. Assess them using the criteria you have found.

Discuss these performances with your mentor/colleagues after sharing the assessment exercise with them.

How much common ground is there between you and your fellow student teachers or mentor?

With some other student teachers try to devise your own criteria for recognising different levels of achievement in performance.

Assessing composition

If assessing performance is problematic then the assessment of creativity, imagination and craft in composition presents arts educators with their biggest challenge. Assessing composition is fraught with all of the inherent problems of making judgements about works of art. Criteria for good or bad art (high and low grades) are notoriously difficult to come by given that we find ourselves confronted by taste, values, subjectivity and other issues. Indeed, the GCSE boards have been bold in laying down criteria which have been usable but have also caused music teachers to reflect on what these criteria should look like. We compare next two different approaches to the problem of setting criteria for composition. The first criterion makes broad statements about compositions and what they must exhibit in order to fulfil the grade criteria. The highest and lowest grades have been included from the WJEC (1999) criteria.

Highest grade   A composition will have utilised a variety of the musical elements in an effective overall form that contains appropriate use of colour and contrast but which has a complete sense of unity. It will contain imaginative musical ideas, a sense of musical development and clear evidence of refinement. It will also reflect appropriate technical knowledge. A composition will have an obvious sense of completeness through the use of an appropriate and consistent style that shows empathy with the medium and its conventions. The style and the musical resources used effectively reflect the nature of the given/chosen brief and the purposes and processes of composition are clear and coherent.

Lowest grade   A composition will include a few of the musical elements in an attempt to achieve some colour and contrast. Musical ideas will be incomplete and will reflect little technical knowledge. A composition will reflect little understanding of the medium and its conventions. The musical resources used will be very limited and the composition will display little sense of purpose.

The second method of describing grade criteria is rather more explicit in the use of the 'elements' as the basis for a composition and are adapted from EDEXCEL (1998); again only the highest and lowest marks are given (see Box 11.4). The marks for each 'element' are added together to give a final mark for each composition out of thirty, in other words, each set of criteria is marked out of five. Three core criteria and three optional criteria are to be used. In each case pupils must produce a score and/or commentary such that these judgements can be made.

There are some critical questions to be asked in relation to both sets of criteria, such as:

- Is it possible for a piece of music to use only a 'few' of the elements?
- Is complexity a measure of musical worth, for example, certain styles of music use limited harmonic resources?
- Are certain styles prejudiced by the criteria, such as, those which do not particularly go in for the extensive development of musical ideas?
- Are notated pieces more likely to be given higher marks than those which rely on a commentary?
- Do we as teachers have prejudices towards certain styles as being more complex than others and therefore of more value?
- Is it possible to break down a composition into the 'elements' to judge its worth?
- Is a shapeless and disorganised melody a poor one?
- What does a well-chosen rhythm sound like?

Swanwick again finds such criteria problematic:

Adding up marks awarded under a checklist seems an odd way to engage in musical criticism. To be useful, criteria statements should indicate qualitative differences rather than quantitative shifts. It is not so difficult to devise these descriptions, provided that there is a serviceable model of musical criticism, *an adequate theory*.

(Swanwick 1988: 151)

Despite the problems noted, practise in using the criteria improves your confidence to make judgements about pupils' work. It is easy to knock criteria down, less easy to build them and the GCSE has been important in focusing our thinking on the nature of assessing music and the arts.

Box 11.4 Grade criteria for assessing composition

Core criteria

Exploitation of medium
5 marks – shows real understanding of medium
1 mark – limited understanding of medium

Use and development of ideas
5 – imaginative use of ideas
1 – characterless, no use of development

Structural interest
5 – interesting structure in total and in parts, imaginative development of basic ideas
1 – structure is unclear

Optional criteria (3 out of 5)

Melody
5 – excellent with style character and appropriateness
1 – lacks shape and purpose

Harmony
5 – appropriate to style, mood showing extended repertoire of chords
1 – very limited harmonic understanding with frequent errors of judgement

Texture
5 – sensitive awareness of textural matters, exploiting texture to good effect
1 – strange textural decisions

Tempo/rhythm
5 – exciting, well chosen and showing some originality
1 – limited awareness of tempo / rhythm throughout

Dynamics
5 – careful, sensitive and appropriate, enhancing the composition
1 – dynamics absent or totally inappropriate

Task 11.5 Assessing composition at GCSE level

Collect the criteria for compositions used by the GCSE board in use by your school.

Apply these criteria to live and taped works from school and the seminar room.

Share your judgements with your mentors and colleagues.

Try to outline some of your own criteria for judging a composition and share them with other student teachers. What makes one composition better than another?

OTHER FORMS OF EXAMINATION COURSES AT 14–16

There are at least three other types of examination course at this level. Two of these offer the possibility of pupils working in variety of arts disciplines in expressive arts programmes. These alternatives have their own syllabi and assessment requirements and offer pupils real choice. Indeed, choice is important at this level because:

- some pupils may not want to study music for a full GCSE
- some may want to develop a wider range of skills and experiences in the arts
- some pupils may have arrived in the arts through more informal routes, such as amateur dramatics, and these courses offer an outlet at GCSE level.

The short course GCSE in music

These courses typically offer shortened versions of the full GCSE and take one year to complete. The reduced content is managed in a variety of ways from less listening content, to a choice of specialising in performing or composing. The course offers the opportunity to study music to GCSE level but with the flexibility of mixing and matching with other subjects, thus offering diversity of qualification for pupils. It has to be said that such courses have not been over popular so far, and this is perhaps related to inherent problems of timetabling.

Expressive arts GCSE

Most GCSE expressive arts courses are explicit in their claims that they are not a replacement for a syllabus in a specific arts subject. They also require that pupils work in a variety of media. Despite offering choice there is some controversy surrounding such courses arising from debates in the wider field of arts education, in other words, whether the arts should be taught as discrete disciplines or as part of a more collaborative, integrated package.

Typically in an expressive arts GCSE, pupils maybe offered art, design, creative writing, dance, drama, music and possibly music technology or production technology. The boards may write into the syllabus certain regulations, for example:

- that pupils must engage with at least three of these areas
- that each assignment must show work in at least two media
- that no area may contribute more that 50 per cent of the total assessment

(OCR 1999)

It is also typical of these courses that the precise content of the course is determined by the school or centre. The assessment procedures *are* carefully laid down by the boards but rarely include any form of terminal paper and pencil test in an examination room. Pupils are assessed through course work using evidence of participation with the expressive arts, and possibly a final task set in much the same way as many art and design GCSE terminal assessments, that is, a stimulus followed by a number of hours to complete (which may run into several days). For example, some boards set the terminal task for expressive arts GCSE as a project to be carried out in the community.

Expressive arts assessment requirements are typically written on the model shown in Figure 11.2, which also informs the course content and assessment criteria.

Teachers can plan content around certain stimuli, for example, poverty, textures, the Greeks, festivals, Aborigines and so on. Students then respond to the stimuli with teacher input in relation to the technique, understandings and knowledge needed for a successful realisation. The performance is then subject to critical evaluation from teacher and pupils. Evidence can be collected during the course in the form of a portfolio which charts the pupils planning, evaluations, and recordings of presentations or performances, for example, tape, video, critical comments, scores and so on. Judgements can then be made about the pupils 'grades' referring to a grid which shows various levels of ability in *planning, realisation and evaluation*. Expressive arts course tend to by-pass issues of good or bad composition/performance by assessing the quality of the pupils *engagement* with these three processes. As may be surmised, given the difficulties of assessing pupils work in one art form, assessing pupils work across media is also problematic. While such criteria are in their early days of development they have been criticised for lacking precision. Perhaps the ephemeral and imprecise nature of the criteria are the price we need to pay for having a system of assessment which is true to the arts themselves.

GNVQ

Music can be used to fulfil part of the performing arts and entertainment industries GNVQ, and this shares with GCSE many assessment procedures.

Figure 11.2 Expressive arts assessment requirements

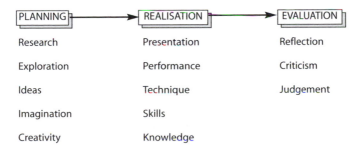

PLANNING	REALISATION	EVALUATION
Research	Presentation	Reflection
Exploration	Performance	Criticism
Ideas	Technique	Judgement
Imagination	Skills	
Creativity	Knowledge	

Task 11.6 Expressive arts course discussion

What are the attitudes to expressive arts courses in your school and among other student teachers?

Is it possible to assess a pupils' engagement with the processes of art-making across several art forms?

What is the role and importance of such examination courses?

The General National Vocational Qualification has been designed to be a work related alternative to GCSE and GCE A level. Since 1993 the courses have offered a vocational pathway where skills and knowledge are used and developed in a practical context. There are a number of areas of study, including the performing arts and entertainment industries and schools, teachers and pupils are encouraged to make links with work related situations. The course is organised into units and pupils are expected to take responsibility for their learning within the parameters of the unit when planning, researching and evaluating their work. In addition all pupils are expected to develop the 'key skills' through contact with the contents of the units, for example:

- communication
- the application of number
- information technology
- problem solving
- working with others
- improving own learning and performance.

GNVQs are becoming increasingly flexible and are able to be taken alongside or instead of GCSE or GCE A level. Different numbers of units 'count' for an equivalent in other qualifications as part of a national qualifications framework (see Chapter 12). However, the levels roughly equate in the following ways:

1 *foundation level* is equivalent to D–G levels of the GCSE
2 *intermediate level* is equivalent to A–C levels of the GCSE
3 *advanced level* is equivalent to GCE A level.

Typically some of the units are 'core' and others optional. Units might have the following titles for the Performing Arts and Entertainment Industries GNVQ:

- Opportunities in the performing arts.
- Skills development.
- Performing work.
- Working on a team.
- Providing quality services to customers.

- Extending performing skills.
- Promoting an event.
- Reviewing performance and entertainment.
- Health and safety.
- Preparing for employment.
          (adapted from EDEXCEL 1999)

The GNVQ shares the 'cross arts' flavour of the expressive arts GCSE and themes such as planning, realising and evaluating are also important. Assessment evidence might include the following:

- working records (plans, research, evaluations and so on)
- observations from teachers
- witness statements from observers outside of school
- records of performance
- materials developed
- externally set tests.

This list represents a wide range of evidence which is then mapped on to grids for each unit and pupils are assessed at pass, merit or distinction levels. The three levels on the assessment grid for 'performing work' might include the following statements:

Level 1: can perform accurately
Level 2: can perform accurately using a range of techniques with some sense of flair and style
Level 3: a fluent technique with a good sense of style and flair.

These levels again present problems to the arts educator, that is, how do we recognise flair and style; what are the criteria for having/not having these qualities? This situation is again part of the ongoing debate about the nature of criteria for assessing the arts. We want our pupils to behave like artists, we want them to present authentic evidence and yet we also want reliable criteria for judging the quality of this behaviour. Valid assessment of the arts is, and has always been, fraught with the problems presented by these issues.

SUMMARY

In this chapter we have suggested that:

- Examination syllabi and assessment procedures have developed over time and have tried to take into account the nature of music as a practical creative subject in school.
- There is controversy over the possibility of moving from one level of study

Task 11.7 GNVQ: questions for a discussion

What work-related experience and contacts might be forged to support the performing arts and entertainment industries GNVQ?

What are the benefits of the GNVQ?

Is it possible for there to be 'equivalence' between GNVQ and GCSE?

List ways in which the GNVQ units might contribute to the development of each of the 'key skills'.

to another but that this is increasingly being addressed by more and more congruence between the national curriculum, GCSE and GCE A level.

- The integration of listening, composing and performing in examination courses is both desirable and possible although coverage of the syllabus needs careful mapping.
- Assessment techniques tend to influence the nature of content in the examination course.
- The assessment of performing and composing is problematic and part of an ongoing debate about the development of 'criteria'.
- 'New' courses offer alternative opportunities at 14–16 and also challenge our assumptions about content, assessment and the teaching of distinct arts subjects at this level.

FURTHER READING

Bowman, D. and Cole, B. (1989) *Sound Matters; An Anthology of Listening Material for GCSE Music*, London: Schott. This is useful collection which can be used to exemplify many aspects of the GCSE listening paper and also be used as stimulus for composing and performing.

Metcalfe, M. (1987) 'Towards the Condition of Music' in Abbs, P. (ed.), *Living Powers*, London: Falmer

Paynter, J (1982) *Music in the Secondary School Curriculum*, Cambridge: Cambridge University Press. In each of these publications can be found important material on the development of music education in the English education system.

Website

www.qca.org.uk Information about GNVQ and all statutory developments in examination courses.

12 Public examinations 2

GCE Advanced Level music and post-16

Chris Carden-Price and Chris Philpott with Mike Lewis

INTRODUCTION

In the previous chapter a brief history of school examinations in music identified some of the ways in which the GCE A level examination in music has changed. The four phases may be summarised as follows:

- Phase 1: the traditional A level with papers on 'classical' western harmony, history of the 'classical' western tradition, set works and aural tests of dictation.
- Phase 2: a broadening of the traditional A level to include other types of questions and papers such as specialist (often minor) options (for example, performance, composition, music technology, twentieth century harmony), some study of works from popular and non-western cultures and aural tests involving a wider range of recognition and perception often within the context of 'real' pieces of music.
- Phase 3: the continuation of phase 2 with the introduction of other types of A level music examination courses such as music technology.
- Phase 4: as part of 'curriculum 2000' there have been more explicit attempts to link GCE A level with the aims and objectives of the GCSE and NC, for example, a clear commitment to an equality between listening, appraising, composing and performing in a wide range of styles and genre, in an integrated examination course.

One of the biggest issues for music teachers and pupils is continuity and progression from one age phase to another, and curriculum 2000 is an attempt to address these issues.

OBJECTIVES

At the end of this chapter you should understand:

- the nature and structure of the A level examination syllabi
- A level within the wider context of music education
- assessment strategies for the A level
- how A level content can be taught musically
- how A level content can be taught in an integrated course
- the nature and structure of other post-16 courses
- the role of music at post-16 in developing the key skills and cross curricular themes.

THE NATURE AND STRUCTURE OF THE A LEVEL

The underlying philosophy of the new A level in music (curriculum 2000) is explicitly related to the national curriculum and GCSE music. The boards have aimed to produce syllabi which are flexible and which allow diversity of approach. They offer a range of possible areas of study which promote pupil choice in relation to their skills, knowledge and interests. The syllabi also espouse a holistic and integrated approach in keeping with current good practice.

The new A level structure for music is made up of 6 units (see Table 12.1), the first three of which form the AS examination content. The AS units are designed to be covered in one year of study post GCSE or GNVQ. The AS syllabus is a discrete course and offers students some flexibility to mix and match with other post-16 courses of study and other AS/A levels. Successful completion of another three units, known as A2 units, will qualify the pupils for the full A level award. The units are described in Table 12.1.

Clear themes emerge from the new music A level, and these include:

- Congruence with the philosophy, in terms of content and assessment of other music syllabi such as NC, GCSE and GNVQ.
- A holistic approach to the teaching, learning and assessment of music with important implications for an integrated approach.
- Inclusion of the 'elements' and associated concepts which underpin a notion of 'musical language' in common with NC and GCSE.
- Opportunities for the study and exploration of a rich variety of style, genre and traditions.
- Opportunities for pupils to tailor courses to cater for their own needs and interests.

While these new courses do allow for some flexibility, choice, diversity and special-isation, it is typical that a certain amount of contact with one or two of the more traditional elements is 'built in', that is, contact with the 'classical' tradition, notation and tests of aural perception.

Table 12.1 Units for the 'new' A level

Some typical units for AS	Possible examination requirements
Performance	solo and/or ensemble can be linked to composition work can be linked to historical study can involve direction and/or rehearsal of an ensemble internal or external assessment (visiting examiner)
Composition	developing musical ideas can be 'open' can be linked to techniques can be linked to style, genre or tradition units score, recording, commentary (analysis) required portfolio of compositions
Listening to and understanding music	aural perception/dictation 'contextualised' aural set work(s) set periods/genre/tradition essays/analysis
Some typical A2 units	Possible examination requirements
Performance	longer recital higher 'standard' expected can involve arrangements/compositions by pupils evaluative commentary often required can be linked to study of style/genre/tradition investigation of interpretations play in/rehearse/direct ensemble
Composition	in response to study of set pieces/style/tradition could involve larger portfolio score, recording, commentary (analysis) if not covered before some boards require that western classical harmony is studied and examined investigation as background
Understanding music	set work period/style/genre/tradition aural perception/dictation essays/analysis

An important dimension to the A level unit structure and an important engine of integration is the feature called *area of study*. Areas of study are broad fields which cut across units in which the elements, musical procedures, social context and aesthetic qualities can be studied in depth. Areas of study allow teachers and pupils to build up an AS or A level course which matches their needs, interest and expertise. These 'areas of study' can be exploited (depending on the board) in any of the units whether through performance, composition, aural or analysis. Typical areas of study might include:

- baroque music
- classical music
- music from 1890–1945
- music from 1954–present day
- form and structure
- music for the media
- words and music
- romantic music
- world music
- a bundle of set works across time or sharing some commonality
- the development of a style/genre/tradition
- the language of Western tonal music.

Typically several areas of study must be opted for, and the aim is to give breadth and balance as well as choice. While it is possible for pupils to specialise in particular areas and dimensions of musical experience it is still expected that at least some contact with the more traditional aspects is maintained, such as 'classical' harmony.

Task 12.1 Finding out about a music A level syllabus

Locate the A level syllabus in one of your placement schools. What is the balance of emphasis between listening, appraising, composing and performing? What are the opportunities for choice and flexibility? Provide a summary for other students.

While there are no formal qualifications needed for pupils to study music at A level, it is recommended that they have one of the higher grades at GCSE (or equivalent) and can perform on an instrument at around grade 5 standard. It is also clear that pupils need to be able to understand and use traditional notation, at least to a certain level. While some 'areas of study' have less emphasis on traditional notation, pupils are required to write scores, notate aspects of aural perception and perform from basic notation. The A level syllabi encourage the use of a wide variety of notations, yet skills in traditional notation are still an important element of the content.

ASSESSING GCE A LEVEL

The styles of assessment noted for GCSE in Chapter 11 are also prevalent in the A level examination. The assessment evidence for AS/A level might include:

- a portfolio of compositions (either taped or digitally recorded)
- scores and evaluative commentaries (analysis)
- performances which are live or audio/video taped
- evaluative commentaries on performances
- investigations and research
- written tests such as essays and technical harmony exercises
- tests of aural perception.

This evidence can be assessed externally, by the teacher (with samples moderated externally) or by a visiting examiner.

The criteria for assessment are again most typically set out in some form of grid (see Chapter 11). When *assessing performance* we again find indicators in the form of statements which embrace technical, stylistic and fluency criteria. There are also ways of adding value depending upon the standard of the piece (grade 4 upwards). As we have seen, these grids are welcome and useful but not without problems, for example what are the *criteria* for recognising that an interpretation is 'rarely convincing' or that an interpretation is 'imaginative'?

When *assessing composition* at A level the criteria are richer and more complex than those used at GCSE. A composition might be assessed on several sets of criteria, for example, creativity and also the relationship of the composition to the 'areas of study'. Criteria might refer to some or all of the following:

- presentation and quality of the outcome in relation to the brief
- realisation of the composition as a problem solving exercise
- investigation as background to the composition
- use of resources
- coherence of the composition
- compositional techniques used (often linked to the use of the 'elements')
- quality of the score/commentary/analysis
- links made with the 'area of study'.

These can be found in the form of either holistic statements for each level of achievement or in the form of marks given to different aspects of the composition (see Chapter 11) for example, use of medium, structure and so on.

Assessment grids with criteria for judging *appraising and analysis* are not currently found in the GCSE syllabi, but are included by some A level boards (see Table 12.2). Such grids are also useful for exposing criteria which has traditionally been the domain of the externally 'marked' written test.

One of the most important dimensions to assessment at A level is the concept of *synoptic assessment*. The examination boards require that a certain percentage of the assessment procedures (for example, 20 per cent) test the application of the full range of skills and understandings developed over all the units. Clearly the 'areas of study' promote such an approach to assessment. Synoptic assessment examines pupils' ability to make connections and to apply their knowledge from all units to possibly unfamiliar areas. An example is when pupils are asked to investigate, report, compose

Table 12.2 A sample of possible criteria for the 'appreciation' of music

Highest mark	Coherent, full, clear insight, clarity, secure grammar/ spelling, clear understanding of use of musical resources in context, perceptive comments, comprehensive research, knowledgeable, well focused and so on.
Lowest mark	Weak organisation, weakness in spelling and grammar, lacking accuracy, relevance and substance, incoherent expression, little exploration of ideas, inadequate appreciation of the use of musical resources in particular contexts and so on.

and perform in relation to a particular theme in an area of study, such as, variation. The examination boards have been consistent in requiring that both the content, delivery and the assessment strategies are integrated, at least in part.

Given the attention we have paid to the assessment of examination syllabi Chapter 11, we now focus in more detail on some strategies for the teaching of A level (and by implication GCSE), which promote an integrated approach to musical learning at this level.

INTEGRATED APPROACHES TO TEACHING MUSIC MUSICALLY AT A LEVEL

Introduction

The notion of the 'area of study' has been developed by the examination boards to promote an integrated approach to teaching and learning. The 'areas of study' require that pupils engage with musical 'themes' across the units when analysing, performing, composing and so on. Synoptic assessment sets out to 'test' the full range of skills and understandings which have been developed by the integrative features of the areas of study. Furthermore, A level music needs to be taught *musically* if integration is to be an effective tool in teaching, learning and assessment.

In order for pupils to develop 'musical understanding' at this level we do not need to abandon the principles of the national curriculum, GCSE or those exposed elsewhere in this book. It is important to conceive of the A level course in terms of continuity and progression from key stages 3 and 4. Being realistic, some of the A level curriculum can (*and must*) be learned as factual and perceptual knowledge and may be unrelated to listening to, composing and performing 'real' pieces of music (for example, here is how we construct a 'French' sixth). However, it is doubtful just how much genuine 'musical understanding' can emanate from exclusively adhering to this approach. Knowing 'how' and knowing 'about' music are indivisible from knowing 'of' music if pupils are to develop genuine musical understanding. For example, just because composition is not part of particular unit does not mean that we cannot engage with this in order to develop musical understanding. Moreover, it is also good practice for an integrative approach. From more intuitive understandings (knowing 'of' music) we can move to a more analytical approach in which these qualities can be described in terms of expressive and technical language. Pupils *will* need to develop a sophisticated perception *and* understanding of musical processes and the musical vocabulary/notations to describe their intuitive experience. However, the process of learning is as important here as it is at other stages of musical development. Having said this, time is not always on the side of a 'musical' approach and rote learning and didactic teaching are sometimes more appropriate.

How is it possible to incorporate knowledge 'of' music within our A level teaching; to place, in Swanwick's (1979) terms, category 1 objectives at the top of our agenda (see Chapter 2.)? In the examples which follow we have not presumed to cover all aspects of the A level syllabus. However, we try to expose some principles for teaching and learning which are congruent with the philosophy advocated in this book (placing knowledge 'of' music at the forefront) and the integrative approach espoused by new A level syllabi. The teaching strategies noted here are also good for GCSE.

Aural perception, singing and harmony

In the widest sense 'listening' is the fundamental act of music-making, learning and development. While all agree that it should be central to any music course it is tempting to teach 'listening' (aural perception) in a barren way which merely encourages the recognition of intervals, chord progressions and so on, with little or no experience of them in a musical context (and this is indeed understandable given the pressure of syllabus coverage). Here, we are concerned with the ways in which aural perception can be taught musically and related to other areas of our musical experience.

Consider the proposition:

The flip side of hearing is singing!

Singers often have to deal with aural training in a manner completely different from instrumentalists. The best instrumental teaching, however, has the student singing as much of his/her music as possible, and this approach can inform A Level teaching. In its simplest form, this might mean that every A Level lesson could include some singing: the notes of simple chord progressions (for example, I-IV-V; I-vi-IV-V-I) can be sung. Any and every line in a madrigal or part-song can be the means to teaching interval recognition and reproduction; and any piece can provide opportunities for practice in harmonic analysis, chord identification and recognition of modulations. Indeed, in the early stages of teaching harmony, an exercise might usefully consist of a given melody and bass, both lines being sung (any student singing either part at any pitch, despite the 'noise' thus produced) before the harmony is agreed and an inner part added by each student for themselves to sing. The end result should work when all sing together if the students have stuck to the agreed progressions; and trios and quartets from within the group could be made to perform. There is also an added incentive here for the students to learn good part–writing: if they know they are to sing the line, they will avoid awkward leaps and make it as 'singer-friendly' as they can. This process is also very good practice for instrumentalists (see Figure 12.1).

- Give the pupils the basic chord progression in Figure 12.1 and play it to them 'live' and on recording.
- Ask them to improvise vocally above the 'feel' of these chords after a teacher model.
- Ask them to sing and/or play one note from each chord with and without accompaniment.
- Ask them to sing and/or play one note from one chord and two from the next.
- Ask them to sing and/or play two notes from one chord and one from the next.
- Ask them to sing and/or play two notes from each chord.
- Ask pupils to add link or passing notes between two notes.
- Freely improvise tunes again for a contrapuntal texture.
- Ask each pupil to compose a melody and notate.

These melodies (plus others provided by the teacher) could form a primitive Kanon!

Teaching points

These include: simple counterpoint, simple chord progressions and cadences, melody writing, sight reading and simple intervals. The pupils will have been part of the music, learning through building a relationship with the music; a knowledge 'of' the music. Teaching points about parallel fifths and octaves can be introduced later! 'Reading' is not essential for much of this exercise providing pupils get to know the 'feel' of the chord progression and are given suitable teacher models.

The example in Figure 12.1 hints at one way in which aural work and harmony can reinforce each other. At the stage when the finer points of chromatic harmony are to be taught, it will appear much more relevant if real musical examples can be sung, and then analysed. Any Bach chorale contains enough examples of secondary dominants to keep most groups happy for a while, and there is a passage from *Messiah* which does a very neat job on two augmented sixth chords. In the second phrase of the chorus *Since By Man Came Death* (Figure 12.2) the students will have no trouble at all analysing the harmony until they come to the Italian sixth on '*came*'

Figure 12.1 Pachelbel *Kanon* exercise

– and the tenor's move to B natural, creating the more acidic French sixth (with its characteristic augmented fourths) will stump them completely. No attempt to explain the chord away in terms of any modulation will work, since the phrase obviously cadences on a chord V in A minor, complete with decorative suspension, so the function of the puzzling chord – to lead firmly to the dominant – is crystal clear. So too is its expressive power, in the context of this short, intensely dramatic moment in the work leading to the next, exultant, chorus.

In conclusion, if we wish pupils to be able to perceive, use and understand the expressive power of harmony they need to experience it in musical contexts. This forms the basis of their ability to name progressions and intervals. You also need to audit your own understanding of harmony through the same process, and Task 12.2 (overleaf) gives you an opportunity to attempt this.

Aural perception, singing and history

We are concerned here to integrate some aural perception with developing an understanding of different styles and techniques in various musical traditions.

Musical history is typically conducted through the study of set works and/or genre, style and tradition. There will, of course, come the time when the nuts and bolts of analysis must be carried out, and students must inevitably be prepared for the classic 'critical commentary/analysis'. This is the focus of much teacher preparation time, when lucid, lively, and luminous notes are lovingly prepared for student consumption. However, aural work may productively be integrated into music history teaching.

To begin once again at the simplest level, this may take the form of ensuring that music of different periods and styles is actually sung by the group. One particularly effective exercise may be to take different composers' treatments of the same text – the settings of the *Ave Maria* by Parsons, Bruckner, and Stravinsky, for example – and learn to sing them, then ask the group to describe in what ways they are different. This can lead quite directly to a developing appreciation that texture, harmony and tonality (and the treatment of dissonance), rhythm (perhaps even harmonic rhythm), and melody were handled differently at different times by different composers – and the group is a long way towards the stylistic analysis grid outlined below (see Table 12.3 overleaf).

Skills of comparison can also be developed by preparing a grid as in Table 12.3, cutting up the sections and asking pupils to arrange them correctly after having

Figure 12.2 *Since by man came death*

Task 12.2 Auditing theoretical knowledge about harmony and understanding Bach through performance

This exercise allows the student teacher to audit his/her theoretical harmonic knowledge after performing the chorale. The principle can also be applied to the teaching of A level harmony.

1   Play or sing (vocalise) the chorale in Figure 12.3.
2   Analyse the cadences.
3   Are there more primary or secondary triads used?
4   Find a II7b, V, I cadence.
5   Find examples of the following: accented passing notes, unaccented passing notes, auxiliary notes, dominant seventh, diminished seventh, cadential leading note falling to the fifth, cadential 6/4: 5/3, suspension, double passing notes, syncopation, augmented chord, diminished triad, Tierce de Picardie, ornamented cadence, examples of 'broken rules'.
6   Analyse the sequence of modulations through which the chorale passes.

performed and/or listened to the pieces. This can be an enjoyable change of strategy; see Task 12.3.

World musics and musical learning at A level

The 'new' A level syllabi have options in which world music can be studied systematically. However, quite apart from this we can learn much from the processes of learning in other cultures, which can help us teach *all* music musically. In particular the oral – aural tradition of many cultures can be put to good use when helping pupils to 'internalise' musical ideas. Many cultures use rote learning, movement and phonetics as the basis for their musical teachings. This suits our purpose by emphasising knowledge 'of' music and by engaging pupils with sound before we provide theoretical models.

Figure 12.3 *By the waters of Babylon*

Task 12.3 Comparing music from different times and places

Prepare a grid such as the one in Table 12.3 and then cut it up. Give the students a blank grid and a stick of glue, and tell them to stick the descriptions in the right place. On this simple theme variations can be played:

- Give each of the students mixed up bundles, so they have to trade bits of paper.
- Make the groups write their own descriptions, then cut them up and give them to another group to re-order.
- Write a couple of bogus descriptions which are irrelevant.
- Have the students criticise each other's descriptions.

It is a strange feeling to sit back and watch a group of students hard at work, requiring very little input from you. The nagging feeling is that their learning at times like this may be far more effective than hours of talking at them!

For example, pupils can learn any simple harmonisations by rote (see Stroman 1998) and experience the tensions and resolutions of simple chord progressions (see also Figure 12.1). When internalised the 'feel' for chords and chord progressions will form the basis of their 'inner ear'.

The example in Table 12.4 is adapted from Kwami (1998) and offers a phonetic approach to the learning of poly-rhythm. He suggests that the rhythms are best internalised by

- saying them
- then adding body movements to them (slapping, clapping, snapping and stamping)
- then playing them on instruments.

The process of reciting mnemonics and adding movements develops an 'inner' understanding 'of' poly-rhythm.

We have much to gain from the processes of musical learning assumed by the music of other cultures, quite apart from the important job of studying them as authentically as possible. The result is an integrated approach which prioritises knowledge 'of' music by direct acquaintance as the basis for musical learning. There are many implications for work across the various units, via 'areas of study' if these principles are adhered to.

Using other aspects of culture to promote musical analysis

However brilliantly-integrated an A Level music lesson may be, there will come those points at which students need specifically to develop their understanding and appreciation of music from different traditions and in various styles in a particular

Table 12.3 Stylistic analysis grid of *Ave Maria*

Genre	Parsons	Bruckner	Stravinsky
	Motet	Motet	Motet
Harmony and Tonality	Modal, through the use of *musica ficta*, especially at cadences, anticipates tonality. Dissonance is carefully prepared: preparation – suspension – resolution	Farily claerly in F major despite the chromaticism, but is not entirely without ambiguity: the opening bars hover between F major and D minor, and the repeated chord of A major at the bottom of the page, suggest D minor. F major again, however, darkened only by the hint of Bb major/C minor as the hour of our death is recalled. A plagal 'Amen' closes the piece.	Chords strike us as dissonances but are clearly treated as consonances in their own right: added fourths and sevenths abound; then after three pages which have hovered between G major and C, the chord of A major is hardly the resolution one might have expected – as if the composer is inviting a reappraisal of the work even in its last moments
Melody	Smooth, moving mostly by step; leaps turn back in on themselves. Derived from plainsong practice, each voice part stays within a narrow range. The *Amen*, in particular, is a wonderful example of the use of *melisma* – lots of notes to one syllable	Dramatic melodic leaps are not uncommon – notably the octave downward leap at 'mortis nostrae'	Short repeated melodic motives, the syllabic setting of the words; incantatory quality
Rhythm	Each part is essentially arhythmic, through the harmonic movement creates a sense of a slow dulpa pulse.	The rhythmic movement is as stately as befits the words.	Lack of a clear sense of pulse – partly as a result of changing time signatures and partly because the relentless progression of block chords negates it

Form	Follows the text	ditto	diito
Texture	Polyphonic counterpoint, in which each new phrase is used as a new imitative *point*, echoed by the other parts. A seamless texture is the result, as parts overlap and interweave	Essentially homophonic; the upper and lower voices are treated as two separate choirs at first,	Relentlessly homophonic

context. This is a common ingredient of all A Level syllabuses, and whether it is to satisfy the examination requirements for study of two or three set topics, with associated set works, or for a wider period of history, the enormity of this undertaking can appear a daunting prospect to the teacher.

One tried and tested starting point has been a comparison with art. Looking at a painting has several advantages over music where instant gratification is what is demanded, which is usually the case with eager young A Level music students thirsting for knowledge. A painting can be viewed, in its entirety, all at once. Bits of it can be easily revisited, peered at for closer inspection. Music, by its very nature, takes place in time; it is a transient experience and can not easily be dissected. But there are techniques at work, obviously, in both art forms, and a teacher's favourite paintings can form the basis for interesting discussion about the relationship between technique and 'meaning'.

Consider, as an example, three paintings: Holbein's *The Ambassadors*, Caspar David Friedrich's *The Lone Traveller*, and Edvard Munch's *The Scream*. All depict, on the face of it, the same subject: a human figure, or two in Holbein's case (ignoring for the moment the fact the figure in the third picture is somewhat androgynous). Ideally, have colour photocopies, blown up to A3 size, and put them before the students. It takes only a few, fairly open, questions to elicit a variety of responses from students: they can all describe what they see. Even the most simplistic remarks – that the two men in Holbein seem aristocratic, that Friedrich's man has his back to us, that Munch's may not even be male – can lead to questions as to *why* they were painted so. More detail emerges as students consider the backgrounds – the instruments of art and science in Holbein, the turbulent landscape confronting the traveller, and the savage lines only vaguely outlining the scene in the Munch – the use of colour, the role of other characters in the picture, and the composition of each picture. Holbein's including the distorted skull across the bottom, Friedrich's character in the centre of our vision, Munch's wild lines accentuating the anguish on his subject's face.

Each painting has demanded different techniques, different treatments of form, colour, composition, perspective – the tools of a painter's trade; *and the same can be said of music*. Now play (or preferably, as suggested above, sing) three pieces from three different eras. Sacred music is a good vehicle here, since the expression of man's

Table 12.4 World musics and musical learning at A level

AGBADZA												
Pulse	1	2	3	4	5	6	7	8	9	10	11	12
Bell	Ken		ken		ke	ken		ken		ken		ke.
Rattle	pa.		Pa	ti	pa	pa	ti	pa	ti	pa	ti	pa
Drum 1		mi-	dzo.		Mi-	dzo,		mi-	dzo,		mi-	dzo,
Drum 2	ko-	ko-	ko-	ko.	Mi-	dzo	gi	di	gi	di,	mi-	dzo
Drum 3	Va		mi-	dzo			va		mi-	dzo	mi-	dzo

Source: Kwami © 2000

faith varied as much in music as it did in theology. One only has to listen to the requiem masses of Mozart, Berlioz and Britten for this to become apparent quite forcefully, though the three settings of the *Ave Maria* mentioned previously will work just as well. Revisit these pieces (Table 12.3) as background to the next paragraph.

The question to be asked, and for the students to answer, is: what *were* these technical features, these tools of the composer's trade, which for various reasons (whether to do with fashion and taste, or politics and religion) were handled so differently from one generation to another? The comparison with art can lead to this discussion quite neatly, and the discussion might try to elicit a framework for under-standing and analysis such as the one suggested previously. The first thing students may notice, having sung the three pieces as outlined earlier (Stravinsky, Parsons, Bruckner) will probably be the harmony, since part of the difficulty in singing the Stravinsky arises from the occasional dissonance. This matter of 'what makes the piece easy or difficult to sing' could be the most obvious starting-point – and the other element of music which is immediately noticeable is the difference between individual melodic lines. Those of the Parsons move quite smoothly; those of Bruckner do not. Texture is another easy element to spot, since the imitative nature of the Parsons presents an obvious contrast with the other two. The end result of all this discussion can be a framework for analysis and understanding. This framework can then be applied to any piece of music – though some headings are more appro-priate than others for different pieces. This becomes immediately apparent when the exercise is repeated with three orchestral pieces from, say, the baroque, classical and romantic eras. Differences of genre, scoring and form become more apparent there. All of these activities can of course be the stimulus for composition which support learning through intimate contact with the problems and processes of creativity.

Composition and historical study

Composition *can* become intimately linked with historical analysis and performance, and, indeed this is a requirement of the new syllabi. There is much scope for compo-sition work as part of historical study, and within the context of an 'area of study'. Indeed, one of the most enjoyable, and musical strategies is to try and integrate some composition, improvisation and arranging into A Level lessons, in order to develop historical understanding (see Box 12.1).

Another approach to composition is through using stylistic 'fingerprints'. Students can be given stylistic 'fingerprints' for a style, period, tradition or genre and these can become the basis of composition exercises. Indeed, composition which is instigated by particular traditions, style and genre is a very important dimension to the 'new' A level, especially in the context of the notion of an 'area of study'.

The examples provided earlier are not an exhaustive study of integration. We have tried to establish some principles of working which encourage you to look for 'musical' approaches to learning and which forge links between pupils' knowledge when listening, appraising, performing and composing music.

OTHER FORMS OF EXAMINATION COURSES AT POST-16

There are several other school qualifications at post-16 in which music can be used to fulfil the examination requirements. Table 12.5 (overleaf) shows the national qualifications framework. An important theme of this framework is the flexibility offered to plot a route by moving between different strands. Another is that there is equivalence between the levels. These possibilities are controversial given that one strand concentrates on a vocational approach while another is more academic. In practice the variety of qualifications allows pupils:

- choice
- entry into arts education from a variety of different backgrounds
- the chance to enter a qualification which concentrates on particular strengths.

How do other qualifications which involve music fit into the framework shown in Table 12.5?

GNVQ performing arts

We have examined the nature of GNVQ in Chapter 11. At post-16 pupils are usually engaged with the intermediate or advanced GNVQ, with the latter having A level equivalence. The *full* advanced performing arts GNVQ consists of twelve units of work and is the equivalent to two A levels. The *single* award of six units is equivalent

---

Box 12.1 *The Rite of Spring*

Composition stimulated by studying *The Rite of Spring* (1913) by Igor Stravinsky

Composition can bring about many gains in understanding through knowledge 'of' the musical resources used in a particular expressive context.

1 Listen to *Auguries of Spring* from part 1 of *The Rite of Spring* (although this could be saved until the end of the exercise).
2 This music has a ritornello of a pounding, percussive rhythmic section (see Figure 12.4).
3 From the episodes of the original the following chord structure can be found (see Figure 12.5).
4 Teach the group the ritornello section and ask them to compose their own episodes based on the chords provided.

Teaching points: The emancipation of dissonance, polytonality, expansion of tonality, primitivism, elemental pounding, dark register of stings, percussive chords hurled out by the horns on the rhythmically dislocated accent, hypnotic insistence of ostinati: a favoured device for Stravinsky and so on.

Figure 12.4 *Auguries of spring*: ritornello

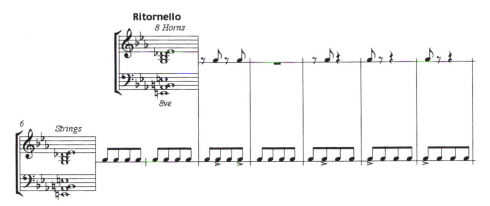

Figure 12.5 *Auguries of spring*: chord structure

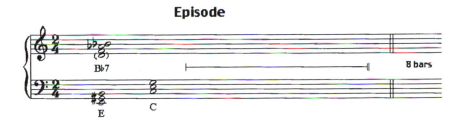

to one A level. In theory both can be taken alongside A levels, AS levels or further GCSEs to form an individually tailored package for pupils. The performing arts GNVQ is aimed at developing pupils in their:

- knowledge and understanding of the performing arts
- practical knowledge and skills for industry
- practical application of learning
- key skills
- independent learning.

Assessment is typically through two-thirds internal assignments and one-third externally set tests, assignments, projects and case studies. The qualification allows pupils scope for specialising in the practical skills of music making in some of the units although many of the units require pupils to show an understanding across the performing arts in relation to the vocational context.

Generic units (which are usually compulsory) might include such areas as:

- investigating the performing arts industries
- skills development
- working in the performing arts.

Table 12.5 The national qualification framework

Quals/levels	Entry level	Foundation	Intermediate	Advanced	4	5
Vocational	common	Level 1 NVQ	Level 2 NVQ	Level 3 NVQ	Level 4 NVQ	Level 5 NVQ
General Vocational	to all	GNVQ Foundation	GNVQ Intermediate	GNVQ Advanced		
General	families	GCSE (grades D-G)	GCSE (grades A*-C)	GCE A/AS level		
--Key skills--						

Source: QCA

The specialist musical modules might include:

- music performance
- music improvisation
- music technology.

It is not possible to complete the examination *only* studying music.

A level performing arts

The GCE A level in performing arts is a development from GCSE expressive arts courses. At least one board offers this qualification and requires the study of 3 AS level units and 3 A2 level units. The syllabus encourages pupils to learn:

- performance styles and genre
- performance skills
- performance processes.

The syllabus also adopts the 'area of study' principle to integrate the various units. For example, pupils might need to both study the performance background to an area of study called 'words and music' and also realise some of the aspects studied in the unit more explicitly in a performance. Again part of the assessment is synoptic in which pupils are required to show their skills and understanding from across the course in certain assessment tasks. For example, in a unit based on a project for the community, pupils might be expected to study, create, practice and perform in relation to a chosen 'theme'. As with the expressive arts GCSE candidates are required to engage with at least two art forms.

A level music technology

At least one board offers a full examination syllabus for music technology (EDEXCEL). It is likely that any teacher who could teach the syllabus for this examination would need additional specialist skills developed beyond initial teacher education. However, the syllabus has a 'musical' emphasis although this is always set within a technological context. The units require pupils to develop their skills and understandings in:

- sequencing
- recording
- arranging
- improvising
- listening and analysis
- producing
- composition.

Typically the 'areas of study' which might pervade the units place technology into a musical context, such as the development of technology in western classical music, technology in pop and jazz, music technology and film. It is clear that candidates need to be both musical and have a good deal of technological expertise in order to be successful.

Other aspects of post-16 qualifications

In common with all other A levels and elements of the national qualifications framework, music needs to address common requirements. The most prevalent of these are the key skills, that is, *the application of number, communication, improving own learning and performance, information technology, working with others and problem solving*, and each examination course is required to map its content in terms of its contribution to these skills.

In addition A level courses need to make a contribution to the following cross-curricular themes:

- spiritual, moral, social and cultural education
- equal opportunities
- a European dimension
- environmental education
- health education.

Independent learning

An important difference between GCSE and post-16 study is that one expects the students to become independent learners. After an introduction to the use of a library, the Internet and effective note-taking the teacher can be placed in the role

Task 12.4 Mapping the key skills

What contribution might A level music make to the key skills? Draw up a table with the following on one side:

- application of number
- communication
- improving learning and own performance
- information technology
- working with others
- problem solving.

Plot these against the following headings:

- possible evidence
- musical context.

Share your findings with other student teachers.

of organiser of students' learning, rather than sole repository and didactic fount of all knowledge. For example you could:

- Ask pupils to prepare presentations for the rest of the group on a topic, either individually or in groups.
- Ask pupils to produce listening exercises, along the lines outlined previously.
- Have the presenters set the rest of the group an essay following their presentation, and even mark it.
- Use pupils' performance work by having them perform a piece from their repertoire (good performance practice) and provide programme notes.
- Have them write critical commentaries on each others' performances and compositions.
- Ask pupils to research and review websites or CD-ROM.

Task 12.5 Music and cross-curricular themes

What contributions might the A level music course make to meeting the cross-curricular themes. Draw up a table as in Task 12.4 replacing the list of key skills with the cross-curricular themes.

How prepared do you feel to teach the A level in relation to key skills and cross curricular themes? What are the strengths and weaknesses in your own key skills and understanding of cross- curricular themes?

Each of these examples shift the focus from the teacher to pupil as active participants in the learning process. This shift must mean more than merely taking notes if independent study is to make a contribution to both the musical course and personal autonomy.

SUMMARY

In this chapter we have emphasised:

- The considerable coherence between A level, GCSE and the NC in relation to content and assessment strategies.
- That current syllabi at all levels require the music teacher to develop strategies which promote integration.
- That it is possible to teach A level musically.
- That music can be used to fulfil other post-16 examination courses.
- That other post-16 courses offer choice, and flexibility.
- That all courses in the national framework need to contribute to key skills and cross curricular themes.

FURTHER READING

Balderstone, D. and King, S. (1997) 'Preparing Pupils for Public Examinations: Developing Study Skills' in Capel, S., Leask, M. and Turner, T. (eds), *Starting to Teach in the Secondary School*, London: Routledge.

Bowman, D. (1998) *Analysis Matters: A Study Guide to London Examinations Advanced Level Musical History and Analysis Papers*, London: Rhinegold

Bowman, D. and Terry, P. (1993) *Aural Matters: Aural Perception at Advanced Level*, London: Schott. Although both of these publications were written for the 'old' style A level they still contain much very useful material for teaching music at this level.

Website

www.qca.org.uk   Important information about GNVQ and all statutory developments in examination courses

13   Beyond the classroom

Charles Plummeridge with Pauline Adams

INTRODUCTION

Most musicians are likely to agree with John Dewey's assertion that the arts are unique realms of meaning through which people share ideas and values, and communicate with each other in special ways. One becomes aware of the power of artistic pursuits in a variety of social settings; it is especially apparent in those schools where importance is attached to concerts, plays, productions and other presentations. These events seem to generate a certain expectation and excitement that has a positive influence not only on those immediately involved, but also on the corporate life of the institution. The nineteenth century reformers in the independent schools were very conscious of this relationship between the arts and social unity. They came to value performances of choirs and orchestras as occasions that brought students and staff together, engendered institutional harmony and reinforced a sense of community identity. A similar idealism has also helped to shape practices in the maintained sector over many years. Consequently, it would nowadays be extremely unusual to find a school where there were no opportunities for students' participation in music other than in class lessons. Most schools have established instrumental tuition schemes and arrange various forms of music-making that take place during lunch breaks, after school hours, weekends and sometimes during holiday periods. There is an assumption that teachers will organise concerts, shows and other events at various times throughout the year, and whenever the school is staging any sort of 'public' celebration it is almost certain that the services of 'the musicians' will be called on to contribute to the proceedings. In recent years, music programmes have been further extended as a result of more direct contacts between educationalists and professional musicians, with orchestras, opera groups and other arts organisations, all promoting educational outreach initiatives. Music education, as it takes place in schools, has become a 'family' of activities and far more than a curriculum subject.

There are, of course, numerous kinds of activities, apart from the arts, that take place outside of school hours. However, surprisingly little has been written about this aspect of schooling. One of the few comprehensive accounts is to be found in an informative volume by Andrews, Vernon and Walton (1996). They report that parents welcome all types of extra activities and see them not simply as pleasant adjuncts to schooling but as an integral part of their children's general education.

According to Smith and Tomlinson (1989) there is some evidence to suggest that students who take part in these activities are likely to make better overall progress in school. Why this should be is not altogether clear, but it may be that through successful involvement in school-based voluntary pursuits students acquire more positive attitudes to school and formal education.

Task 13.1 The benefits of the extra-curricular

What are the benefits of extra-curricular work for the pupils and the school? What do you perceive to be the issues and problems for the music teacher in relation to extra curricular work? Discuss your answers with colleagues.

Activities that are additional to the timetabled curriculum are described variously as extracurricular, after-school, out-of-school, extended, twilight and so on, and there has been some debate over suitable terminology. The Subject Working Group for the national curriculum (DES 1991b) recommended 'extended activities' as the most appropriate term for further musical pursuits since this implies a link with curriculum programmes. In the past, any such links have often been far from clear or secure. This has led to many misunderstandings regarding the nature and purpose of musical studies within the context of education and to a situation that has sometimes been detrimental to the general development of music in schools. Our intention, in this chapter, is to re-examine the aims and values of extended activities in music, and consider factors relating to their organisation.

OBJECTIVES

After having studied this chapter you should be able to demonstrate a knowledge and understanding of issues relating to:

- instrumental teaching in schools
- choirs, orchestras and ensembles
- concerts and public presentations
- links with musical bodies beyond the school
- organisational factors.

INSTRUMENTAL TUITION

There is a long and much respected tradition of instrumental teaching in British schools with lessons being provided through a combination of local authority music services, private organisations and self-employed music teachers. Some ten years ago, and following two decades of expansion, Caroline Sharp (1991) estimated that approximately half a million children were receiving tuition. However, as a result of changes in the funding of services it is generally accepted that more recently there has been some decline in provision. Not surprisingly, musicians and educationalists have reacted sharply to what is regarded as a worrying state of affairs; many express the fear that one of the most valued and successful post-war developments in school music education is in danger of being irrevocably damaged by short-sighted financial policies. In actuality, it is quite hard to determine exactly how far instrumental teaching services have suffered as a result of new financial and administrative structures. In a review of services conducted by Coopers and Lybrand (1994) it was concluded that there was 'no evidence to suggest a decline in the number of pupils receiving instrumental tuition'. However, findings from other research studies suggest otherwise. West and Pennell (1995), for example, have shown a marked restriction in services in the London boroughs during the 1990s, and there have been numerous reports of similar trends in other parts of the country. Music educationalists argue that limiting students' access to instrumental tuition is a regressive step and contrary to the principle of equal opportunities; the point is also made that lack of provision will ultimately have a negative effect on the musical life of the nation. In 1998 the Secretary of State for Education and Employment responded to these much publicised, and not infrequently sensationalised, anxieties and re-affirmed the government's commitment to music in schools, promising funding to ensure that all children would be able to pursue and develop their interests and talents. Subsequently, the Department of Culture, Media and Sport (DCMS) launched the Youth Music Trust (now the National Federation for Youth Music), and allocated substantial sums for the improvement and expansion of music services. The findings of an investigation carried out by the Performing Right Society (1999) seem to suggest that throughout the country there has been a recent increase in the numbers of children learning instruments, but there is still considerable local variation in provision which causes concern for teachers, students, parents and members of the music profession. This has been acknowledged by the newly appointed National Advisory Committee on Creative and Cultural Education (NACCCE 1999) which has accordingly recommended a major review of instrumental teaching services as a necessary basis for their better organisation and more effective operation.

In those schools where provision is limited, teachers frequently find themselves in the unenviable position of having to make decisions as to which students should be selected for tuition. This is never an easy task and one that inevitably presents professional and ethical dilemmas. There are some people who favour selecting students according to their performance on musical ability tests. Nowadays, most teachers would regard this procedure as unsatisfactory largely because of the obvious limitations of these tests which seem to measure only one aspect of musical operations, namely, aural acuity. While this sort of information might be of some educational relevance, and especially useful for diagnostic purposes, there are clearly many other significant factors that have a bearing on the learning of an instrument: students' motivation, level of interest and parental support being the most obvious examples. A rather more sophisticated type of selection procedure is recommended by Ben–Tovim and Boyd (1990) who maintain that it is possible, and indeed desirable, to identify personal dispositions, physical characteristics and cognitive abilities that are required in the learning of particular instruments. They suggest that in order to be reasonably sure of some future success it is vital that teachers and parents choose the 'right' instrument for the individual child. These writers provide much helpful and sensible advice but again there is a need for circumspection. In a very elegant piece of research, Mills (1988) has demonstrated how people often overcome what may appear to be physical constraints to the playing of instruments. According to Mills, motivational factors seem to be far more significant than is frequently supposed; learners are remarkably adept at working out strategies to solve technical problems related to personal physical characteristics. Advice on how to select students for instrumental tuition can certainly be useful to teachers, but as with any guidance it has to be used cautiously. Ideally, of course, all children should have the opportunity of learning a musical instrument of their choice and then selection would be far less of an issue. While there are grounds for optimism regarding the re-instatement and improvement of instrumental services it is likely that teachers will, at least in the immediate future, have to make decisions over which students should receive tuition.

Although much attention is quite rightly given to provision (or lack of it) there is rather less professional discussion about the aims of instrumental teaching. This is an issue that can, in fact, lead to quite serious differences of opinion among practitioners. It is often taken for granted that the teacher instructs students on an individual basis, with the aim being to develop each student's performance skills to the highest possible standard. In these circumstances, grade examinations tend to feature prominently and are often used as achievement benchmarks. To some extent, this view of instrumental teaching is underpinned by the notion of the virtuoso solo performer as the paradigm of musical achievement and excellence; it is the conservatoire ideal. Of course, teachers realise that the vast majority of their students do not become star performers or professional musicians. Even so, the performing paradigm, with its emphasis on the progressive development of technical proficiency and musical insight continues to exercise a strong influence in music teaching circles. Consequently, there are those teachers who maintain that if students do not practice regularly and systematically and demonstrate steady progress then tuition is largely pointless. There are others, however, who see their aims differently, focusing more on group tuition and regarding the playing of an instrument as part of students' general musical education. In this case the concentration is not so much on the individual's performance attainments but on the qualitative musical experiences of members of the group. It does not follow from what is more of a brass band perspective that students are not required to practice, nor is there any abandonment of principles relating to musical standards. But the teacher who is working with a group of children and sees their instrumental playing as one aspect of a broader musical education has somewhat different aims and expectations, and therefore different practices, from the teacher who sees his or her intention as developing the solo performer. Further relevant discussion on the aims of instrumental teaching is to be found in materials produced by the course team of the Music Teaching in Private Practice Initiative based at the University of Reading (see Plummeridge 1994). In school, these musical and educational issues, which are by no means uncontroversial, need to be carefully considered by the music staff in the process of developing a coherent music policy. Consequently, it is most important that visiting instrumental teachers are given opportunities to attend meetings and contribute to that policy. This is not always easy to organise, but an effort has to be made to ensure that part-time colleagues feel part of the school's music department. There is nothing worse for a visiting instrumental teacher than going to a school week after week and having little or no contact with the full-time staff. Regular meetings, rather than a quick word in the corridor, are required if staff are to feel that they are working as a team and pursuing common goals. The extract below, from a document produced by the Music Advisers National Association (MANA 1995), could provide a starting point for the formulation of an instrumental teaching policy.

Box 13.1 A framework for learning in music

Traditionally, much instrumental teaching and learning has been based around the framework provided by graded examinations. While recognising the purpose and value of these examinations, structuring schemes of instrumental work entirely in this way may limit the nurturing of a wide range of musical skills. Perhaps a more holistic approach could be considered which would encompass and accentuate the relationship of instrumental with classroom music. While there are differences in emphasis the following areas of study, drawn from the national curriculum Orders for Music, are entirely compatible with those for a rounded instrumental curriculum.

Aural awareness: the ability to recognise and identify musical elements (pitch, duration, dynamics, tempo, timbre, texture and structure) and their interaction.

Technique: the ability to perform a variety of music (from memory or notation) with fluency, expression and control via the development of such aspects as co-ordination, posture, breathing, articulation, tone quality. Manipulative and technical skills.

Interpretation: the ability to perform in a range of musical styles and traditions, and demonstrate considered interpretations.

Composing: the ability to compose, arrange and improvise, and develop ideas within musical structures.

Communication: the ability to communicate musically, verbally and non-verbally within an ensemble, to an audience and individually.

Critical awareness: the ability to listen with understanding; to describe, discuss, compare, evaluate and critically assess their own and others' performances and compositions.

Ideally, students attend for lessons throughout their school years but it has to be admitted that, in fact, quite a large number 'drop out' of instrumental tuition schemes. There are many reasons why students do not persevere with their playing. Hallam (1998) points out that while some factors are beyond the control of the teacher, it is always necessary to be aware that students need much positive feedback and assurance so that they can succeed. This support is especially helpful when students are experiencing those usual difficulties that everybody encounters in the process of playing. Hallam goes on to suggest some useful strategies to encourage students when interest is on the wane; in particular she emphasises the motivational effect of working towards some type of performance. In the school setting, full-time music teachers can assist the work of instrumental colleagues by arranging additional and complementary performance activities and by monitoring the progress of students. It is always regrettable when a student decides to discontinue with instrumental lessons and there is much talk of 'wastage'. However, it should not necessarily be concluded that by not continuing he or she has a wasted an opportunity. Learning to play an instrument, even though for a short period, is always of some musical value and one of the many encounters that contribute to the individual's educational development. This is not to suggest a laissez-faire attitude to dropping out. Teachers obviously want to encourage students, help them to achieve their musical potential and realise the pleasure of making music as an instrumentalist. However, one always has to accept that this form of musical experience does not appeal to everybody.

Task 13.2 Instrumental teaching

Review the arrangements for instrumental teaching in your present school. Bearing in mind the issues referred to in this chapter, discuss the following topics with colleagues in other schools and exchange ideas and information about policies and practices:

- students' choices of instruments
- the aims of instrumental teaching
- support for visiting instrumental teachers
- the timetabling of instrumental lessons.

Make notes on each topic as the basis for your discussion.

CHOIRS, ORCHESTRAS AND ENSEMBLES

Most teachers would wish to emphasise that school choirs, orchestras, bands and other ensembles are musically and educationally worthwhile in that they offer opportunities for experiences which are additional to, and in some ways different from, those of the normal curriculum. The Subject Working Group for the national curriculum makes the point thus:

> These [extended activities] provide opportunities to bring together pupils of different ages and stages of musical development in activities which extend and challenge their skills in ways which are not always possible in class lessons.
>
> (DES 1991b, section 14.2.)

From their own experiences, teachers know the satisfaction and pleasure of working with others who share their musical interests and enthusiasm for group music-making. They therefore want to arrange activities that enable students, and very often members of staff, to participate together in a musical venture. In a number of schools, parents are encouraged to take part in choirs and orchestras, and where this happens music beyond the curriculum is likely to assume a rather wider educational and social function. There may also be parents with a particular musical specialism who are prepared to organise and direct certain types of ensembles which would not otherwise be available in the school.

Since music is not compulsory beyond key stage 3, extended activities provide the opportunity for older students to continue with their musical education. There are always those who do not choose music as an examination option but nevertheless retain an interest in the subject and enjoy participating in some form of instrumental or choral group. In fact, Bocking (1985) has suggested that voluntary music making might be of greater educational value for many older students than any compulsory programme. He maintains that allowing students to 'opt in' to musical activities is likely to be more fruitful than attempting to cater for whole classes in which interests, experiences and attainments are increasingly diverse. Bocking accepts that his position may not meet with universal approval, but his type of curriculum organisation arises from a practical reality that is appreciated by many teachers.

While there are clearly good reasons for supporting and encouraging musical activities that are additional to class programmes, it is nevertheless the case that teachers have, on occasion, been criticised for giving too much time and attention to this side of their work. It has been suggested that there are teachers who only find a musical 'fulfilment' through directing choirs, orchestras and bands. A more severe and rather mischievous observation is that teachers concentrate on activities beyond the curriculum in order to secure personal recognition and thereby enhance their promotional prospects; on this view, musical groups assume a somewhat sinister image. It may be that both of these observations are not entirely without foundation, but it would be quite wrong to take them too seriously and assume that they have any sort of general applicability. However, it is perhaps fair to say that there has not always been an appropriate balance between class programmes and the extended activities. In a major survey of music in schools carried out some twenty years ago as part of a Schools Council Project (Paynter 1982) it was found that undue focus on highly accomplished choirs and orchestras sometimes led to a situation in which music was regarded as an exclusive pursuit and therefore of interest to only a small minority. There is, of course, no reason why this should be the case; in many schools, students of all abilities take part in a range of activities. The task for the teacher is to arrange various types of music making so as to cater for different levels of interest and achievement. In this way music loses any elitist image that it may have acquired in the past and is regarded as an area of experience for all students. Even so, class music programmes and regular activities such as choir and orchestra may still be regarded as separate forms of musical education. To some extent this cannot be avoided since many extended pursuits are designed for those students with a certain penchant for music. But there can be opportunities for all children to take part in music beyond the curriculum. This happens when students are able to demonstrate their classwork in concerts and other presentations (see Box 13.2).

Providing for a wide variety of extended activities inevitably presents considerable organisational, musical and pedagogical challenges. Teachers take on numerous roles including those of conductor, composer, arranger, accompanist and repetiteur, all of which require particular skills and expertise. It would, of course, be unreasonable to expect people to be specialists in every branch of music and teachers in school have to become general practitioners. They are required to be versatile musicians who have wide tastes and interests and can work confidently in different musical settings. Extending this versatility is central to their professional development.

Task 13.3 An inclusive approach to extra-curricular activities

In what ways can extra curricular work be seen to be owned by more and more pupils?

How can links be made between the curriculum and what goes on out side of the curriculum? You might like to think about:

- the use of classroom work outside of the curriculum
- the use of extra curricular projects for classwork
- the use of instrumental teachers in the classroom
- the use of visiting artists
- sharing aims and objectives.

Prepare an oral presentation on your ideas to other student teachers.

Box 13.2 Extra-curricular events

Schools usually arrange a number of events during each year which provide opportunities for workshops and public performances by groups – and by talented individuals. These events may be concerts, religious services, official school occasions or social functions; sometimes they take place on school premises, sometimes outside the school. Whatever the nature or venue of the events, they give pupils valuable experience in public performance as well as helping to project the school's image and to forge links with parents, governors and the local community in general. Wherever possible, the opportunity should be taken for whole classes to participate in the presentation of performances and of pieces composed in music lessons, so that these events can constitute a part of the curriculum.

(DES 1991a)

CONCERTS AND PRESENTATIONS

'Public' presentations range from the performance of operas and musicals to more modest events such as year-group concerts, presentations of work resulting from combined arts projects, and performances of students' compositions. Quite frequently, teachers arrange for students to perform outside the school, and many children have the experience of making music in venues such as senior citizens residences, hospitals and community centres. Naturally, these different activities require careful planning, organisation and management; they also involve a range of value issues.

From a musical point of view the most valuable thing about taking part in concerts is that it helps students become more aware of what it is to be a musician. Over time they come to learn something of the precise demands inherent in the processes of music-making and so develop their musical thinking and understanding. They also acquire an awareness of the many social factors that make music a meaningful and expressive form of human endeavour. Consequently, there is a strong argument in favour of all students participating in concerts during their years of compulsory schooling; such experience may be seen as a central element in their musical education. Not every child will be a member of one of the music groups that meets on a regular basis. As suggested earlier, however, work undertaken in the classroom can be performed in a concert situation. Such presentations are always of interest to parents and one of the best ways of illustrating justifications and aims in music education. Furthermore, class music lessons are likely to become much more important to students when they are given the incentive of working towards a public performance.

It is often suggested that taking part in a large musical performance is a means of enhancing students' confidence and self esteem. An individual may make only a small contribution as a member of a choir, chorus or orchestra, but can nevertheless feel a great sense of pride and satisfaction through having been part of the corporate venture. This aspect of artistic experience is emphasised by Hargreaves (1982) who maintains that because so much schooling focuses on individual academic success, many students acquire a poor self-image and sense of failure. This is one of the causes of alienation. Through arts activities involving large numbers, children can develop a feeling of solidarity and personal dignity; music and the arts thus contribute to personal and social education. From their own professional experiences most teachers are likely to find themselves very much in agreement with Hargreaves's observations and able to identify students who have grown 'as persons' through participation in musical activities beyond the classroom.

While it is possible to make these sorts of general points about the value of concerts, shows and other presentations, it is always necessary to be aware that these musical activities cannot be viewed solely from an artistic perspective. They have to be related to the culture of the school. In an extensive review of school cultures, Hargreaves (1995) makes the point that in all institutions there is a concern both for academic achievement and human relationships. The culture of the school is determined by the relative importance attached to one or the other. In what Hargreaves describes as a 'formal' culture there is an emphasis on high academic standards and the maintenance of traditional values; relationships within the school are likely to be distant although there is a certain commitment to institutional loyalty.

In this type of school, extended musical activities and public presentations may well be frowned on by some staff if these are seen as getting in the way of academic objectives. However, within the formal culture, concerts and productions might be encouraged if it was felt by those in authority that such presentations would be good for the public image of the school. It is sometimes implied by those concerned with the politics of education that music and other arts activities are used for the purpose of advertising the school's achievements in what is an increasingly competitive educational climate. To what extent this may or may not be the case is difficult to say, but it is not hard to see how such an attitude could have an influence on the content and style of any artistic venture which was for public consumption. A very different type of school culture is what Hargreaves refers to as 'survivalist' where there is little emphasis on either academic achievements or human relationships and there is danger of institutional breakdown. In this culture, any activities initiated by the music staff, no matter how enthusiastically, might well founder because of indifferent attitudes and practices on the part of the headteacher and other staff. The ideal culture is where there is an appropriate balance between the academic and the inter-personal. This is the culture of what is often called the 'effective school' and according to Barber (1997) extended activities and public presentations are likely to flourish in this type of environment.

Connections between public performances and school cultures are very complex, and the comments above are only of an introductory nature. The point is, however, that teachers always have to work within a particular culture which has a bearing on the operation of extended musical activities; some understanding of these issues is part of the music teacher's professional knowledge and expertise. Music, like any other school subject, is but one element of a wider academic and social system. Whatever guidance may be offered in connection with the organisation and operation of musical activities and presentations teachers always have to make decisions which they judge to be appropriate in their own school context.

> ### Task 13.4 The versatile music teacher
>
> Music teachers have to be versatile 'general practitioners' who can operate in a variety of musical settings. Nobody can be a specialist in every area, but when compiling your Career Entry Profile (CEP) you may be aware of musical skills and techniques that you feel you need to develop. Make inquiries about the availability of resources and services that could be of assistance to you in your professional development. You could start by discussing the matter with mentors and tutors.

PARTNERSHIPS WITH ARTISTS IN THE COMMUNITY

It is an ever-increasing phenomenon that schools are using expertise from the community to contribute to music and arts education. This might involve working with artists (composers) in residence, community arts groups, professional musicians, workshops (one off or a series), orchestras and so on. This work is also clearly important to the artists themselves. A survey undertaken by the Arts Council for England (Hogarth *et al.* 1997) revealed that 78 per cent of publicly funded arts organisations were involved in education work, and that 63 per cent of these had a dedicated education officer. In the report 'The State of the Arts' (Ross and Kamba 1997), the results of teacher assessment of influences on the quality of arts provision in five secondary schools, revealed that visiting artists came top of the list. Much evidence, therefore, suggests that partnership between schools, professional artists and community arts organisations is welcome and well established.

The value and benefit of community partnerships

Teachers have recognised that broadening the curriculum content required by the national curriculum for music, alongside the influences of cultural diversity, and the development of technology, has redefined the body of musical knowledge and range of skills required for classroom teaching. The so-called 'traditional' curriculum is being re-worked to incorporate 'popular' music, jazz studies, musics other than western, an awareness of contemporary music and composers, and information and communications technology. Expertise across such a broad range of styles and traditions is unrealistic for any teacher, but nor can teachers and schools afford to isolate themselves from their local communities and the wider society.

The spin-offs from any community partnership project, what ever the duration, can be valuable to all those involved. Ideas and procedures can feed into curriculum development and design, thus extending the scope of the music syllabus. Both visiting musicians and teachers have opportunities to share and learn new skills alongside pupils, and from pre-project workshops and discussions.

A visiting African dance and drumming group was invited to work alongside a predominantly English caucasian community in Dorset. This project brought a new and different cultural perspective to children who would not otherwise have interacted with people of different ethnic descent. Such a project confirms Peggie's view that:

> There is one important assumption: that musicians can make a significant contribution to the life of the school and to the education of its pupils. This is most likely to be achieved by aiming to create an experience of musical reality which could not be achieved in any other way
>
> (Peggie 1997: 9)

For the secondary music specialist there is a real opportunity to function as teacher, musician and participator.

Planning and funding partnership

Planning for partnership has many of the features of your regular planning, and needs to embrace:

Task 13.5 The benefits of partnerships with the community

What are the benefits of working with the community for:

- the pupils
- the artists / musicians
- the teacher and school?

Make a list of the types of artists or group with whom you could forge a partnership of benefit to the music curriculum.

- choosing the artist or project in relation to pupil needs and prior learning
- having clear aims and objectives
- writing a brief for the project for example, type of involvement of the participants
- raising and working to a budget for materials and resources.

However, an added dimension is the need for shared and mutual understandings between school and artist in relation to these points.

The funding for such collaborations comes from a number of sources, including national funding bodies, arts education agencies/organisations and business and industry. National Lottery funding has also opened fresh possibilities for broadening and strengthening the arts within both schools and community. There is also a firm commitment from the government to secure public money for the arts. Schools, as prospective bidders for National Lottery funding, have become more business oriented, with heads and teachers having to learn the skills of fund-raising and marketing. A number of schools have secured performing arts status, some gaining newly built arts centres and setting-up allowances for resourcing. There is an opportunity here for schools to share these resources and engage with the wider community.

Evaluation and feedback

Evaluating projects is essential and it is inevitable that when a number of different agencies are involved there may be challenges and difficulties to overcome, and recommendations to be made. Orchestral players face similar challenges to those experienced by music teachers, when trying to evaluate and measure the success of project outcomes, that is, they find qualitative measures 'much harder to agree' than quantitative. In any case documentary evidence should be kept, such as videos, tapes and scores.

The Spitalfields Festival based in London was one of the first festivals in the UK to appoint an education officer to its Education and Community Programme in 1989. The programme was built around the June music festival and since 1996 the Festival has provided all-year-round projects. The commitment undertaken to maintaining a worthwhile Education and Community Programme is exemplified by the way the festival is developing its approach to monitoring and assessing individual projects. An education committee meets on a regular basis to discuss past and future projects, and responds to the Education Officer's written reports, as well as to teachers', pupils' and participating musicians' responses. It is at such meetings that consideration is given to quality assurance in the setting up of projects, and procedures for monitoring and evaluating them. Feedback to arts funding providers and schools is essential to inform any planning of future projects. Recommendations based on evaluations and subsequently implemented by Spitalfields Education Committee have included the following:

- Cross-phase projects and partnerships should be negotiated initially with primary headteachers and secondary heads of music, ensuring projects have clear aims and objectives and are incorporated into curriculum planning and pitched at levels appropriate to different age groups.
- Preliminary meetings are vital to which clarify the different, but equally important roles of the arts providers and the teachers.
- Long-term planning with schools is needed to enable projects and partnerships to be included and prioritised in school development plans.
- Evaluations which encourage a qualitative as well as quantitative response are important.

As a student teacher you should begin to consider the role that the different kinds of arts organisations can play in contributing to the school music curriculum and what is already on offer within your teaching practice area. Future pupils will benefit from your initiatives and from your willingness to be involved in arts projects. It is all too easy for music teachers to spend their time exclusively in the music department, as they try to meet the demands of the classroom curriculum and extended curricular activities. However, music departments are often small and therefore limited in resources. The opportunity to work alongside other artists and musicians can be instrumental in furthering teacher professional development, as well as enriching the musical education of the pupils.

Task 13.6 Community partnerships in placement schools

There are many different organisations offering projects and workshops related to the arts. Find out if your teaching placement music department has been involved in

- a local community project
- a project involving a professional orchestra or ensemble
- a combined arts project.

Find out ways in which other arts subjects have been involved with outside agencies such as in theatre or art gallery based projects.

SOME ORGANISATIONAL FACTORS

One of the duties that occupies a good deal of the full-time music staff's time is the organisation of the school's programme of instrumental tuition. Arrangements vary from school to school and there is no one ideal formula that can ensure a foolproof organisational system. What works in one school may not do so in another. In many instances lessons operate on a rota, thus enabling students to attend for tuition during normal curriculum hours but at a different time each week. The rota system can work well but practising teachers are only too aware of its shortcomings and limitations. Students can get confused over their timetable and it is not uncommon for some colleagues to be unhappy about students being absent from their lessons. It is unfortunate that in many cases the rota functions in an uneasy and somewhat disputatious manner. If such systems are to work smoothly it is absolutely vital to have agreed procedures. This is a matter for the whole staff and part of the school's management policy.

In order to avoid these types of complications, instrumental lessons are sometimes held during lunch breaks or after school. In these circumstances difficulties arise regarding the availability of teachers for relatively short periods of time and programmes of tuition organised along these lines may prove to be limited and unsatisfactory. The organisation of instrumental teaching can present awkward problems for all concerned and it has to be acknowledged that the time-tabling of instrumental programmes is never properly resolved in some schools. Music teachers often spend many hours attempting to deal with these organisational difficulties which can be frustrating and an apparently inefficient use of valuable time. Even so, organising instrumental work is part of the music teacher's managerial function.

In most schools, students have opportunities to take part in a wide variety of extended activities in the arts, sports and numerous other areas of interest. Ideally, a proper timetable for these activities ensures the avoidance of clashes. However, in a study of fourteen schools Barber (1997) found that in only three schools did head teachers state that they had developed a formal policy on the organisation and management of the extended curriculum. There is often a common agreement that certain days and times are 'reserved' for particular pursuits. Even so, teachers have to be prepared to be flexible and accommodating when, for example, the same students are required for different activities. Confrontation with colleagues is never helpful; tact and diplomacy are much more likely to lead to satisfactory outcomes. It always has to be remembered (although it is often forgotten) that extended activities are for the benefit of the students; they should not be placed in the position of feeling troubled over what they might see as divided loyalties.

One of the points that teachers stress about running choirs and orchestras is that these activities need to be held on a regular basis. Cancellations of rehearsals are to be avoided wherever possible; pupils are likely to quickly lose interest and commitment if they feel that such pursuits are not regarded too seriously. It is also the case that any activities held after school may involve quite complicated arrangements for some pupils and often the parents of the younger children. When changes do have to be made to the normal routine it is necessary to make quite sure that all students are informed in good time and given an adequate explanation. It is also important to see that parents are given advanced notice of changes in the normal schedule and particularly about late rehearsals. These points may seem obvious but they are easily overlooked.

Large-scale projects such as a major orchestral concert or the production of a musical are inevitably complex enterprises and involve numerous artistic, financial and logistic factors, all of which have to be considered well in advance of the first rehearsals. It is usually the case that the success of these ventures is dependent not only on the obviously essential combination of students' commitment and teachers' enthusiasm, but very much on the co-operation and support of colleagues working together as a team. Projects of this type can also provide opportunities for the involvement of those students who do not wish to participate as performers but are very willing to undertake various types of support duties. The operation of extended programmes also depends on the co-operation and goodwill of non-teaching staff. It is necessary to be aware of the fact that activities taking place after school or at the weekends often means extra or inconvenient duties for those responsible for the school premises. The services of ancillary staff are vital and should never be taken for granted. Although there are stories of conflicts between teaching and non-teaching staff it would be quite wrong to assume that such cases are likely to be the norm. Research carried out by Swanwick (1988) and others in some forty schools revealed that caretakers, secretaries, cleaners and other support staff showed considerable interest in what students were doing in activities held out of school hours. They enjoyed musical events which they regarded as being part of the social life of the school.

Because of the scope of school music there are many demands on teachers and it is very easy, especially in small departments, to fall into the trap of trying to run too many activities. There is a limit to how much any one person can do single-handed and over-commitment can all too quickly result in negative outcomes. This is not a new problem but it is one that always needs to be borne in mind. It is often the case that there are colleagues with musical interests who are willing to assist with extended activities and, of course, visiting instrumental staff can make an important contribution in this area. The music teacher new to a school needs to find out about the staff's musical expertise although this is something that should always be done with discretion.

The full-time music specialist has many responsibilities and often has to take on a managerial role rather earlier in his or her career than colleagues teaching other subjects. Consequently, it is sensible to become acquainted with some basic topics such as principles of leadership, team building and management styles. A knowledge of management theories does not provide solutions to all the problems of running a music department but such theories can shed light on some of the organisational complexities that teachers have to deal with on a daily basis. A very useful and thought provoking book is *Reflecting on School Management* by Gold and Evans (1998). All music teachers would benefit from a study of this volume or another similar introductory text.

SUMMARY

In this chapter we have seen that:

- Extra curricular music can bring educational and social benefits to pupils and their schools.

Task 13.7 Planning a production

Your head teacher suggests that a very good arts project for the school would be a production of *South Pacific*. Under the following headings, draw up a list of factors that you would need to bear in mind in relation to:

- pupil musical resources
- timetable: performance dates; rehearsal schedules
- finance
- staff involvement and collaboration
- the school culture
- accommodation
- publicity.

Discuss your lists with a music teacher who has experience of a similar production.

- There are ways in which work inside and outside of the classroom can be integrated.
- The modern music teacher needs a broad base to her musicianship, to cope with the many demands of curricular and extra curricular work.
- Involvement with community projects can provide important and authentic musical learning.
- The music teacher needs to develop many organisational skills in order to cope with their wide remit.

ACKNOWLEDGEMENTS

We are most grateful to colleagues in schools who kindly found time to talk to us and provide information for this chapter. In particular we would like to thank Sally Yarrow, Louisa Hodgson and Scott Gibson for their extremely helpful comments, observations and suggestions, although, naturally, responsibility for the content (and any shortcomings and limitations) rests with the authors alone.

FURTHER READING

Andrews, K., Vernon, G. and Walters, M. (1996) *Good Policy and Practice for the After School Hours*, London: Financial Times Pitman.
Everitt, A. (1997) *Joining In: An Investigation into Participatory Music*, London: Calouste Gulbenkian Foundation.
Hallam, S. (1998) *Instrumental Teaching*, London: Heinemann.

14 Three curriculum issues in music education

Chris Philpott

INTRODUCTION

In this chapter we examine three curriculum issues which are currently important to the teaching of music:

1 ethnomusicology and music education
2 gender and music education
3 creativity and music education.

As well as teasing out the issues surrounding these topics we also explore some ways in which they can be addressed in the classroom. However, it must be emphasised that there are many dimensions to these topics which are still problematic for music educators. For this reason each section of the chapter is based upon reflective activities which attempt to draw out your attitudes and perceptions, before moving on to some practical possibilities. Some of the views exposed are intentionally controversial and reveal conflicts within the literature of music education itself.

ETHNOMUSICOLOGY AND MUSIC EDUCATION

Ethnomusicology and the music national curriculum

Ethnomusicology is the study of music from different cultures and on this definition both teachers and pupils need to become ethnomusicologists as part of the national curriculum for music. At key stage 3 pupils are expected to be taught how to 'identify the contextual influences that affect the way music is created, performed and heard for example, intention, use, venue, occasion, development of resources, impact of ICT, the cultural environment and the contribution of individuals.' In addition

---

OBJECTIVES

By the end of this chapter you should:

- understand the issues surrounding an inclusive approach to the teaching of musics.
- be able to develop some strategies for addressing these issues in the classroom.
- understand the issues surrounding gender and school music.
- be sensitive to the strategies which can be employed to promote equality of opportunity.
- understand the issues surrounding creativity in the music classroom.
- understand how you can create the conditions for creativity in your classroom.

---

they need to study 'a range of live and recorded music from different times and cultures including music from the British Isles, the 'Western classical' tradition, folk, jazz and popular genres, and by well-known composers and performers' (DfEE QCA 1999a: 20–1). One of the basic tenets of ethnomusicology is that all music is folk music, in as much as all music has a social and historical context surrounding its production. Having said this, the inclusion of music from 'other cultures' has been problematic in recent times. Issues include questions about the need to include other musics at all, the possibility of teaching them successfully, charges of a tokenistic multi-culturalism and the value of music outside the 'western canon'.

Issues in ethnomusicology and music education

In Box 14.1 are some quotations showing a range of attitudes to the use of music from 'other cultures' and traditions (sometimes called world music as distinct from pop, jazz). Read the quotations and consider the issues in relation to Task 14.1. There are several issues which seem to arise from these quotations, which include:

- The relative value of music from all cultures and traditions which is usually seen in terms of western classical versus the rest.
- The possibility that teachers can teach musics which are largely outside of their own experience.

Box 14.1 Ethnomusicology and music education

For the sake of all children, whatever their ability, we need to recover a sense of values in music. If children are to learn to appreciate music for its own sake, they need to understand the complicated grammar of Western music. This can only be done if students are given a musical education which cuts through the dross.

(Chew, quoted in the *Guardian*, 5 March 1991)

Box 14.1 (continued)

The requirements that teachers should cover world music evenhandedly will mean (that) much school music will be based on abysmal ignorance on the part of the teacher.

(Chew, quoted in the *Guardian*, 5 March 1991)

Too often in schools these days, concentration on the readily accessible results in the initially inaccessible remaining so, particularly when ... there is no suggestion as to how the ascent from the top 10 to Mozart is to be made. If the ascent cannot be made – as some claim – then, in my view it would be better to have no music at all, rather than pandering to the lowest and commercially exploited tastes of the young.

(O'Hear, quoted in *TES,* 22 February 1991)

Blacking (1976) maintained that all music is folk music and that an analysis of the surface complexity cannot tell us anything useful about the expressive power of the music in the context of the people who created it.

the real sources of ... all culture, are to be found in the human body and in the coopera-tive interaction between bodies.

(Blacking 1976: 116)

Blacking noted that literacy and notation are clearly important factors in generating extended musical structures, yet these are not necessarily more clever or sensitive: 'under certain circumstances, a "simple" "folk" song may have more human value than a "complex" symphony.'

(Blacking 1976: 116)

The task of education is to reduce the power of ... stereotypes through a lively exploration of musical procedures, phenomena which can be relatively independent of cultural ownership. . . . It is by working with musical processes themselves as though they had a degree of autonomy that transcendence of these culturally restricted worlds becomes a possibility. . . . Musical procedures can be absorbed and reused over centuries of time, between vastly different cultures.... The fact that musical procedures can to some extent be free-standing, transferable, negotiable is vital to any sense of individual freedom.... Without such scope education is unthinkable.

(Swanwick 1988: 107)

any particular kind of music can only be understood in terms of the criteria of the group or society which makes and appreciates that music.

(Shepherd 1977: 1)

Interculturalism favours cultural mixing while multiculturalism suggests cultural divisive-ness ... the school music curriculum should have a pluralistic and intercultural, rather than multicultural, focus.

(Kwami 1996: 60–1)

Box 14.1 (continued)

reference to non-western musics as 'ethnic' implies that western musics are not ethnic. Also, the term 'primitive music' suggests that music which is inferior. Although the link between 'ethnic' and 'primitive' music may not be explicitly stated, the inference is clear: Western musics are superior to non- Western musics.

(Kwami 1996: 63)

- The notion that all music is folk music.
- That there is a universal biological origin to music, and that musical processes are free of cultural ownership.
- That musical procedures have a cross-cultural currency and are to some extent transferable; this is important in the process of transcending our own cultural context and in combating blind prejudice.
- That music can only really be understood by the society from which it came, in the same way as language.
- That intercultural is not the same as multicultural.

Task 14.1 Ethnomusicology and music education

- Is there any sense in which the 'western canon' represents the best music ever written?
- Are there ways in which we can judge the relative value of different musics?
- Should we study the music of 'other cultures'? Why?
- Can we really understand the music of unfamiliar cultures?
- Are there universal musical processes which transcend cultures?
- Can you think of examples where musical ideas and processes have been 'borrowed' from other times and places?
- Do you feel equipped to deal with the implications of the requirements for the NC noted above? How can you develop your skills and knowledge in this area?

We now turn our attention to possible justifications for the use of 'other' musics in the music curriculum.

Why include the music from 'other cultures' in the curriculum?

Justifications for the use of many musics in the curriculum tend to be based on the assumption that through the study of *authentic* material (from our own and other cultures) we can arrive at *universal* musical benefits. The argument follows (see Blacking 1976), that given the biological and social origins of all music, by studying the music of other cultures we can:

- understand our own music more clearly
- reassess what constitutes musicality
- notice the deep structures and processes which transcend individual cultures
- transcend our own individual culture by creatively embracing new ideas or reformulating old ones
- understand our own 'encultured' habits and conceptions of music
- learn to live in a multicultural society.

Quite apart from the universal musical benefits there is of course the justification of studying authentic material for its own sake. Pupils are less likely to have negative feelings about a particular culture if they have positively engaged with its music.

However, it must be said that the multi-cultural argument, that 'we have many of our own cultures and so need to cater for them', is one of the weaker reasons for including a wide range of musics in our curriculum. The implication is that if we did not live in a multi-cultural society than we would not need to explore the music of other cultures. On the contrary it can be argued that the music of other cultures offers a critique of our own society and education system when confronting us with models of musical learning which are largely lost from our own society, such as the oral/aural tradition.

> ### Task 14.2 Why include music from 'other' cultures in the curriculum?
>
> Read the arguments in support of using music from other cultures.
>   Can you think of any other reasons for or against treating all music as 'folk' music?
>   How would you justify your curriculum choice to a parent who questioned the reasons for her child studying and playing music of the gamelan?

Despite the arguments for and against the place of various musics in the curriculum you do have a statutory duty to include examples from different times and cultures. You need to develop strategies for an inclusive curriculum at all levels, although you retain control over the relative balance of musics studied in your classroom.

How can we use the music of other cultures to bring about musical learning?

When devising strategies for dealing with 'folk' music in the classroom (in the ethnomusicological sense) the concepts of the *authentic* and the *universal* are important. There is a certain tension which exists between these two concepts. For example, to what extent is it possible for us to achieve authenticity in the classroom, and without authenticity is the experience devalued for the pupils? If we deal with universal processes is there a danger that we compromise the authentic, and see all music in terms of our own cultural assumptions? Having said this each concept is a useful starting point when designing curriculum materials in both the short and long term.

There are arguments against trying to be *authentic*, for example, the need for music of all cultures to be taught by highly trained and skilled musicians (including our own, see Fletcher 1987), and that it is impossible to really understand music from another culture unless we are fully immersed in it. However, you can achieve some authenticity by employing the following strategies:

- Visit professional workshops, for example, a gamelan centre and base work around this.
- Buy in professional workshops (either musical or on a collaborative arts basis).
- Hire authentic instruments or buy them for use in class.
- Use pupils with particular skills (although I did hear a cautionary tale from one school who recognised that the Indian community were 'fed up' with the assumption that they can in some way help with the arts curriculum).
- Build up sources and resources.
- Develop your skills and knowledge base.

Stock (1996) feels that in order for our studies of music to achieve authenticity we need to embrace an understanding of cultural, historical, social and educational differences of those that make it. For example, definitions of music are fluid and some African tribes cannot conceive of music without dance; some cultures do not have *a* word for 'music'. Western definitions can be suspect and not very useful when dealing with music from other cultures. The Kaluli people of New Guinea associate certain falling intervals with the songs of birds. They believe that when we die we turn into birds and thus these usually colourful sounds prompt feelings of loss, loneliness and abandonment. In African culture high drums and horns are associated with the male and low sounds with the murmuring of women. Stock feels that if we are to understand the music then we need to understand the cultural and social context of its production.

Swanwick (1988) argues that *universal* musical processes are the only rational basis of music education if we are to avoid the 'noise' of cultural stereotypes. Our own expectations may hinder our listening to other types of music, yet if we are aware of our conditioning then we can overcome its effects. Most importantly if we concentrate on musical processes then such problems will be limited and at best will help us to transcend cultural boundaries, both at the level of reception and creation. One possible way to do this is through the exploration of cross cultural 'borrowings', for example, Stravinsky and jazz; Debussy, the gamelan and 'exotic' scales; the music of Peter Gabriel; Afro-Irish fusion and so on. Box 14.2 shows an analysis of potential cross–cultural musical processes which can be used in the analysis of music and the generation of curriculum content.

Box 14.2 Universal musical processes

There seems to be certain things that we can say about all musics. That is they all contain:

- Musical time: the tempo can be free, flexible or strict.
- Melody and musical space (pitch and performers): for example, absolute, relative pitch; not necessarily equal temperament.
- Modes and scales: in some cultures these can be the basis of distinctive melodic progressions, patterns of ornamentation, instrumentation, cadential stress and performing technique, such as an Indian raga; also the concept of 'key note' is recognised in some cultures.
- Musical instruments: how the instrument is built may dictate the patterns of music available; although our western classifications of these are not always useful to other cultures.
- The process of music making: composing, performing, improvisation, reception and appraisal; these may overlap and have a different emphasis.
- Musicians: not always specialists and different musicians may have different functions.
- The structural processes of repetition and contrast (and variation and transformation): which seem to be common across the world.

These categories suggest the notion that there are *UNIVERSAL MUSICAL PROCESSES WHICH TRANSCEND CULTURES.*

Source: adapted from Stock 1996

Whether we are prompted by authenticity or universality it is certain that both the national curriculum, GCSE and current good practice require that teachers and pupils alike engage with music of many traditions. This does not mean that teachers and pupils becoming ethnomusicologists is not without its difficulties or controversies.

Task 14.3 Universal musical processes

Can you think of any other examples of cross-cultural 'borrowings'? Design a worksheet for the appraisal of one piece of music you know or have discovered, for KS 3 pupils.

Design a unit of work in which you use two different musical traditions or cultures for a GCSE group. Parts of the scheme might explore comparisons, for example, in appraisal while others might ask for fusions to be made, such as in composition.

Discuss your lesson plan with your mentor.

GENDER AND MUSIC EDUCATION

Gender and the national curriculum

The equality of access to musical achievement for both sexes is an issue of individual needs. The national curriculum for music states that 'teachers should set high expectations and provide opportunities for all pupils to achieve, including boys and girls...' and that they should 'should plan their approaches to teaching and learning so that all pupils can take part in lessons fully and effectively.' (1999b: 25) The national curriculum is a basic entitlement and the only difference between boys and girls that we can be sure of is the fact that boys voices break at puberty! This fact alone is unlikely to account for the different patterns of attitude and musical achievement that we find among boys and girls. It is clear that there are wider, and powerful social influences which delineate gender attitudes to and achievement in music. This is not to suggest that we should not try to reconcile two seemingly contradictory needs:

- for both boys and girls to pursue their own interests and inclinations
- for boys and girls to have equality of access to all types of musical achievement.

You can begin to address the individual needs of boys and girls through an understanding of the issues involved, and the development of potential teaching strategies.

Issues in gender and music education

In Box 14.3 (overleaf) are some quotations which have been collected to stimulate your own thoughts in relation to gender issues, that is, gender and society, gender and music, gender and music education. Read the quotations and consider them by carrying out Task 14.4.

From these quotations the following issues seem to arise:

- the general under-achievement of boys in music at school
- the apparent paradox that boys are disproportionately over-represented in the music profession
- the stereotypical patterns of achievement and attitude among boys and girls at school
- the gendered meanings placed on music which are determined by the structure and nature of society
- the 'loss' of a female history of music.

Processes involved in gender stereotyping

It must be said that the issue of gender and equality of opportunity is a hugely complex (and sometimes paradoxical) issue and that awareness and sensitivity is the baseline for

Box 14.3 Gender and music education

Boys have traditionally been under represented among those learning to play an instrument. Approximately twice as many girls play instruments as boys. Girls also do better in school music examinations. Despite this there appear to be no gender differences in measured musical ability on music tests.

(Hallam 1998: 55)

Historically, men have dominated the music profession as composers, conductors and performers and in jazz and pop groups – It is therefore perhaps surprising that, given the predominance of successful male role models, the explanation for the greater numbers of girls learning to play instruments, singing in choirs and being involved in other musical activities is seen as reflecting stereotyped views of music as being a 'feminine' activity.

(Hallam 1998: 55)

Green's research (1996b) into music teachers found that they said the following things about *girls*: they sing, prefer keyboard or orchestral instruments, are better at playing classical music, are committed, are conservative composers, are less imaginative than boys, are in the main mediocre.

Green's research into music teachers found that they said the following things abut *boys*: they don't sing, prefer electric guitars and drums and attendant pop music, are aesthetically adventurous in composition, are a rare breed yet often gifted and creative.

It is now known that women have been involved as performers and composers in all periods of history from antiquity to the present day – one consistent factor is that women have tended to work in specialised areas of music rather than across the whole musical field as represented by the men of their era.

(Green 1996a: 41)

But the women singer not only appears sexually available, for in her private capacity she conjures up an inversion of this public image, that of the idealised mother singing to her baby. Pivoted upon the binary division between whore and madonna, harlot and virgin – is one of the reasons why – women have been more abundant and successful in singing than any other single musical role.

(Green 1996b: 124)

[The final variation] subsequently plunges passionately and boldly on and becomes so violent, that one has quite forgotten by the end that the composer is a woman; indeed, one could think that one were dealing with a capable man, who can truly strike earnestly and hard as here.

(a critic's view of Louise Adolpha Le Beau quoted in Green 1996b: 126)

Box 14.3 (continued)

A great deal of music by women composers has been denigrated for its effeminacy; other music has been more favourably received as displaying positive feminine attributes such as delicacy or sensitivity; a tiny amount of music by women has been incredulously hailed as equal to music by men.

(Green 1996b: 127)

Task 14.4 Gender and music education

Consider your own experience as a musician and music teacher.

In your experience are there any gender patterns to those who become professional musicians/teachers/composers?

In what ways is the behaviour of boys and girls similar and different in music lessons?

What sorts of things do boys and girls say about music?

In your experience are there any differences in achievement between boys and girls across the various areas of musical practice, for example, in perform- ance and composition?

Which instruments do boys and girls tend to choose? Do boys and girls learn in equal numbers?

Is there any pattern to choice at GCSE music level related to gender?

Do you or your mentors use female composers/performers as part of the lesson content?

Use your answers as part of personal reflection, discussion and a presentation to your group.

all teachers. Clearly, there are some fairly powerful influences which can cause major gender differences and paradoxes in musical achievement. It seems that girls participate and succeed in school music with few role models, as opposed to boys under achieving with many! Girls do well at school in the context of curriculum materials which barely recognise the existence of women musicians, and the few boys who do partic- ipate succeed even though many others spurn school music. Subsequently it is boys who seem to progress disproportionately to high status roles in music. This is, of course, a vast generalisation and yet it represents a pattern observed by many teachers and researchers. A common perception is that boys and girls see certain forms of music making as being inherently feminine especially those which can be loosely termed as 'classical–light'. However, other styles such as pop, rock and jazz are seen as being inherently more masculine and thus attract the boys. Given that many school music departments have a 'classical–light' emphasis, the patterns of achievement noted above should not surprise us. However, more and more music departments are becoming eclectic in their attitude to style, and we should expect to see rather more equality of numbers, in both sexes, participating in various areas of music making. However, why are boys and girls drawn to particular forms of musical participation and achievement? What social forces are at work to create the stereotypes?

Clearly, the forces at work are the same as those for any issue of gender in society. Themes of male under achievement, positive female attitudes and overall male success, are common to many walks of life. Green (1996b) offers an analysis of the processes behind the construction of musical stereotypes for women and by inference for men. She notes that the most abundantly successful job for a female in all styles of music in the western world is that of singer. Females, she maintains, predominantly perform on an instrument which is their body, which is an affirmation of their femininity. For centuries the singing woman has been associated with the sexual temptress and yet also the idealised mother singing to her child. These socially constructed visions structure the way in which we see the female role both in society, and as a participant in music. As further evidence of the social processes which structure female achievements she asks us to consider our attitudes to female composers, who have often been written about in terms of an idealised vision of the male composer (see Box 14.3). Women composers have been denigrated for their effemininity, praised for their sensitivity or said to be the equal of men! This analysis might explain how perceptions of girls are channelled by society and thus the types of success they achieve in school. Having said this times are changing and there are an increasing number of role models from the world of pop (girl power), and classical music (composers and conductors) for girls. Also, there is anecdotal evidence which suggests that patterns for the choice of instruments to learn is becoming less stereotypical. Perhaps music teachers should take some of the credit for these perceptible shifts in the equality of access to musical achievement for all.

Task 14.5 How are gender differences maintained?

Read Green's analysis of gender stereotyping in music. What is your response to her? To what extent is it possible for society to structure our individual attitudes towards gender?

Is it possible to explain the apparent differences in attitude and achievement (both in and out of school) between boys and girls?

Are there any physical and psychological differences between males and females which determine the activities they can do well at?

How can we deal with issues of gender in the music classroom?

What practical measures can teachers take to address the issues of equality of access to all types of musical achievement for both sexes? Short of restructuring the gender stereotypes of society, understanding and sensitivity seems to be our best armoury.

You can at least be aware of the processes of society which channel perceptions of boys and girls (ours and theirs). Also, you can be sensitive to the fact that by your own actions you can confirm or challenge gender stereotypes. Some possible strategies for addressing the gender issue in the classroom include:

1   Making sure that you value a wide range of style, genre and tradition both in and outside of the class, and, if possible, offer opportunities for all to participate and pursue their interests.
2   Being sensitive to the possible perceptions of boys that making classical-light music is a feminine activity. Promote singing among boys (some have tried boys only choirs) and provide opportunities for them to explore all types of musical instruments.
3   Providing access to a wide range of role models including, for example, male singers and female drummers.
4   Being sensitive to the 'lost' history of the female in music and to curriculum materials which explore women's role in music.
5   Being open to the possibility that the history of music is an opportunity to explore the gender issue as part of the lesson. Green (1996a) suggests that the history of women as musicians should be told 'as it is' with no positive discrimination, and that the issues which emerge should become topics in their own right.
6   Looking for opportunities to play music by women composers when illustrating a musical point to a class. Green suggests that it is just as easy to illustrate ostinato through the music of Francesca Caccini as through the music of her father!
7   Being sensitive to the fact that making music can itself become a challenge to gender stereotypes, and that some pupils will vigorously pursue aspects of music, which resist these stereotypes.

Task 14.6 Gender and strategies for the classroom

Read the list of strategies for addressing gender stereotyping.
Can you think of any other possible strategies?
What measures are in place for equality of opportunity at the individual, departmental and school level in your placement school?

Gender stereotyping is a complex and difficult area, not least because attitudes to gender are deeply embedded in our experience of society, education and music. While developing curriculum materials is important the most important resource of all is the sensitivity and awareness of teachers themselves.

CREATIVITY AND MUSIC EDUCATION

Creativity and the national curriculum for music

The concept of creativity has traditionally been associated with the acts of composing, improvising, arranging and indeed, the national curriculum requires that pupils 'produce, develop and extend musical ideas, selecting and combining resources within musical structures and given genres, styles and traditions' (DFEE 199b: 20–1). However, pupils are also required to behave creatively when they perform and re-create music, and again the national curriculum asks that they are given opportunities for 'exploring and developing musical ideas when performing' (ibid.). There is also a creative act involved in responding to a piece of music in audience when pupils 'communicate ideas and feelings about music using expressive language and musical vocabulary to justify their own opinions' (ibid.). Having said this, we must acknowledge that creativity is a slippery concept and there is little in the way of common consent about its nature. For example, is creativity a gift or something that we can all engage with? However, most might agree that creativity is often employed to solve a problem (composer and performers are problem solvers) and that the imagination needs to be applied in order for this to happen.

What is creativity?

In Box 14.4 are some statements made about creativity which exhibit a wide range views on its importance and nature. Read these quotations and then attempt task 14.7.

Arising out of these quotations, the following tensions seem to appear in relation to the concept of creativity. These tensions are identified in Figure 14.1, and represent differing attitudes to the possibility of creativity and the conditions under which it can take place. It is important for you to explore the tensions shown in Figure 14.1, for your attitudes to these determines the extent to which you believe creativity a possibility in the classroom.

Having briefly examined the concept of creativity, we must also explore ideas on

Figure 14.1 Tensions in creativity

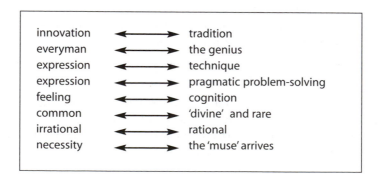

Box 14.4 Creativity and music education

What possible virtue can there be in pretending that creativity, an attribute not possessed by towering geniuses until childhood is past, can and should be generated in the pupils of primary schools … re-creation, that's the thing. But re-creation is surely also the apposite term for so many of the activities of that highly imitative being, the human child.

(Sherratt 1977: 34)

There is a continuum in the creative act which moves from the ordinary to the extraordinary, from daily perceptual vision to deep anological vision, to the rhythmic babblings and repetitions of the pre verbal utterance to the regular beat and syntactic echoing of epic poetry.

(Abbs 1989: 8)

In contrast, on this approach (i.e. creativity = novelty), 'true' creativity arrives when individuals breaks rules or invent new ones..

(Pateman 1991: 33–5)

artistic activities which offer the greatest scope for the majority of pupils to develop their innate sensitivity, inventiveness and imagination might have a strong claim for a place of importance in the curriculum.

(Paynter 1977: 5)

composing is one of the most difficult things it is possible to undertake: there have been less than thirty composers over the past two hundred and fifty years in Europe who are generally remembered with any deep sense of gratitude now.

(Fletcher 1987: 41)

Marx maintained that all making was creative.

the text is a tissue of quotations drawn from innumerable centres of culture.

(Pateman 1991: 40)

Martha Graham once said that it takes at least five years of training in the discipline to be spontaneous in dance, which brings out how misconceived is the notion that creativity is inhibited by learned technique. On the contrary, although of course technical competence does not necessarily give creative flair, it is a necessary precondition for such flair, in any subject discipline or activity.

(Best 1992: 96)

'When people ask me what comes first, the tune or the lyrics', said the well known popular songwriter Sammy Cahn, 'I say the thing that comes first is the phone call.'

(Hargreaves 1986: 146)

Box 14.4 (continued)

When the muse is upon him, he works frantically, without food or sleep, until the work has been produced. According to this view, creativity is mysterious, unconscious, irrational, and anything but ordinary.

(Hargreaves 1986: 147)

The painter Max Ernst claimed to exert no conscious control over his work … whereas the writer Edgar Allen Poe insisted that the creative involves no more than conscious planning and rational decision making.

(Hargreaves 1986: 147)

Task 14.7 What is creativity? (discussion and reflection)

Use the ideas in Box 14.1 and Box 14.4 and any others from your reading to answer the following questions.

- What have you witnessed in the music classroom thus far that you consider to be evidence of creativity (during appraisal, composition, improvisation, performance)?
- Which of the views discussed above have the most resonance for you?
- Can four year olds compose music?
- What is the relationship of composing to notating?
- Attempt a definition of creativity for yourself, or with a fellow student teacher.

how it takes place, in other words, the process of creativity. Understanding the creative process also further enhances our understanding of the concept of creativity itself.

What is the process of creativity?

Three models of the creative process are presented next. They are not designed to be definitive, but are introduced to illustrate a range of thinking and to stimulate your own thoughts on the creative process.

Model A

Wallas (1926) suggests that the creative process has four stages:

- *Preparation*: researching the problem
- *Incubation:* conscious attention is turned away from the problem and unconscious processes dominate, irrelevant conditions may act as stimuli, imagination plays a large part.
- *Illumination:* the 'eureka' experience when a creative solution is defined.
- *Verification:* formalisation of the solution, refined and adapted to meet practical constraints.

Model B

Ross (1980) proposes four stages to creativity:

- *Initiating* the creative impulse by exploring, doodling and playing.
- *Acquainting* oneself with a particular medium, with the potential and possibilities of sounds for particular purposes; further playing around with ideas.
- *Controlling* the medium through the mastery of basic skills and techniques; understanding constraints and limitations.
- *Structuring* the ideas into a satisfying and comprehensible whole; can also involve reviewing.

Model C

Abbs' (1989b) model of the creative process has many elements contained in the above.

- The release of impulse; a stirring of the psyche.
- Working in a medium; representative embodiment.
- Critical judgement moves towards a realisation of final form.
- Presentation and performance; taking the work into the community.
- Responses and evaluation of the community.

He also explores the interplay between innovation and tradition, the conscious and unconscious in the creative process as shown in Figure 14.2 (overleaf).

An important issue which arises out of studying the creative process is the relationship of technique to creativity. Is it necessary to develop technique before we can become creative? If so it might be that creativity is a state only be achieved after a technical 'apprenticeship'. Is it possible for technique to develop along side the use of the imagination? In this case technique can develop out of the problems posed by the creative process itself, in other words, new technique becomes a means to solving the problem.

Through understanding something of the concept of creativity and the process which takes place when we are being creative, you are in a better position to encourage the emergence of creativity in your lessons. You, after all, are expected to promote creativity through the national curriculum for music.

Figure 14.2 Abbs' model of the creative process

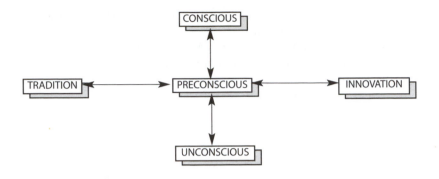

> **Task 14.8 The process of creativity**
>
> After examining the three models outlined on page 253, answer the following questions.
>
> - What evidence have you seen of these processes at work in relation to appraisal, composition and performance in your placement school?
> - Consider your own creativity in relation to music making. Do you recognise any features of the creative process in your own work? Illustrate any comments you make.

How can we encourage creativity in the classroom?

It is possible for you to create the conditions in which creativity can flourish, although like any flower you cannot guarantee that it will grow. Despite producing a suitable environment for creativity to flourish we have to accept that *sometimes* little creative activity emerges from a situation and at times we cannot be over-critical, for there will be failures. However, despite the necessary risks, it is only by allowing pupils to make music in many different ways that opportunities for creativity will appear, in other words a pupil's entitlement to music is also an entitlement to be creative. You can enhance the potential for creativity by building up rich and stimulating resources which can be used to both initiate and support the creative process. As a teacher you can also plan suitable challenges in relation to a pupils developmental stage, in other words, challenges which stimulate the pupils and set them a problem which they have a realistic chance of solving. These challenges can range from

- free choice (expression)
- to open ended tasks

- to solving specific expressive problems in which the expressive and structural ingredients have been limited, for example a Bach chorale, or the whole tone scale.

It is appropriate to include various levels of structure when promoting creativity depending on the pupil, the task and the desired musical learning. You also need to be a role model and set up opportunities for other role models to be seen and heard, for example, other pupils and external groups. This might require *you* to be creative, such as 'jamming' with pupils or composing for the class or group yourself. Creativity in music cannot be given limitless time and yet when solving problems pupils often need 'space' in which to satisfactorily complete the work. You need to be sensitive to this and be prepared to give the type of support pupils need in order to complete tasks, such as help with the technical skills which enhance the work in progress.

> ### Task 14.9 Creating the conditions for creativity
>
> Can you think of any other conditions which will enhance creativity in the classroom?
>
> Share an example of your planning (or an observation) in which you feel that creativity has been promoted. How did you stimulate the pupils? What support did you give them? Describe the outcomes of the lesson and your reflections on them.

It is important that as a music teacher you develop for yourself a concept of creativity. This concept will define what counts as creativity in the classroom and how you can plan for an environment which promotes its development.

CONCLUSION

In this chapter we have seen that:

- The use of music from many cultures in the classroom is problematic, particularly in terms of training and resources.
- There are many musical and social benefits to be gained from the study of a wide range of musics.
- The concepts of authenticity and universal processes are useful when considering classroom strategies for teaching music from other cultures.
- There are complex processes at play which impinge upon the different musical achievements of boys and girls.
- Awareness and sensitivity to gender issues is one of the teacher's most important resources when developing classroom strategies.

- Creativity is an essential component of the national curriculum for music.
- A well-reasoned concept of creativity should underpin practice.
- Much sensitivity and planning from the teacher is required for creativity to flourish.
- The issues in this chapter are representative of many which impinge upon the teacher of music.

FURTHER READING

Plummeridge, C. (ed.) (1996) *Music Education: Trends and Issues*, London: Institute of Education.

Spruce, G. (ed.) (1996) *Teaching Music*, London: Routledge. Both of these books have useful chapters/articles on many issues related to music education including the ones addressed in this chapter.

Stock, J. (1998) *World Sound Matters: An Anthology of Music from Around the World*, London: Schott This is an invaluable listening and study resource from which you can devise your own performing and composing activities.

Appendix A

A step-by-step guide to planning your own professional development in music-related ICT

Bill Crow

This guide takes you through the following areas and provides some tasks which audit and address your training needs. It can also be used alongside Chapter 9.

- Self-assessment of *music-related ICT*: audit and target setting.
- Gaining a practical knowledge of the *common ICT tools* available to you in your teaching practice school and in your ITT institution.
- Developing a personal proficiency in the use of *common ICT tools*.
- Auditing the *music-related ICT* available to you in your teaching practice school.
- Developing a growing awareness of how *music-related ICT* might effectively be applied in the classroom.
- Beginning to make use of *music-related ICT* in the classroom at a level that is appropriate to your current competence.
- Continually reassessing your training needs in relation to *all types of ICT* and working at a level beyond the competence that you might need in the classroom
- Developing a depth of classroom experience in the use of *music-related ICT*.

Self-assessment of music-related ICT: audit and target setting

You should complete the following self-assessment in tandem with the audit of common ICT tools supplied by your provider. Try to indicate your performance on a scale of 1 to 5 (unsatisfactory to excellent) and complete the audit at three points during the year. Don't be too daunted by the depth of detail in the following table. It is designed to make you aware of the wealth of the music-related ICT that is available to teachers. You should aim in the first instance to become proficient in the ICT offered by your placement school.

Having completed your assessment you should use the information to set targets and to plan appropriate action.

Task A.1 ICT in the music classroom

Complete the self-assessment in Table A.1 using the following assessment rating:

1   Unsatisfactory
2   Weak
3   Satisfactory
4   Good
5   Excellent.

Table A.1 ICT in the music classroom

ICT in the music classroom 1: *General presentation and monitoring*	Assessment rating Audit point		
	1	2	3
Music cassette playback and record			
Compact disc playback and record			
Digital tape/disc playback and record			
Photocopier			
Overhead projector (OHP)			
Video tape playback and record			
Video camera			
Projector			
Presentation software			
ICT in the music classroom 2: *Using specific music technology*	Assessment rating Audit point		
	1	2	3
Electronic keyboards w/ auto accompaniment features			
As a pupil resource			
As a teacher resource			
The MIDI music computer in the classroom			
Setting up and loading MIDI software			
Accessing sounds on a GM sound card/module			
Using the system as a pupil resource			
Using the system as a teacher resource			

Table A.1 continued

	Assessment rating		
	Audit point		
	1	2	3
Using MIDI sequencing software			
Using MIDI scoring software			
Using other types of MIDI software			

	Assessment rating		
Creative sound: sampling, synthesis, processing,	Audit point		
recording	1	2	3
Handling sound basics			
Using a microphone			
Amplifying sounds			
Recording sound in layers (into 1 of the following)			
Stand alone multi-track recorder			
Computer based recording software			
Creating new sounds (using 1 of the following)			
A special effects unit			
A synthesiser			
A sampler			
Manipulating recorded sound (in 1 of the following ways)			
Sound mixing: placement and balance			
Sound editing: copy, loop, cut, replace			
Sound enhancement: adding reverb, echo			
Importing recorded sound (from 1 of the following)			
Sampling CD			
CD ROM/Internet			

	Assessment rating		
ICT in the Music Classroom 3:	Audit point		
Using CD ROM and the Internet	1	2	3
Setting up and loading a CD ROM			
Using CD ROM as a pupil resource			
Using CD ROM as a teacher resource			
Access the Internet			
Construct a 'search' and visit a music related site			
Download text and graphics into a word processor			
Download a MIDI file and play it back on a sequencer			
Using the Internet as a pupil resource			

Gaining a practical knowledge of the common ICT tools available to you in your teaching practice school and in your ITT institution

Task A2 Availability of common ICT tools

Try to find out the following from your placement school:

- Where are the photocopy facilities and how do I access them?
- Where can I access a word processor?
- How can I gain access to the Internet and e-mail?
- Are there other computer-peripherals that I can use such as scanner, digital camera, etc?

Developing a personal proficiency in the use of common ICT tools

Task A3 Developing ICT skills

You will need to develop a foundation of common ICT skills that will have application in the classroom.
Try to complete the following tasks in the first term of your course:

- Set out some of your planning ideas on a word processor.
- Design a classroom worksheet that manipulates font style and size and places these alongside graphical elements. Cut and paste from other sources or use Clip art.
- Create an Overhead Transparency (OHT) using a photocopy machine.

Audit the music-related ICT available to you in your teaching practice schools

Task A4 Auditing ICT resources

Using Table A1 as a guide, audit the resources available to you in your placement school.

- Are they all in working order?
- How does the music department in your placement school use the resources?

Developing a growing awareness of how music-related ICT might effectively be applied in the classroom

You need to foster an awareness of how music-related ICT might be successfully applied in the classroom. You should also try to consider where ICT is less appropriate or where its inclusion will limit skill development or musical understanding. In addition you need to reflect on how it can best support you as a teacher.

The ICT chapter provides you with starting points for your professional development in ICT, but you also need to make the commitment to keep yourself informed of statutory requirements, new developments and current thinking. The supportive resources and websites quoted at the end of Chapter 9 should be a good starting point for your explorations.

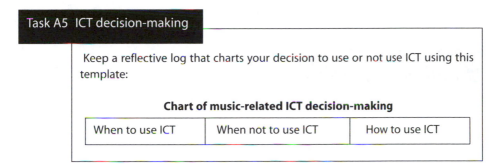

Task A5 ICT decision-making

Keep a reflective log that charts your decision to use or not use ICT using this template:

Chart of music-related ICT decision-making

When to use ICT	When not to use ICT	How to use ICT

Begin to make use of music ICT in the classroom at a level that is appropriate to your current competence

There is a continuum of competence in ICT that takes you from novice to expert and all the stages in between. It is important that you try out your ICT music skills in the classroom as soon as you feel competent enough to do so. This might be as simple as starting and stopping a keyboard rhythm. More tasks of this nature are provided in Chapter 9. Remember that, whatever your level of competence, it is certainly tested under 'classroom pressure'. You need to 'rehearse' your interaction with the technology in the same way that you would prepare for a musical performance.

Continually reassess your training needs and work at a level beyond the competence that you might need in the classroom

As a teacher you need to continually reflect upon your practice and its effectiveness in the classroom. This is especially true of the application of ICT in the music lesson. Throughout your career you should attempt to identify your personal training needs in the light of current technologies. As always you need to assess their appropriateness in relation to musical learning and their application in the classroom.

The BECTa support materials (see Further Reading in Chapter 9) – in particular the MIDI sequencing section – offer good models for reviewing skills and setting goals. Other documentation – for instance the exam requirements outlined in the Music Technology 'A' level syllabus – also indicate the scope of knowledge and understanding required at this level.

Developing a depth of classroom experience in the use of music-related ICT

Depth of experience only comes with time. For the present you should be conscious of when you are using ICT to further the musical learning of your pupils and when you are using it to support your own teaching.

Task A6 Identifying usage of ICT

Identify where you are making use of music-related ICT in your lesson planning. Consider:

- How it is being used to meet teaching and learning objectives:
  - as a teacher resource?
  - as a pupil resource?
- How it is being used to assess and monitor pupils' attainment and progress.
- How it will impact on the organisation and conduct of the lesson.
- Why it is appropriate to the subject-related objectives.

Appendix B

Another lesson and unit plan pro-forma

Chris Philpott

Figure A1 Lesson plan no. 2 in a scheme on 'variation'

Subject: Music	Class: Year 7 Date: 10.2.00 (1 hour)

Lesson outline/NC PoS:

Second lesson in 'variation' unit in which they will learn a simple tune in order to compose their own 'versions'.
NC POS :1b, 1c, 2b, 3b, 3c, 4b, 5a, 5c, 5d

Prior learning

Work on the song *Shalom* and how it can be 'changed'. Some pupils are aware of 'cover versions' from the 'charts'.

Objectives:

- to develop further understanding of how musical ideas can be changed through mood and expressive use of the musical elements
- to learn how to play *Twinkle Twinkle Little Star*
- to be able to compose a variation on *Twinkle Twinkle Little Star*
- to develop skills of playing in ensemble such as playing together, basic technique of melodic percussion (holding beaters, where to hit notes)
- to be able to use and recognise change to produce variation.

Teaching strategies for bringing about learning:

- musical models for recap
- didactic input (for example, tell them about changes they 'miss', technique)
- question and answer discussion for all activities
- rehearse class ensemble in *Twinkle, Twinkle*
- differentiated stimuli for composition i.e. use of *Shalom*, learned last week, for vocal variations or *Frere Jacques* for a more complex instrumental variation
- problem solving in relation to musical change
- formative help during composition .

Use of ICT

Two groups to use [the software program] Cubase VST to produce sequenced variations to explore e.g. tone, tempo and layered changes .
Use of keyboards to explore sound changes and rhythm changes as variations on *Twinkle, Twinkle.*

Materials and resources

Acoustic instruments, electronic keyboards, 2 computer workstations, notations of the tunes

Sequence of teaching activities and tasks:

- greet
- recap with musical models on piano for example, how can idea can be changed?
- briefly revise song (*Shalom*) and the 'changes' made
- move class to a 'horseshoe' and distribute melodic instruments
- teach and rehearse *Twinkle, Twinkle* with individual practice if required
- how can we change this tune to produce a new version (pupil suggests – teacher plays)
- form friendship groups with 5 maximum in a group and 3 minimum
- set task, that is, produce two versions (variations) of *Twinkle, Twinkle* (or differentiated stimuli)
- send groups one by one to practice rooms to begin composition
- circulate with formative help
- back into class and listen to some of the ideas
- recap the 'problem' set and how they have solved it
- dismiss.

Pupil teacher development of language

Development of pupils' use of intuitive/literary language to describe change. Development of subject specify vocabulary, such as, variation, ornamentation, mood, style arising out of pupil responses and compositions. Teacher to use subject-specific vocabulary only when pupils have engaged with 'sonic' events.

Assessment strategies (collecting evidence of musical achievement)

- formative assessment during whole class Q+A sessions, ensemble work
- feedback during composition
- listening to ensembles and composition (recording if time)
- notable aspects can be collected in rough notes on a pupils' 'record page'
- pupil self assessment/appraisal

Evaluation (for example, management issues, issues of musical learning, the relationship between these two)

Did the pupils learn in relation to the objectives? If yes, how do I know? If no, then why not? What can I change/try in the next lesson to improve the musical learning? How could I improve this individual lesson next time?

Figure A2 Unit plan pro-forma

Title: Variation (versions)	Length: 5 weeks		Year/class: 7	Term: 1	
Aims and main AT focus	Week 1	Week 2	Week 3	Week 4	Week 5
To develop an understanding of the expressive and structural potential of musical change.	Learn how to sing *Shalom Cheverin*. How can we change this to produce different versions? Listen to Ives's variations on *America* (grid analysis). Produce a simple inventory of possible musical changes.	Recap 'changes' with musical models (use *Shalom*). Whole class ensemble to learn a simple tune such as *Twinkle, Twinkle*. Group composition to produce 2 versions of the tune. Possible differentiation for example, use *Shalom* (for voices) or a more complex tune such as *Frere Jacques*.	Continue with compositions. Record (some could be responsible for their own recording), perform. Others appraise 'live' in books to an agreed format (grid analysis). Play selected bits of Dohnanyi version (if time). Q+A appraisal of this.	Finish Dohnanyi variations. Listen to recording again. Groups notate one variation; tune is presented in large format to all pupils and this can be annotated with words, graphic or traditional notation. Decorate and display. Self-assessment of the compositions.	Return to *Shalom* and other songs known by the class applying ideas from compositions. Introduce the notion of cover versions to lead into next unit; brainstorm examples. Listen to and appraise *Help* by Beatles, Tina Turner, Bananarama (grid analysis). Presentation by those who have researched 'covers' on Internet

Detail of NC POS: 1abc, 2a, 3abc, 4ab, 5abcde

Assessment opportunities: collecting evidence	Formative feedback on song; Q+A; marking grid analysis	Formative, for example, technique on instruments; appraisal during group work	Appraisal of composi-tions; marking books.	Marking notation; self assessment sheet.	Formative during singing; evidence from worksheets.
Resources	Ives recording, worksheets, song sheets	Instruments, some to use ICT, notations of tune(s)	Recording equipment (some portable) ; books; Dohnanyi variations recording.	Notation sheets, tape, instruments, self-assessment guidelines.	Recordings, worksheets, use of Internet research on cover versions.

Appendix C

A basic audit of subject knowledge and musicianship

Chris Philpott

The areas of subject knowledge and musicianship listed here are derived from examining a common GCSE syllabus for music. They are by no means exhaustive, but give you some idea of the areas in which you need to develop skills, knowledge and expertise, if you are to teach music at this level and beyond. However, it must be emphasised that no music teacher comes to, or leaves a PGCE with the 'full set'. You have a professional responsibly to develop yourselves further during your NQT year and beyond. The grid below can also be used as a pre-course needs analysis such that you can set targets before commencing the programme. Be honest about each element, in other words, have you the skills and knowledge to engage musically? This audit does not include music specific ICT.

1   I am confident in my skills, knowledge and understanding.
2   I am sound in my skills, knowledge and understanding.
3   I have some skills, knowledge and understanding here but need to develop further.
4   I have no confidence in my skills, knowledge and understanding.

Table A2 A basic audit of subject knowledge and musicianship

Knowledge, skills, understanding and musicianship	1	2	3	4
Conducting/directing				
Playing in ensemble				
Singing in ensemble				
Solo performance				
Keyboard skills				
Keyboard harmony				
Singing voice				
Composing (any style)				
Improvising (any style)				
Arranging				
Grade 5 theory				
Harmony (for example, analysis of 'classical' harmony)				
Harmony (for example, writing in the style of Bach)				
Musical analysis (written)				
Musical analysis (dictation)				
Musical analysis (verbal)				
Aesthetics				
Jazz (any style)				
Blues				
Folk music (any style)				
Pop (any style)				
Indian music				
African music				
Caribbean music				
South American music				
Chinese music				
Gamelan				
Other world music (state)				
Other world music (state)				
Medieval music				
Renaissance music				
Baroque music				
Classical music				
Romantic music				
Twentieth century music				
The development of western 'classical' music				
Instrumental families				
Instrumental ensembles				
Vocal combinations				
Musical textures (polyphonic, homophonic etc.)				
Musical forms, structures and techniques of development				
The teaching of individuals in music				
The teaching of groups in music				
Others (state)?				

Appendix D

An induction guide to a school music department

Chris Philpott

OBJECTIVES

- To experience the change from graduate/mature student to that of music teacher in a secondary school.
- To gain some understanding of how to interact with pupils, teaching and non-teaching staff at your school.
- To become familiar with the physical environment, materials and resources of the music department.
- To understand the various roles of the music teacher.
- To gain insight into classroom management and organisation strategies.
- To gain insight into the planning and delivery of the music curriculum.
- To place these insights into the whole school context.
- To gather materials and reflections which will be of use in future subject studies sessions/discussions.

Schools are happy to have students, although the period in early September can be extremely busy. It is important that you recognise how occupied music teachers can be and that, where possible, you should try to make a positive contribution in both the classroom and the school. Often you may need to sit quietly and observe, but there will be other times when the best way of fitting in will be by assisting the teacher. Diplomacy is very important and you should consult before embarking on anything independently. However, there will come a time when you need to use your own judgement about offering your services without being asked. The balance between being proactive and diplomatic is a delicate one and you should always bear this in mind.

The following guide to the collection of initial data about your department can be used in the first weeks of your school experience. Some of the information arises quite naturally as part of your immersion in a music department, other data you need to actively seek.

Teachers use many skills to successfully manage a lesson and to ensure that effective learning takes place. For example, mastery of the teaching material, organisation of equipment, planning and preparation, choice of appropriate strategies and the management of pupils through effective relationships and interactions.

The environment

- What sizes of group do you notice and how does this change in relation to age?
- How many music staff are there and how many visiting specialists?
- What range of facilities exist in terms of buildings, rooms, practice rooms and so on? In what condition are they?
- What audio visual resources are there? What ICT facilities are available to the music department?
- What musical instruments for classroom use exist?
- What is the stock of instruments available for 'learning' outside of the classroom?
- Does the school loan any of their musical instruments? Which ones and how many?
- How is the furniture organised and is this flexible?
- Are there displays on the walls? Describe these and their effect on the classroom environment.

Ethos

- In the context of the rest of the school does the music department have any local rules or policies?
- Does the department have any of its own rewards and sanctions?
- Which extra curricular groups exist and how many pupils are involved?
- What links exist with the local community?
- What access do pupils have to the music facilities of the school outside of classroom time?

Classroom organisation and management

Observe some lessons with the following in mind:

- *Beginnings:* how do the children enter the class? How promptly does the lesson begin? Do pupils have easy access to their books and materials? Are the objectives clear to the pupils?
- *Transitions:* how do the classes change from one activity to another? Are these moves smooth? Does the furniture need reorganising?
- *Endings:* how is the lesson brought to a conclusion? Is there a summary? Are

pupils told about the next lesson? Is any home work set? How were the class dismissed?

Relationships and interactions with pupils

In relation to teacher–pupil interactions, observe some music teachers and make notes on the following:

- The teacher's use of voice, that is, the 'performance' during presentation.
- Eye contact and body language.
- How much encouraging, praising, organising, explaining, discussing goes on with pupils.
- How much individual help is given and feedback is given to pupils.
- How much work is marked.
- How much reprimanding takes place.

Strategies

Strategies are best seen as planned approaches to learning. Which of the following do you note during your early observations:

- Whole-class teaching (when and for how much time)?
- Whole-class discussion?
- Group discussion?
- Problem solving, for example in composition?
- Performance and rehearsal?
- Listening to music?
- Talking about music?
- Other strategies?

Children learning

For one or two lessons try to carry out the following tasks.

- What are the lesson's objectives, that is, what knowledge, understanding, skills and attitudes is the lesson designed to develop?
- What work do the pupils produce? How would you describe the quality of the work? How do the pupils feel about their work?
- What strategies are used to achieve the objectives?
- Are the pupils on task?
- Do they interact successfully with each other?
- Is there any special help for those who learn more slowly?

- How are the most able catered for?
- Can you tell whether pupils have made progress during the lesson?

Assessment

Assessment can happen in a variety of ways:

- Formally, by the teacher recording, testing or examining what the pupils know, understand and can do.
- Informally, by the teacher talking over pupils work and discussing issues which arise.
- Pupils can also assess themselves.

You might also consider the following questions which are important issues in arts education;

- What are the purposes of assessment in music education?
- How can we assess compositions?
- How can we assess performance?
- How can we assess a response to music?

The curriculum

- Try to collect departmental lesson plans, units of work, schemes of work, philosophy and policies (these may come in the form of a handbook).
- What assessment procedures are in place? Collect the relevant documentation.
- How is the timetable organised; who teaches the various classes and where?
- Begin to make a list of curriculum materials and resources held by the department.
- Which 'boards' are used at examination level?
- Does music collaborate with any other subjects during lesson time?

SUMMARY

Try to sketch some answers to the following questions:
- What makes a good music teacher?
- What makes a good music lesson?
- What are the ingredients of the ideal music department in terms of resources and accommodation?
- What is the greatest challenge that you feel you will face in your development as a music teacher?

Appendix E

Subject-specific tasks for primary experience

Chris Philpott

Does the school have a music co-ordinator?

- Try to interview him/her to ask about their role.
- Which classes do they take for music?
- How do they support other colleagues?
- What are the constraints on their role?
- Do co-ordinators exist for other subjects?

Try to observe some music lessons at key stages 1 and 2

- What is the balance of listening, appraising, composing and performing?
- What are the typical resources for music found in the key stage 1 and 2 classrooms, in terms of printed materials, home-grown resources and hardware (including music specific ICT)?
- Is there any use made of broadcasts?
- What are the differences between music at key stage 1 and key stage 2?
- What do you notice about the things that pupils write or say about music?
- What do you notice about their singing voices and other performing skills such as control and technique?
- Describe some of their compositions (creativity, imagination, structure, expressive qualities and so on).
- Describe their skills of notation.
- What differences do you notice in the musical achievement of pupils at key stage 1 in comparison with those at key stage 2?

Try to obtain a copy of a policy statement on music and samples of any lesson plans or units of work (in other words, a collection of lesson plans)

- What importance is attached to music in the policy (in other words, why study music)?
- Is there any INSET provision for staff?

Try to talk to a teacher who is a non-specialist (generalist)

- How much time do they spend on music?
- How important do they consider it to be?
- What opportunities do they perceive for making music?
- What are their constraints?
- Have they taken part in any music INSET?

Try to interview some pupils about music

- How important is music to them?
- What music do they enjoy at home?
- What aspects of music lessons do they enjoy in school? Why?
- Do they compose their own music?

Extra-curricular work

- Do any of the pupils have instrumental lessons from visiting teachers?
- Are there any groups or choirs?
- What extra curricular music are they currently engaged with?
- Does music feature in any productions or concerts?
- Is music used in any topics, projects or to support other subjects?

Appendix F

Moving on and professional development in music education

Chris Philpott

There is much excellent generic advice in the 'parent' book (Capel *et al.* 1999). Here is a brief guide to some issues of 'musical' significance for moving on and professional development.

LETTERS OF APPLICATION: A SUGGESTED STRUCTURE

1 A sentence about the job being applied for and where you saw it advertised.
2 Where you have come from and where are you at present. What sort of musician are you? What has attracted you to apply for this particular post?
3 What are your main experiences of teaching in music thus far (curricular, extra-curricular)? What skills and qualities can you bring to the job as a result of this experience and your own music education?
4 Briefly write on your beliefs about music and arts education, for example its role, purpose and your approach.
5 What other teaching experiences have you had (or hope to have) and what skills have you (will you have) developed as a result of this, for example second subject, PSE, form tutor.
6 Other relevant skills, interests, qualities, experiences.
7 Conclusion, for example, thanks and 'would like to expand at interview'.

It is important that you read the advert or job description, carefully picking out the specific requirements and qualities sought. Each application will require a particular 'spin'. Try not to regurgitate your CV and keep the letter short and to the point (two pages maximum). Finally, show your letter to as may people who will look at it! In particular headteachers are experts at identifying letters which will make an impression; after all they spend much of their time looking through them.

INTERVIEWS

You need to get used to sharing experiences about interviews, for they are all very different. What experiences can you pass on about the structure and nature of interview days? What questions are likely to be (have been) asked? How have you negotiated the balance between being keen, energetic, enthusiastic and yet humble and respectful?

It is increasingly likely that music teachers are seen teaching during the interview process. If so make sure that:

- You are certain what is required of you.
- You become aware of the basic philosophy of the department such that you can 'tweak' the lesson.
- You do not try to cover too much.
- You make the lesson as musical as possible (this can only impress!).

You might also prepare some answers to these questions.

- Why do you want to teach music?
- Why do you want to teach music in a secondary school?
- Why should we teach music in schools?
- What can you offer to our extra curricular programme?
- What can you offer us; why should we employ you?
- Tell us about your musical skills and expertise.
- What sorts of things would you do in a music classroom?
- Can you play the piano? (Have a positive answer!)
- How has your college course prepared you for a position in school? What are your current strengths and weaknesses?
- How has your school experience prepared you for this job?
- Can you teach to A level?
- How would pupils of all abilities be catered for in your lessons?
- Others?

Always talk positively about your experience, skills, knowledge and understandings. Even if they ask you about weaknesses reply in terms of being proactive and enjoying the challenge of developing.

PROFESSIONAL DEVELOPMENT IN MUSIC EDUCATION

Figure A3 (overleaf) illustrates some of the options for professional development in music education.

Figure A3 Professional development in music education

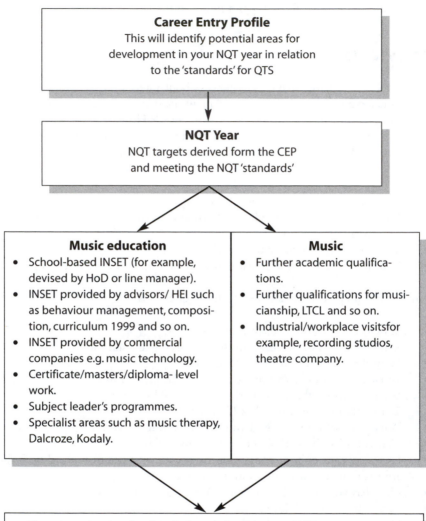

Career Entry Profile
This will identify potential areas for development in your NQT year in relation to the 'standards' for QTS

NQT Year
NQT targets derived form the CEP and meeting the NQT 'standards'

Music education
- School-based INSET (for example, devised by HoD or line manager).
- INSET provided by advisors/ HEI such as behaviour management, composition, curriculum 1999 and so on.
- INSET provided by commercial companies e.g. music technology.
- Certificate/masters/diploma- level work.
- Subject leader's programmes.
- Specialist areas such as music therapy, Dalcroze, Kodaly.

Music
- Further academic qualifications.
- Further qualifications for musicianship, LTCL and so on.
- Industrial/workplace visits for example, recording studios, theatre company.

- There is money in schools to help you develop as an NQT.
- All schools have INSET budgets above and beyond this.
- Use the CEP and NQT standards to identify and promote your professional development as a priority.
- Much professional development can now be accredited by HEIs (including NQT work), with the potential for credit transfer.
- Commitment to professional development is important, but only take on courses you feel you have the energy and enthusiasm to sustain. For example, a masters programmes can become a chore if you are not totally committed, especially after a full day's work.

References

Abbs, P. (ed.) (1987) *Living Powers: The Arts in Education,* London: Falmer.
—— (ed.) (1989a) *The Symbolic Order,* London: Falmer.
—— (1989b) *A is for Aesthetic: Essays on Creative and Aesthetic Education,* London: Falmer.
—— (1994) *The Educational Imperative,* London: Falmer.
ACAC Curriculum and Assessment Authority for Wales (1997) *Music, Optional Test and Task Materials* developed by P. Adams, J. Coplan and K. Swanwick in consultation with the Curriculum and Assessment Authority for Wales, Cardiff: ACAC
Andrews, K., Vernon, G. and Walters, M. (1996) *Good Policy and Practice for the After School Hours,* London: Financial Times Pitman.
Aspin, D. (1990) 'The Problem of Aesthetic Education', in Swanwick, K. (ed.), *The Arts and Education,* London: National Association for Education in the Arts.
Auker, P. (1991) 'Pupil Talk, Musical Learning and Creativity,' *British Journal of Music Education* vol. 8, no. 2, Cambridge University Press.
Bannon, N. and Cox, G. (1997) 'Music', in M. Wilkin *et al.* (eds), *The Subject Mentor Handbook for the Secondary School,* London: Kogan Page.
Barber, M. *et al.* (1997) *School Performance and Extra-Curricular Provision,* London: Department for Education and Employment.
Barrett, M. (1990) 'Music and Language in Education', *British Journal of Music Education* vol 7, no. 1, Cambridge University Press.
Bennett, N. and Dunne, E. (1994) 'How Children Learn and Implications for Practice', in Moon, B. and Shelton-Mayes, A. (eds), *Teaching and Learning in the Secondary School,* Milton Keynes: Open University Press.
Ben-Tovim, A. and Boyd, D. (1990) *The Right Instrument for Your Child. A Practical Guide for Parents and Teachers,* London: Gollancz.
Bernstein, L. (1976) *The Unanswered Question: Six Talks at Harvard,* Cambridge, Mass.: Harvard University Press.
Best, D. (1992) *The Rationality of Feeling,* London: Falmer.
Blacking, J. (1976) *How Musical is Man?,* London: Faber.
Bocking, G (1985) 'Opting into School Music – A Philosophy for the Upper School', *British Journal of Music Education* vol. 2, no. 2, Cambridge University Press.
Boyson, R. (1974) *Oversubscribed: The Story of Highbury Grove School,* London: Ward Lock Educational.
Bruner, J. S. (1966) *Towards a Theory of Instruction,* Cambridge, Mass.: Harvard University Press.
—— (1986) *Actual Minds, Possible Worlds,* Cambridge, Mass.: Harvard University Press.
Calouste Gulbenkian Foundation (CGF) (1982) *The Arts in Schools,* London: CGF.

Campaign for Music in the Curriculum (1998) *The Fourth 'R'*, London: Campaign for Music in the Curriculum.

Capel, S., Leask, M. and Turner, T. (1999) *Learning to Teach in the Secondary School: A Companion to School Experience,* 2nd edn, London: Routledge.

Chew, G. (1991) 'Putting Beethoven before Chuck Berry', *Guardian* (25 March).

Cooke, D. (1959) *The Language of Music,* Oxford: Oxford University Press.

Coopers and Lybrand (1994) *Review of Instrumental Music Services,* London: Incorporated Society of Musicians.

Davies, L. (1993) *Take Note: A Music Handbook for Primary Teachers,* London: BBC Publications.

Department for Education (1995) *Music in the National Curriculum,* London: DFE.

Department for Education and Employment (1998) 'ITT National Curriculum for the use of ICT in Subject Teaching', in *High Status, High Standards,* London: DfEE.

Department for Education and Employment/Qualifications and Curriculum Authority, (1999a) *The National Curriculum for England: Citizenship,* London: QCA/DfEE.

—— (1999b) *The National Curriculum for England: Music,* London: DfEE/QCA.

Department of Education and Science (DES) (1985) *Music from 5 to 16, Curriculum Matters 4,* London: HMSO.

—— (1991a) *National Curriculum Music Working Group Interim Report,* London: DES.

—— (1991b) *Music for Ages 5 to 14. Proposals to the Secretary of State for Education and Science and the Secretary of State for Wales,* London: HMSO.

—— (1992) *Music in the National Curriculum,* London: HMSO.

Dickinson, C. and Wright, J. (1993) *Differentiation: A Practical Handbook of Classroom Strategies,* NCET.

Durrant, C. and Welch, G. (1995) *Making Sense of Music: Foundations for Music Education,* London: Cassell.

EDEXCEL (1998) *GCSE Music (1425), Syllabus 2000,* London: EDEXCEL.

—— (1999) *GNVQ Performing Arts,* London: EDEXCEL.

Elliot, D. J. (1995) *Music Matters: A New Philosophy of Music Education,* Oxford: Oxford University Press.

Everitt, A. (1997) *Joining In: An Investigation into Participatory Music,* London: Calouste Gulbenkian Foundation.

Fiske, R. and Dobbs, J. (1956) *The Oxford School Music Books,* London: Oxford University Press.

Fletcher, P. (1987) *Education and Music,* London: Oxford University Press.

Flynn, G. and Pratt, G. (1995) 'Developing an Understanding of Appraising Music with Practising Primary Teachers', *British Journal of Education* vol. 12 no. 2, Cambridge University Press.

Fryer, M. (1996) *Creative Teaching and Learning,* London: Paul Chapman.

Gardner, H. (1993) *Frames of Mind: The Theory of Multiple Intelligences,* 2nd edn, London: Heinemann.

Gold, A. and Evans, J. (1998) *Reflecting on School Management,* London: Falmer.

Green, L. (1996a) 'The Emergence of Gender as an Issue in Music Education', in Plummeridge, C. (ed.), *Music Education: Trends and Issues,* London: Institute of Education.

Green, L. (1996b) 'Gender, Musical Meaning and Education', in Spruce, G. (ed.), *Teaching Music,* London: Routledge.

Green, S. (1998) *Doing Things Differently: How can Teachers Really Meet Pupils' Individual Needs in Music?* Yamaha Educational Supplement 27 (Autumn/Winter).

Hallam, S. (1998) *Instrumental Teaching,* London: Heinemann.

Hargreaves, D. H. (1982) *The Challenge of the Comprehensive School,* London: Routledge and Kegan Paul.

—— (1995) 'School Culture, School Effectiveness and School Improvement', *School Effectiveness and School Improvement* vol. 6, no. 1: 23–46.

Hargreaves, D. J. (1986) *The Developmental Psychology of Music,* Cambridge: Cambridge University Press.

Harris, R. and Hawkesly, E. (1989) *Composing in the Classroom,* Cambridge: Cambridge University Press.

Harvey, E. (1988) *Jazz in the Classroom,* London: Boosey and Hawkes.

Hogarth, S., Kinder, K. and Harland, A. (1997) *Arts Organisations and their Education Programmes,* London: Arts Council of England.

Kushner, S. (1991) *The Children's Music Book, Performing Musicians in School,* London: Calouste Gulbenkian Foundation.

Kwami, R. (1995) *Music File,* Series 8, Issue 1, Cheltenham: Thornes.

—— (1996) 'Music Education In and For a Multi-Cultural Society', in Plummeridge, C. (ed.), *Music Education: Trends and Issues,* London: Institute of Education.

—— (1998) *African Songs for School and Community: A Selection from Ghana,* Mainz: Schott.

Kyriacou, C. (1991) *Essential Teaching Skills,* Cheltenham: Thornes.

—— (1998) *Effective Teaching in Schools,* Oxford: Blackwell.

Langer, S. K. (1957) *Philosophy in a New Key,* 3rd edn, Cambridge, Mass.: Harvard University Press.

—— (1978) *Philosophy in a new Key,* Cambridge, Mass.: Harvard University Press.

Lawton, D. (1988) *Education, Culture and the National Curriculum,* London: Hodder and Stoughton.

Loane, B. (1982) 'The Absurdity of Rank Order Assessment', in Paynter, J., *Music in the Secondary School Curriculum,* Cambridge: Cambridge University Press.

Lowson, S. (1999) *Orchestral Education Programmes: Intents and Purpose, Report of the Consultation Process,* London: Arts Council Of England.

Major, A. (1996) 'Reframing Curriculum Design', *British Journal of Music Education* vol. 13, no. 3, Cambridge University Press.

Manhattanville Music Curriculum Project (1970) Bardonia, New York: Media Materials.

Metcalfe, M. (1987) 'Towards the Condition of Music', in Abbs, P. (ed.), *Living Powers,* London: Falmer.

Mills, J. (1988) 'Tips for Teachers as Traps', in Salaman, W. and Mills, J. (eds), *Challenging Assumptions: New Perspectives in The Education of Music Teachers,* Exeter: Association for the Advancement of Teacher Education in Music (AATEM).

—— (1991) *Music in the Primary School,* Cambridge: Cambridge University Press.

—— (1994) 'Music in the National Curriculum: The First Year', *British Journal of Music Education* vol. 11, no. 3, Cambridge University Press.

—— (1996) 'Starting at Secondary School', *British Journal of Music Education* vol. 13, no. 1.

Music Advisers National Association (MANA) (1995) *Instrumental Teaching and Learning in Context,* London: MANA.

National Advisory Committee on Creative and Cultural Education (NACCCE) (1999) *All Our Futures: Creativity, Culture and Education,* London: DfEE.

National Curriculum Council (NCC) (1990a) *The Arts 5–16. A Curriculum Framework,* London: Oliver and Boyd.

—— (1990b) *The Arts 5–16. Practice and Innovation,* London: Oliver and Boyd.

—— (1990c) *The Arts 5–16. A Workpack for Teachers,* London: Oliver and Boyd.

O'Brien, T. (1998) *Promoting Positive Behaviour,* London: David Fulton.

O'Hear, A. (1991) 'Out of Sync with Bach', *Times Educational Supplement* (22 February).

OCR (1999) *GCSE Expressive Arts,* OCR

OFSTED (1993) *Music, Key Stages 1, 2 and 3, First Year, 1992–93. The Implementation of the Curricular Requirements of the Education Reform Act,* London: HMSO.

—— (1995a) *Music: A Review of Inspection Findings 1993/94,* London: HMSO.

—— (1995b) *Guidance on the Inspection of Secondary Schools,* London: HMSO.

—— (1998) *The Arts Inspected,* Oxford: Heinemann.

Packer, Y. (1987) *Musical Activities for Children with Behavioural Problems,* London: Disabled Living Foundation.

—— (1996) 'Music with Emotionally Disturbed Children', in Spruce, G. (ed.), *Teaching Music,* London: Routledge.

Parsons, M., Johnston, M. and Durham, R. (1978) 'Developmental Stages in Children's Aesthetic Responses', *Journal of Aesthetic Education* 12.

Pateman, T. (1991) *Key Concepts: A Guide to Aesthetics, Criticism and the Arts in Education,* London: Falmer.

Paynter, J. (1977) 'The Role of Creativity in the School Music Curriculum', in Burnett, M. (ed.), *Music Education Review: A Handbook for Music Teachers vol. 1,* London: Chappell.

—— (1982) *Music in the Secondary School Curriculum,* Cambridge: Cambridge University Press.

—— (1992) *Sound and Structure,* Cambridge, Cambridge University Press.

Paynter, J. and Aston, P. (1970) *Sound and Silence,* Cambridge: Cambridge University Press.

Peggie. A, (1997) *Musicians go to School: Partnership in the Classroom,* London Arts Board.

Performing Right Society (1999) *Musical Instrument Tuition in Schools – A Survey,* London: Price Waterhouse Coopers.

Plummeridge, C. (1994) 'Education and Training: Criteria and Processes' Unit 1A. Module 1 Principles and Processes of Music Teaching, *Music Teaching in Private Practice Initiative,* Reading: University of Reading International Centre for Research in Music Education.

—— (1991) *Music Education in Theory and Practice,* London: Falmer.

Pratt, G. and Stephens, J. (eds) (1995) *Teaching Music in the National Curriculum,* London: Heinemann.

Rainbow, B. (1989) *Music in Educational Thought and Practice,* Aberystwyth: Boethius.

Reid, L. A. (1986) *Ways of Understanding and Education,* London: Heinemann.

Reimer, B. (1989) *A Philosophy of Music Education*, New Jersey: Prentice Hall.

Rogers, R (1998) *The Disappearing Arts: Report for the Royal Society for the Encouragement of Arts, Manufactures and Commerce*, London: Calouste Gulbenkian Foundation.

Ross, M. (1975) *Arts and the Adolescent*, Schools Council Working Paper 54, London: Evans/Methuen.

—— (1980) *The Arts and Personal Growth*, London: Pergamon.

—— (ed.) (1982) *The Development of Aesthetic Experience*, Oxford: Pergamon.

Ross, M., Radnor, H., Mitchell, S. and Bierton, C. (1993) *Assessing Achievement in the Arts*, Buckingham: Open University Press.

Ross, M. and Kamba, M. (1997) *The State of the Arts*, Exeter: University of Exeter School of Education.

Rowntree, D. (1977) *Assessing Students, How Shall We Know Them?*, Harper and Row.

Schools Curriculum and Assessment Authority (SCAA) (1996) *Exemplification of Standards: Music*, London: SCAA.

—— (1997) *Music and the Use of Language*, London: SCAA.

Sharp, C. (1991) *When Every Note Counts: The Schools Instrumental Music Service in the 1990s*, Slough: National Foundation for Educational Research (NFER).

Shaw, P. (1996) *Mapping the Field: A Research Project on the Education Work of British Orchestras*, London: Association of British Orchestras.

Shepherd, J., Virden, P., Vulliamy, G. and Wishart, T. (1977) *Whose Music? A Sociology of Musical Languages*, London: Latimer.

Sherratt, R. G. A. (1977) 'Who's for Creativity, in Cox, C. B. and Boyson, R. (eds), *Black Paper*, London: Temple Smith.

Shuter-Dyson, R. and Gabriel, C. (1981) *The Psychology of Musical Ability*, London: Methuen.

Simpson, K. (ed.) (1975) *Some Great Music Educators*, London: Novello.

Skilbeck, M. (1976) 'Ideologies and Values', Unit 3, Course E203, *Curriculum Design and Development*, Milton Keynes: Open University.

Sloboda, J. A. (1985) *The Musical Mind: The Cognitive Psychology of Music*, Oxford: Oxford University Press.

Small, C. (1977) *Music – Society – Education*, London: John Calder.

Smith, D. and Tomlinson, S. (1989) *The School Effect: A Study of Multiracial Comprehensives*, London: Policy Studies Institute.

Spruce, G. (1996) 'Assessment in the Arts: Issues of Objectivity', in Spruce, G. (ed.), *Teaching Music*, London: Routledge.

Stock, J. (1996) 'Concepts of World Music and their Integration within Western Secondary Music Education', in Spruce, G. (ed.), *Teaching Music*, London: Routledge.

Stroman, S. (1998) *Developing the Inner Musician*, NAME Conference Report.

Swanwick, K. (1979) *A Basis for Music Education*, Windsor: NFER-Nelson.

—— (1988) *Music, Mind, and Education*, London: Routledge.

—— (1992) *Music Education and the National Curriculum*, The London File, University of London Institute of Education, London: Tufnell.

—— (1994) *Musical Knowledge: Intuition, Analysis and Music Education*, London: Routledge.

—— (1999) *Teaching Music Musically*, London: Routledge.

Swanwick, K. and Tillman, J. (1986) 'The Sequence of Musical Development: A Study of Children's Composition', *British Journal of Music Education* vol. 3, no. 3, Cambridge University Press.

Swanwick, K., Plummeridge, C., Taylor, D., Winter, J and Whithead, S. (1988b) *Music in Schools: A Study of Context and Curriculum Planning*, London: University of London Institute of Education.

Tate, N. (1996) 'The Role of the School in Promoting Moral, Spiritual and Cultural Values', *Educational Review* vol. 10, no. 1: 66–70.

Vincent, A. (1992) 'Behind the scenes of the National Curriculum', in *Music File* series 4 issue 2, Mary Glasgow.

Vygotsky, L. S. (1986) *Thought and Language* (rev. edn), trans. A. Kozulin, Cambridge, Mass.: MIT Press.

Wallas, G. (1926) *The Art of Thought*, London: Watts.

West, A. and Pennell, H. (1995) 'Survey of Inner London Headteachers: Educational Expenditure and Out-of-School and Extra-Curricular Activities', *Educational Research* vol. 37, no. 2: 159–76.

Weston, P., Barrett, E. and Jamison, J. (1992) *The Quest for Coherence: Managing the Whole Curriculum 5–16*, Slough: NFER.

Witkin, R. (1974) *The Intelligence of Feeling*, London: Heinemann.

WJEC (1999) (1998), *GCSE Music*, WJEC.

Index